Synthesized Organization

Björn Paape
Drago Vuk
(eds.)

Synthesized Organization

PETER LANG
Frankfurt am Main · Berlin · Bern · Bruxelles · New York · Oxford · Wien

Bibliographic Information published by the Deutsche Nationalbibliothek
The Deutsche Nationalbibliothek lists this publication in the Deutsche Nationalbibliografie; detailed bibliographic data is available in the internet at <http://www.d-nb.de>.

ISBN 978-3-631-59215-1

www.peterlang.de

Synthesized Organization

Preface

This book has been published to present in one place the results of years of research in the field of organization and management from our colleagues at the Kranj Faculty of Organizational Sciences, University of Maribor.

The majority of contributions published in this edition cover the problem of organization and management in the Republic of Slovenia, prior to or after joining the EU. Some contributions come from foreign practice. Therefore, the most important aspects of the Slovenian transition period, starting in the 1990s after the disintegration of Yugoslavia, have been covered scientifically. The majority of contributions deal with specific aspects of the transition period on the basis of concrete research carried out in that period by individuals and research groups. Most of the research work was performed in the last few years, meaning that the results obtained are all the more significant not only for Slovenia, but for all the countries that have come into existence on the territory of former Yugoslavia, and for their neighbours. Some research work was performed with their cooperation.

Owing to the fact that the Republic of Slovenia has been developing at an impressive rate in the last decade, the content of this scientific monograph presents a good model and a sample of research in this field for our neighbouring countries, which have yet to undertake such a development procedure.

Last but not least, the book is aimed at graduate and post-graduate students of organization and management studies, both in Slovenia and abroad (as a theoretical starting point and as a practical guideline for individuals and companies entering the Slovene market and the markets of transitional countries of the south-eastern Balkans).

Drago Vuk
Björn Paape

Table of Contents

The Synthesized Organization

Antun Vila

antun.vila@zg.htnet.hr

Abstract

In theory and in practice, a so-called organizational gap is known in the hierarchical organization, as well as the gap of not understanding between functions and departments. Each function creates its own optimums, which are often opposed to one another. It took a long time to understand that are organization functions in processes that have to be coordinated. Finally, it was realized that the process is a basic organizational unit, which needs to be organized and led. This is simple when it is possible to organize clean organizational processes – when the process is completed in a way that can satisfy the final user (see picture 2), but this is only possible in rare cases, meaning that the different departments must be left so they can be put into some sort of chain, one after another. This kind of organization needs the existence of a definite constant and temporary interfunctional teams, as shown in figure 3. The author suggests that such an organization will more easily accept new organizational methods and principals, such as a learning organization, knowledge, workers, team work, continuous education and knowledge management. This is how a type of synthesized organization is created. One of the possibilities of such an organizational structure is also shown in figure 3.

Keywords: business structures, business processes, transfunctional organization, synthesized organization

1. Introduction

1.1 Fragmentation of an Organization

According to the definitions of "synthesis"[1], an organization is always synthesized, i.e. fragmented and consisting of numerous elements which verify into a whole. Organizational science consists of a number of theories, schools, principles, methods and techniques, all of them jointly forming a very complex organizational science. A business organization is supposed to adopt more or less the best of it all, or at least - to chose the ones producing solutions which are closest to the practice in real terms. In fact, a business organization adopts whatever convenes it best at any given moment and does not consider it a specific problem.

How successful it would be in practically implementing the acquired, depends on the knowledge, skills and competencies of the high level managers and their closest collaborators.

A synthetic organization is an artificially formulated notion maintaining that an organization should be studied as a connection of its elements, as well as the connectedness existing between theory and practice. It needs to be demonstrated that it is not a kind of a phantom, understood only by a few highly educated individuals entangled in their masters' and doctors' theories, far from the reality of actual life. If they really are such, then the task of academic circles is to bring them nearer to the experts working in practice and to demonstrate that many facets of an organization can be satisfied simultaneously.

Although it is hard to avoid a "mosaic" type of lecturing (if we can call it that) at universities, teaching subject by subject with all their theories and specifics, the basic idea of this edition is that there should be something linking them into a whole, demonstrating how it could all be practically

---

1 **Synthesis:**

a) the combining of the constituent elements of separate material or abstract entities into a single or unified entity.

b) a complex whole formed by combining simpler elements.

c) a thinking process resulting in conclusions based on known and supposed principles.

A method of studying a subject as a whole, as a unity and interrelations of its compounds.

to synthesize – make whole, gather in one [Rozman, 1999].

unified in an organization capable of bringing all the effectiveness and efficiency principles into real life. This would be a kind of comprehensive synthesized organization – encompassing the best of it all.

Fragmentation can also be observed in business practices. It is best illustrated by the structure of an organization, although it has to be noted that, at present, we are incapable of dealing with it otherwise. Depending on the size of a company, an organization can be fragmented into a large or even an enormous number of functions, departments and services, plants, workshops or groups of workers and the most important problem is that of their co-ordination and synchronization. In addition to that, each and every larger organizational unit strives to find the best solutions for problems it is faced with and makes its decisions accordingly, although it can all be in direct opposition to the best solutions found by another organizational unit with which there is no co-ordination at all.

Most managers have never been specifically educated to cope with organizational and management problems. A large majority of them have a university education, but with varying specializations. That is not to say that they should all be experts in organization and management, but it would be essential for them to occasionally indulge in some additional training in this sphere. Some of the most recent ideas in the sphere of organizational sciences are presently unknown to a large number of managers, although they might substantially reflect in a company's effectiveness and efficiency. In present times of very unstable business environments and substantial changes, this fact should be seriously considered.

Disregarding the sphere of human activity, such fragmentation is enhanced by high specialization in all the fields of modern life, leading to various solutions that have not been co-ordinated among different specializations and professions. This occurs in technical, as well as in other spheres, such as health care for example, where medicines prescribed by one specialist can often cause important or even life-threatening complications in quite a different health sphere. In organizational terms, we can state that the so-celebrated and promoted team work results in a new kind of splitting-up of a large number of teams, thus creating the need for forming new co-ordination teams, because various solutions are not being co-ordinated.

Considering these problems, we are especially alarmed by the fragmentation of business systems' organization. Therefore, it would be necessary to point this out at universities, and transfer this awareness into business organizations themselves. Let us try to synthesize things, let us demonstrate to the people the **wholeness of diversity**. This would be the main topic of this paper.

In order to make the whole idea of fragmentation of an organization clearer, let us have a look at present approaches to an organization and organizing.

2. Present Approaches to Organization and Organizing

2.1 Theoretical approach

When studying the theory of organization at universities, lecturing to undergraduate and postgraduate students, or teaching courses to professionals, we usually find our starting points among some of the already developed theories and schools of organization, such as:

- Contingency theory
- Resource-dependence theory
- Institutional theory
- Population-ecological theory
- Systems theory
- Decision-making theory
- Management theory
- Etc.

Or we talk about certain organization schools, such as (Vila, 1994, p. 164ff):

- Organizational Behaviour School
- Empirical School
- Decision Making School
- Quantitative School
- Management Processes School

And some authors list even more theories and various other schools. Some specific topics are also being studied separately:

- Work organization, i.e. technical organization
- Human resources management
- Co-ordination – an essential element of management
- Influence of the environment on an organization
- Organizational structures
- Process organization
- Organizational culture
- Organizational communication
- Etc.

There are probably some unmentioned theories, schools and methods of organization and organizing, as different authors apply various classification, but all of those ideas, principles, methods etc - although not quite explicitly – serve the same goal: the increase of organization's effectiveness and efficiency (Vila, 1994, p. 24).

It has to be admitted that, due to the above abundance, it is not easy for all the practical managers to successfully introduce all these theories, schools and methods into practice. This should be facilitated by a kind of a practical synthesis and some other forms of organizational structure.

2.2 Design of an Organization – How to Structure an Organization in Practice

When setting-up an organization, *its organizational structure* is usually defined at the very start. First of all, the basic units of an organization or a new company, referred to as the "basic functions" of the company, are defined and then they are further divided vertically, up to the basic executive groups and individual executives. That is how hierarchy of an organization is formed within its structure of divisions, departments, particular groups up to executive officers (Vila, 1994, p. 234). Each executive officer, a service or a department has a higher department above it and, finally, there is the general manager. The higher the position of the department within the organizational structure, the more important the tasks it deals with and, therefore, its range of activities is wider as well as its powers. Every such division, subdivision, service etc. has its own manager with competencies corresponding to his or her position and *adequate powers*, which has been one of the most significant aspects of management throughout history. This phenomenon is still being studied by contemporary management and is also important for our further deliberations.

2.3 Principle of Structure and Hierarchy

The principle of structure and hierarchy has been known for thousands of years at the level of states, but especially in armies. It is well known that various war formations of ancient times knew a certain hierarchy: the number of subordinates at each level was fixed, as were certain co-ordination methods in wartime.

The first mention of organizational structure is to be found in the times of Moses[2], who led his nation from Egyptian slavery and complained to his father-in-law of being unable to cope with the burden of leadership, because he was obliged to solve all of his people's problems. The father-in-law advised him to select leaders for groups of 1000, 100, 50 and 10 people, who would be in charge of all the lesser problems, so that he would only have to deal with the most complex ones (Vila, 1994. p. 168). All this can be well illustrated by an organizational scheme, i.e. a hierarchical organizational structure.

The first written documents on organization and management in industry date from the 19th century. In the 50s and the 60s of the 20th century, a number of studies on problems of organizational structure in industry appeared. These also dealt with the problems of formalization and complexity of organization, i.e. the vertical and the horizontal differentiation (dealing with the height and the width of the organizational structure), the use of committees etc. Various classifications of particular types of industrial enterprises, as well as of small and large serial manufacturing and processing industry plants were also invented.

It was believed that it would be possible to *invent an **optimum organizational structure** to be applied for various types of industrial enterprises, but it is quite clear today that this is **impossible***. Until the very end of the 20th century this was a very significant manner of setting-up an

2 *He led the Israelites from slavery in Egypt back to the Promised Land around 1300 B.C. This event is described in the second book of the Bible containing an account of the Exodus – The Road to Sinai 18:17-23*

organization and there are still many experts who are firm believers in this theory.

Organizational structures that are studied and lectured at various universities and especially at the faculties of organizational sciences, are the following:

- Line (hierarchical) organizational structure
- Line-Staff
- Functional
- Matrix
- Project
- Divisional
- Ad hoc
- Likert's organization of linking pins
- Mintzberg's organizational structures (Mintzberg, 1989)

Likert's, organizational structure, presented in Figure 1, is very interesting for our studying purposes (Vila, 1994, p. 196ff). It deals with structure in a specific manner, as it understands an *organization as a structure of groups* within which the head of the group represents a linking pin with the higher groups in the hierarchy. He or she belongs to his or her own group, as well as to the higher group, and an important part of that person's function is *to link the groups vertically and horizontally.* Likert was most certainly aware of the problem and the difficulties with communication and co-operation, which to a large extent exist within all known organizational structures.

The system 4, that he developed later on, is certainly very interesting. It is connected to the illustrated organizational structure and he establishes the following 4 management systems:

1. System 1 is distinctly autocratic and there is no trust in subordinates
2. System 2 is less autocratic with a low level of confidence in people
3. System 3 is not yet based on complete trust, but confidence is already at a high level
4. System 4 is a very democratic one, demonstrating complete confidence among the management and the subordinates, and we could even say that there is a certain degree of their participation in decision-making, with the accent being put on responsibility and self-control.

Likert's structure is based on his System 4.

According to the systems stated above, Likert has observed

> ***A certain organizational gap between various divisions and services and a low level of mutual co-operation and communication, which should be prevented by his type of organization.***

These observations are all of essential value for our further deliberations.

Figure 1: Likert's organizational structure of linking pins

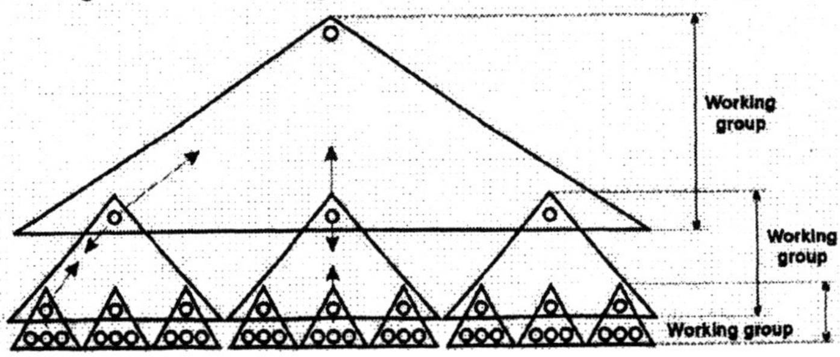

2.4 Choice of Structures in Practice

The presented list of organizational structures failed to mention the one among the organizational structures which is most frequently applied, especially in industrial practice, which means that we usually apply

a functional – linear organizational structure

without specifically mentioning it.

When functions of an enterprise are defined, they become a company's divisions, basic units of an organization, which are still vertically divided into departments and services or into industrial plants, workshops, teams of workers and – finally, there are individual workers.

These functions-divisions are headed by professionals familiar with the method of work within a particular function. They have to choose their collaborators, define the divisions and subdivisions, and thus the organization of such an organizational unit will function vertically, following the principle of linear hierarchical organization. However, this is not the rigid organization that existed within the first half of the 20th century, but it remains a hierarchy in which the heads of higher divisions maintain higher powers, which are used as much as circumstances of a particular case permit it. This is where misunderstandings occur and they are further transferred to the lower levels of the organization, sometimes reaching into individual functions.[3]

All this is due to a lack of knowledge of the problems that other functions and their departments are faced with, their methods of work, their tasks, priorities, problems and difficulties. Our own practice, as well as the practices of the most developed industrial states, such as the USA, has demonstrated that there is often a huge gap existing between functions, divisions and services. It is an interfunctional gap. There is a syndrome of "Us" and "Them"[4], whereby "Us" refers to our function or division, or "Us" experts of a particular profession, which further accentuates the interfunctional and intersectional gap.[5]

Nevertheless, it is clear to everyone that they have to act together in order to produce products and sell them at the market, that the quality and the price have to be acceptable and at the same time they have to have one common and substantial goal of every enterprise, which is its effectiveness and efficiency. There are various opinions as to how this could be achieved. Some of the functions – divisions believe that they hold the key to the solution of this demanding task, indicating that their solutions would have to be adopted by others, and thus they consider themselves the most important part of the company. This is especially true of the four essential functions of an industrial enterprise: marketing, sales, procurement and production.

This fact is caused by

---

3 *This may occur among development and production engineers who might consider certain development demands to be too pretentious, complicated and useless.*

4 *A manager of an important American company stated that, in their mutual relationships, his function managers behave like enemies.*

5 *This deficiency in organization is best solved in Japan, where young professionals are rotated throughout the company for quite a while – five years or even longer - and they do not expect to get their final positions any sooner. That is how they learn about the problems of all the functions and services in their company.*

- The growth of an enterprise. As long as enterprises remain small, such problems are almost non-existent, but as the company grows, so does the number of employees within specific functions and the experts heading the functions keep studying and introducing new and better work methods within a particular function and they are often successful in doing so. But, some of the goals of particular functions are in opposition to the goals of other functions, for example: the goal to sell as much as possible within the shortest possible period of time can lead to total disturbance of the time scheduling in the production department. As all the other functions are behaving in the same manner, *it might lead to an increasing lack of knowledge and understanding of other horizontal parts of the organization.* It thus becomes obvious ***that there are vertical and horizontal barriers (boundaries, frontiers) within an organization*** which block its successful functioning and the question arises of how to overcome these barriers. Figuratively speaking, we could say that particular functions – divisions keep locking themselves within their own courtyards.
- Lack of interdisciplinary education in the sphere of organization and management where - in addition to the basic subjects of particular professions, which are interesting for the economy (and are usually part of the curricula of faculties of technical sciences and economics), sciences dealing with some other significant spheres should also be read, such as: common technical, economic, sociological and organizational sciences, which should result in better understanding among the various professions coexisting in every organization.

3. Relationship between Practice and Theoretical Premises of a Scientific Organization

Basically speaking, the attitude of the economy to the aforementioned theories, schools, methods and principles of a scientific organization could be described as a significant lack of interest, or a deeply set-in belief, that all of them are highly unpractical and useless in reality.

In order to bring science closer to practice, organizational scientists have, since World War II, developed over 50 various methods and techniques intended to increase effectiveness of organizations in specific fields of activities, among which: goal-oriented management, network planning, decision-making tree, operational research, value analysis, excellency-driven enterprise, just in time delivery, team work, kanban, quality circles, total quality etc. The list is extensive. Some authors write ironically that there are actual pilgrimages to seminars held by various management gurus, while some others state that we have reached the phase of MBMA – management by magazine articles method.

In spite of all the theories, methods and techniques developed by contemporary organizational sciences, we are witness to the fact that enterprises are not often capable of effective reorganization. Some outstanding ideas fall in ruins in the very beginning, implementation of some ideas is actually started and soon becomes victim of corrections that everybody likes to introduce, or the initial enthusiasm quickly deflates and some of the ideas degenerate in time, while others are never taken seriously or even understood.

There is also a certain gap between university and practice. It is frequently said that curricula of universities should be brought closer to practice, which resulted in the creation of new 3-year curricula intended to produce engineers for practice, in addition to the existing 4-year curricula. Therefore, new colleges are being established with their own hierarchy, administration and lecturers taken from the original faculties. The question arises as to what might be the difference in lectures held in a 3-year machine faculty university programme and a 4-year university programme specializing, for example, in internal combustion engines at both institutions. In some private discussions, the responsible persons admit that no such difference exists. Upon introduction of the Bologna Declaration on the European Space for Higher Education, special attention should be given to synthetization of organization in practice and within itself, as well as the synthesis between theoretical education and practice.

4. Practical Functioning of an Organization

4.1 Business Processes

During the past twenty years, it has been noticed that many organizational levels tend to hinder effective functioning of an organization. There is a large number of middle managers, while transfer of information is hindered and time consuming. Delays in decision-making as well as in adoption of decisions coming from higher hierarchy levels resulted in a sudden decrease of the number of levels in practice without any influence of new scientific theories. This was also assisted by information technology, which successfully replaced the work of many middle managers. On the other hand, the already mentioned interfunctional gap also functions as an impediment to the horizontal functioning of an organization.

It had not been noticed until recently that the basic functioning of an organization is horizontal, sequential, consisting of a number of tasks to be performed by various individuals and/or groups working in various divisions dispersed through various functions. These are the precisely defined chains of activities that are being performed within every hierarchic organization without even being noticed or given special attention as a whole. THEY ARE BUSINESS PROCESSES. In fact, it has not been noticed that an organizational structure in no way defines the practical functioning of an organization and that it only represents its static part.

It is interesting to note that, regarding the question of functional organization in relation to process organization, an equivalent is to be found in medicine, where the same relationship exists between anatomy and physiology6. According to the definitions listed under footnote 7, it is quite clear that anatomy as such does not explain the functioning of organs, nor does it explain their mutual relationships within the functioning of the human body as a whole. This is an exclusive task of physiology, which studies processes in human and animal bodies.

On the basis of the above stated, we can conclude that it is necessary to develop certain new theories on design of organizations, as well as some new structures. Basically, we are dealing with a horizontal process organization, without any barriers or boundaries that exist between functions, divisions and services. This was introduced with the ideas of Hammer and Champy, who maintain that an organization (Hammer, Chapy, 1993):

> Has to be changed ***thoroughly, radically and dramatically,***
> if we are to progress in critical spheres of activities,
> such as: expenses, quality, services and swiftness.

---

6 ***Anatomy*** *- the science dealing with the structure of animals and plants.*
Physiology *- the branch of biology dealing with the functions and activities of living organisms and their parts, including all physical and chemical processes.*

According to the authors of the a.m. book, this type of reorganization is called Business Process Reengineering (BPR) and it is the most frequently applied one. There is a very well-known translation of this expression into the Slovene language: **»Radikalna prenova Poslovnih Procesov« (RPP).**

Figure 2 illustrates the basic idea of a transformation of a functional organization within a process (Vila, 2000, p. 154). The process has been defined as:

> **a number of linked activities forming a whole; it starts with an input and results in an output. A process-oriented organization does not recognise borders between functions, departments and services and simply does not acknowledge them. The process itself is the basis of the new organization.**
>
> **This is a transfunctional organization**

In certain concrete cases, it is possible to form complete processes, which has already occurred in practice. For example: in specific cases of industrial production, it has been known that there are certain organized wholesome processes extending from placement of an order up to delivery, with all the necessary activities involved in the process, with their own management, complete staff and all the necessary ancillary means for the production and finalization of a given output.

This is the topmost form of process organization, which can also take some other forms of »un-wholesome« organizational processes (Vila, 1998).

In most of the cases, it will not be possible to set up such an organization of wholesome processes, but even then we would like to organize at least a hybrid of a process organization in order to avoid problems that have been established in hierarchic organizations; our aim is to create an organization without boundaries and barriers even in cases where a certain unavoidable form of functions still remains.

Figure 2: Illustration of the transformation of a functional organizational structure into a process one

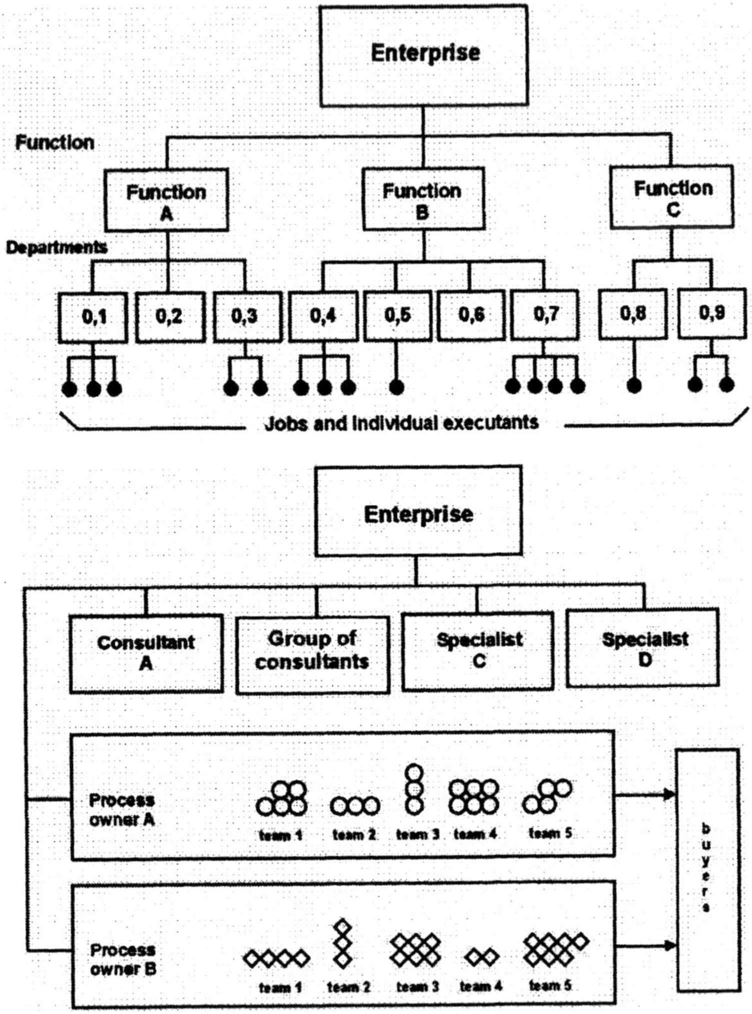

Disregarding the organizational structure, **team work** has recently become the success-story of a scientific organization. There is a lot of literature dealing with it, hundreds and thousands of books, articles, case studies, and reasons for failure analyses etc. The books advise that multifunctional and therefore multidisciplinary teams be organized, as they would be able to absorb the power of functions and their discrepancies. One such option is presented in Figure 3, where some of the previously main functions, as well as divisions of certain functions, have been set into a sequence following the logical succession of their tasks, with built-in ad hoc or permanent teams. In this way, certain process organization, as well as team work could be achieved.

Figure 3: Variation of a process organization of functions

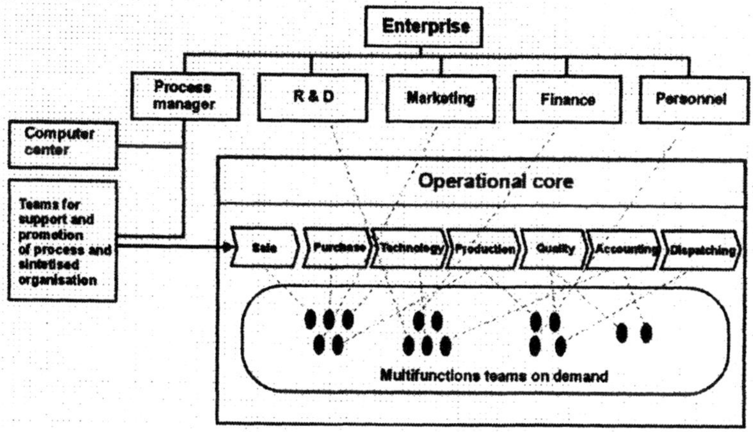

The substance of this organization lies in the fact that previous functions have been put in a chain, one after the other. These are previous functions which co-operate at an operational level, therefore their common name is an OPERATIONAL CORE.

What will remain on the top and directly under the competency of the executive manager remains a question to be answered in each specific case separately. These are all important functions which are not in charge of operational tasks, as they are dealing with long-term goals. Among them we can place various headquarters, consultants etc.

It is quite insane that a larger number of varieties of such an organizational structure may exist and certain elements of this idea can be found in Henry Mintzberg's work (Mintzberg: 1983). What specific organizational structure would be accepted for such an organization depends on various factors influencing particular situations. Therefore, it is good to consider that, in such an organization, certain wholesome sub-processes might exist that would play an important role in the whole functioning of the organization.

Within the operational core, a number of teams could exist and they would be formed according to actual needs, but some of them could also be of permanent nature. The permanent teams would have an opportunity to meet more frequently and in the same composition, which would most certainly increase the cohesion among experts, and result in better co-operation.

It should be pointed out that the importance of particular units within an organizational structure, shown in Figure 3, would not be reduced when compared to the classical hierarchy, where these units were representing functions at a higher level of organization. The fact is that the notion of importance, significance or value has to be changed within this structure and moved away from the hierarchy. A new philosophy of significance and importance has to be defined and spread throughout the organization.

But, academic deliberations and theories also have to submit to it!

4.2 Paradox of Process

By reengineering business processes, important rationalization of the process itself can be achieved, such as speeding up the flow, cutting short the delays between particular activities and work tasks, achieving more logical re-grouping of work posts, reducing the number of work posts etc. But, it would be quite unreasonable to believe that better efficiency and effectiveness of general business operations would be guaranteed just by reengineering business processes. The huge problem is that many people are of that opinion, but it is a serious delusion. Many among the improved processes have not brought any improvement into general business operations, nor have they increased the profit. For quite a while, the literature had been acknowledging the results of substantial investments into the reengineering of entire organizations in the USA, but tens of billions of US$ were invested and the resulting reorganizations were considered unsuccessful. The question arises: how is this possible?

Obviously, the reengineering of business processes was not followed by other changes in business operations, which, even prior to the reengineering, had hindered the efficiency. Unfortunately, there is a long list of possible reasons: the image of the company is dwindling, the quality does not reach the international level, too-slow responding to customers' demands, poor after-sales services, new products seldom appear on the market, improvements of existing products are not frequent enough, customers' satisfaction is very poor, staff structure is weak, various regulations in force within an organization are not complying with international standards, information support to the organization is weak and not co-ordinated with the newly formed processes, the top management of the company does not trust the methods of organizational reengineering, the management is not familiar with the main processes of the company, relationships within the company are poor, supporting processes are never considered, insufficient support to staff education and rewarding of successful employees etc.

Everyone could add a lot to the above list. But how to deal with it all?

First – The basic issue is that the reengineering of business process should be started at the top management level, because they have to offer the project the highest possible support. Throughout the implementation of the business processes reengineering project, the top management has to actively monitor the evolution of the situation and the progress of the project. Many a reorganization has failed because top managements were convinced that this was the task for the lower levels of organization and selected consultants. Following the example of uninterested top management, the lower levels considered that no substantial engagement was required in the matter. It is quite clear that, in addition to a top management team, there should also be a team (or even teams) of experts involved, as they would professionally plan and manage the whole project (Mintzberg, 1983, Chapter 3.3.6).

Second – It is wrong to consider reengineering of business processes only in view of rationalization of a particular process. An organization has many facets (aspects) that have to be considered simultaneously.

- Eventual changes of processes have to be followed by adapting the organizational structure, including all the requirements that were mentioned in previous sections.
- People who are working within the renewed processes have to be adequately qualified and at the right work posts (playing their proper

roles!). It is very important that the competences granted to people who implement such processes correspond to necessary knowledge, skills and abilities that are essential to the process. That is why systemization has to be regulated and the staffing aspect of an organization has to be re-thought.

- Systemic and other regulations that are usually linked to quality management within a business system have to respond to actual requirements of the processes. The standards involved have to be adapted to achieving efficiency and effectiveness instead of reaching imaginary bureaucratic standards that are often nothing but excuses for employing more staff for working on tasks which bring no added value or for hiring new consultants.
- Information support has to be adapted to actual requirements of the processes. Specific segments have to be unified and not just connected subsequently. It is important to achieve a high enough flexibility of information support, such as promised by the state-of-the-art tools of Workflow and IT.
- The environmental aspect also has to be considered, as it has always been a limiting factor of business system development. But, at the same time, it also offers us an opportunity to implement better organization in order to satisfy the requirements of ever stricter laws and regulations in this field, thus acquiring additional competitive advantages.
- Safety at work and health protection are also aspects to be considered when renewing a company. They too can be a kind of a limiting factor, but also a tool for improving satisfaction of employees, when this aspect of organization is adequately set up.
- The legal aspect of organization also has to be considered. Work legislation regulates relationships among employees and the company (as well as reward systems) and the company's relationships with other legal entities. Nobody can succeed in the modern business world without properly set up regulations, which also contribute to lowering not only the risk of legal actions against the company but other risks as well.
- An adequately set up change management system is probably the most important for a company. It is probably the hardest challenge of organizers nowadays. A relatively high formalization of the a.m. aspects of organization on one side, and the need for frequent and immediate adapting to the needs and demands coming from the environment on the other, are two mutually exclusive requirements, unless a company has established adequate flexibility mechanisms in order to adapt all the organization's aspects to the ever changing

processes. Only recently have experts and managers discovered that a common and manageable business model is also required for that purpose and it can only be managed on a long-term basis by an adequate business repository and a large enough critical mass of internal and external users (Vila, 1994, p. 196f).

Third - There are many principles, theories, schools, methods and techniques. Especially interesting are some of the new ideas in the field of organizational sciences that have proved to be very useful and practical and that have been tested in some very large American and European companies, such as:

- Learning organization, from which the need for
- Continuous training of all the company's staff arises
- On the basis of which the company acquires the so-called knowledge workers at all levels – up to the task executants
- Joint efforts of all the company's employees towards complete customers' satisfaction is achieved by active involvement of
- All the employees in keeping the existing customers and
- Striving to attract new ones
- While being flexible in all business fields
- Expecting the unexpected at all times
- An organization based on team work
- Can ensure effectiveness of varied relationships with customers, suppliers, legislators, financial institutions and many other contemporary institutions in the society
- And many similar statements remain to be added.

These ideas have to be built into a process organization, but also into any other existing organizational structure.

Fourth – Monitoring of processes has to be introduced. »Key process indicators« (the so-called KPIs) have to be established as well. Special attention has to be given to financial indicators. In the event that a process has negative financial impacts, the whole organization or reorganization becomes senseless.

4.3 And Where Am I in All This?

When observing a wholesome process-based organization it becomes obvious that advancing through hierarchy is quite impossible, as there is no such thing as a hierarchy and Figure 3 shows that it is minimalized and exists only within the operational core.

So what happens with my salary and its increasing with the years of service? New organizational theories and methods are expected to answer such questions as well. Some new theories, methods and techniques have been invented and are still being born, such as: learning organization with additional professional training, knowledge workers and granting of extended powers based on newly acquired knowledge and skills, rewarding better engagement in promotion of the company, performance in the sphere of customers' satisfaction, excellent implementation of tasks, intense engagement in team work and similar efforts, acceptance and ability to perform increasingly demanding tasks and all that would guarantee better salaries to capable individuals. This is true for the whole operational core, as well as for the maintained functions.

Therefore, promotion would not occur following the hierarchy, but by acquiring a new status based on the abilities and skills of an individual who has acquired them by additional training and experience. Such individuals can be given certain titles to indicate their status, such as: Assistant, Staff Member, Senior Staff Member, Consultant, Senior Consultant, Instructor, Trainer etc. which would also result in financial benefits.

By stating that a hierarchy merely exists within such a structure, we mean that certain hierarchies can still exist, depending on the size of particular units. Within individual units, shown in the organizational structure depicted by Figure 3, certain groups of executants may exist and certain divisions and services as well. Heads of such units would be the leading professionals within the group, having certain competencies to co-ordinate executants and to independently decide upon activities within their sphere of action, resulting in higher income. In fact, we are talking about a very flexible organization within which formalization should remain at the lowest possible level.

5. Conclusions

The basic idea of this publication is to:

- Put an accent on a process-oriented organization which should be given utmost attention and increase a company's efficiency based on the best possible structuring of business processes
- Point out that an organization has been studied in fragments during the past hundred years, by academic circles, as well as in its practical implementation, which resulted in our losing sight of its wholeness
- Jump across the gap existing between theory and practice
- Give special attention to numerous very important principles and aspects of an effective organization and build them into business process (as described in chapter 4.2)
- Bring the university curricula closer to practical needs.

This in fact means that organization should be studied further from various aspects, aiming towards new knowledge and deeper understanding of any theory, school or method, while searching for new theoretical and practical methods of organization of business systems.

At the Faculty of Organizational Sciences, activities in the sphere of organization synthetizing have been ongoing for quite a while. Within the subject entitled »Process Management« the carrier of which is the author of the present article, we strive to present various facets of an organization as a given whole. Thus, while studying reengineering of organization, based on analyses of processes, we also present some other organizational aspects that we consider essential for the efficiency of a process organization, such as: learning organization, knowledge workers within a process organization, process organization and customers' satisfaction, management and leadership, team work, new organizational structures. In addition to this, we offer an overview of various important aspects of organization, so that our students would understand that, in practice, an organization is subject to many other organizational methods that have already been developed in the most developed states of America and Europe or in Japan (some companies belonging to more developed economies).

Therefore, an opportunity was given to some of our former postgraduate students who had produced outstanding master's theses, to lecture about learning organization and knowledge workers, as well as on process organization and customers' satisfaction, as their expert knowledge of these topics is also based on their own practical experiences. Thus we have partly managed to achieve good co-operation among scientists and practitioners. We intend to continue in this direction and to further widen such co-operation.

In this manner, we shall be able to synthesize organization

- Within academic circles;
- Within companies:
- Between academic circles and practice.

Bibliography and References

Hammer, M., Champy, J. (1993): Reengineering Corporation – A Manifesto for Business Revolution: Harper Business – New York, NY.

Mintzberg, H. (1983): Structure in Fives – Designing Effective Organizations; Prentice Hall Inc.

Mintzberg, H. (1989): Mintzberg on Management - Inside our Strange World of Organization – The Free Press, A Division of Macmillan Inc. New York.

Rozman, R (1999): Teorije organizacije (Theories of Organization – in Slovene), Založba Moderna organizacija, Kranj.

The Random House Webster's Unabridged Dictionary.

Vila, A. (1994): Organizacija in organiziranje (Organization and Organizing, Chapter 14 – in Slovene), Založba Moderna organizacija, Kranj.

Vila, A. (1998): Nova organizacijska revolucija (New Organizational Revolution – in Slovene), Organizacija, Vol.31, No. 6, pp. 319-329.

Vila, A. (2000): Organizacija v postmoderni družbi (Organization in the Post-Modern Society – in Slovene), Založba moderna organizacija pri FOV, 2000.

About the Author

Antun Vila is a professor at the University of Maribor, Faculty of Organizational Sciences, in active retirement. His current activities involve lecturing in 3 postgraduate courses, and his current research activities are in the field of knowledge management.

The Feasibility of Using the Combustible Fraction of Municipal Waste as a Primary Source for Generating Thermal and Electric Energy

Marko Agrež

marko.agrez@tet.si

Drago Vuk

drago.vuk@fov.uni-mb.si

Abstract

Waste is a by-product of human life. We must live with it and, in the event of its inappropriate disposal, we pollute the environment and leave the problem to our descendants. This paper presents one possible efficient waste management solution – the collection, sorting and conversion of waste into useful energy, together with the control of atmospheric emissions and non-combusted products (Agrež, 2006).

Keywords: municipal waste, energy, incineration, environmental protection.

1. The Conversion of Combustible Municipal Waste into Heating and Electrical Energy

An integrated approach to waste management has been designed on the basis of the achievements of industrially developed countries and comprises three hierarchically ranked systems (Vuk, 1997, p. 15):

- reducing the quantity of waste,
- using waste (as a prime energy source),
- depositing unavoidable residue.

All three systems are interlinked into one integrated whole.

1.1 Reducing the Quantity of Waste

This area of waste management aims at the abatement of waste generation. The quantities and environmental impact of waste should be reduced by means of changes in production programmes, changes in material processing, the development of more environmentally-friendly products and technologies and by a more ecologically aware behaviour of consumers.
The following requirements should be met, as far as technically and economically possible (Rules for Waste Management, 1998, 2000, 2001).

- products should be designed, manufactured and used in such a manner that the balance of the materials and substances can be maximally re-used,
- the sale of new products and the collection of used products should be arranged in such a manner that the quantity of waste remaining with the final consumer is as low as possible,
- products should be designed in such a manner that the quantity of waste and hazardous substances remaining after their use should be low as possible,
- products should be used in such a manner that as little waste as possible remains.

Such an approach also requires the development of waste reduction programmes, including:

- pure technologies in manufacturing,
- the ecologically aware behaviour of customers (including rejecting products that cannot be recycled),
- reducing packaging and the introduction of ecological packaging material (packaging material regulations),
- incentives for manufacturers to use less packaging material or to introduce ecological packaging material (tax benefits),
- activities to inform the public of the consequences of inappropriate waste management.

1.2 Using Waste

Prior to any beneficial use, a decision must be made regarding waste material as to whether to focus on material or energy recovery. Any waste recovery or recycling is accompanied by two favourable side effects:

- a reduction in waste management costs,
- a reduction in the quantity of residual waste that needs to be disposed.

The following are the procedures applied for waste recycling or energy recovery from waste:

- primary recycling,
- composting,
- the incineration of waste with energy recovery.

1.2.1 Primary Recycling

Primary recycling actually entails the sorted collection of useful waste and separate collection of special, i.e. hazardous waste (Decree on Management, 2001).

In practice, the term primary recycling covers the sorted collection of paper and glass, as well as of metals and mineral resources, plastic material, textiles, vegetable waste and bulky waste such as old cars, furniture, white goods, etc.

Primary recycling also covers the separate collection of old accumulators, batteries, unusable medicines, waste oils, products with mercury, pressurized containers and other dangerous waste.

Primary recycling is carried out at collection sites with suitable special containers.

Such collection sites are sometimes called **ecology islands**. In Ljubljana, such ecology islands consist of three clearly distinguished coloured containers: a blue one for paper and cardboard, a green one for glass and a yellow one for packaging material made of plastic, and cans. Containers are placed near residential buildings, shopping centres, schools and kindergartens. The placement of such containers in 2002 was the beginning of organized waste management in our capital city.

The placement of containers alone, however, is not the end of the selected waste collection chain of activities. The efficient recovery of municipal waste also requires the selected collection of biological waste (the wet fraction) and other waste (the dry fraction).

1.2.2 The Composting of Waste

The process of composting total quantities of municipal waste has proven to be inappropriate for the following reasons (Operational Program, 2003):

- there exists an imbalance between compost production (ongoing throughout the year) and compost sales (only seasonal),
- non-compostable components (metal, glass, plastic...) are present, which impede production in any compost plant,
- harmful substances in waste material (heavy metals...) are present, which make the sale of such compost more difficult or even impossible.

For these reasons, exclusively the "green" vegetable waste matter without the above-mentioned negatives has been used for composting in industrially developed countries. High-quality compost can be produced from this "biological fraction" of waste. The quantity, that is, the mass of biological waste, is very important in this production – and the results of municipal waste analysis have shown that this fraction makes up 40% of total municipal waste. Such waste sorting has yet another positive effect - the use of separately collected biological waste for composting also results in a higher specific combustion heat of the dry fraction in comparison to unsorted waste.

1.2.3 Waste Incineration with Energy Recovery

The incineration of waste is a technological process in which municipal waste is converted into heating energy. It can then be effectively used for district heating and industrial steam production, or as an energy source for driving a gas turbine and, consequently, as an electricity generator – to produce electricity from waste. The process also generates adverse combustion by-products which are emitted into the atmosphere in gaseous form (CO2, NOx, SO2), water vapour, dust particles and particularly harmful dioxins and furans. In addition to harmful exhaust gases, the combustion process produces "fly ash" and slag (possibly containing heavy metals), which have to be disposed of on properly arranged dumping sites. Regretfully, only some of these pollutants can be reduced (Rules for Waste Incineration, 2000).

- carbon dioxide (CO_2) is a combustion product that cannot be reduced – such can only be compensated for by wood biomass,
- nitrogen oxides (NO_x) can be reduced by installing additional oil burners and gas burners,
- sulphur dioxide (SO_2) can be reduced by installing desulphurization devices (dry or wet procedure),
- the emission of dust particles can be reduced by installing sack (mechanical) or electrostatic filters,
- dioxins and furans must be neutralized by chemical or catalytic processes.

Regulations on emissions from such energy recovery installations are very strict (Decree on Emissions, 2000).

Waste has a certain energy potential bound up both in the mass (m) of the material and in the specific combustion heat (heating value – q_s). Thermal energy (Q), generated by combustion equals (Tuma, Sekavčnik, 2004):

$$\mathbf{Q = m \times q_s}$$

Q – heat (J – joule)
M – mass (kg – kilogram)
q_s – specific combustion heat (MJ/kg) – heat generated by the combustion of 1 kg mass of material)

Caloric value q_s

The lower caloric value of municipal waste, that is, the heat produced by the combustion of 1 kg waste, is a very important physical quantity which defines the energy potential of waste. It changes through the year, depending on the composition and humidity of the waste. The lower caloric value of municipal waste is estimated on the basis of:

- an approximate calculation that takes into consideration the morphological composition of waste,
- an approximate calculation that takes into consideration flammable substances and the humidity of the waste,
- a comparison with previously established and proven data on waste from other comparable towns.

The average lower caloric value is approximately 11 MJ/kg, with variations from 2 to 20 MJ/kg.

The table below lists some sample values derived from a laboratory thermal analysis of various types of waste (The Report on Collected and Disposed Waste, 2001-2003; Vuk et al., 1996):

Table 1: Caloric values of various fractions of waste

Type of waste	Caloric value (MJ/kg)
Synthetic materials, textiles	18 – 20
Paper, cardboard	16
Wood-chips	8 – 16
Dried activated sludge	12
Waste from households	2 – 6

Such a **non-homogenous nature** of various types of waste causes big problems in the energy regulation of combustion chambers. They are resolved by feeding in other primary fuels (wood biomass, gas…), and by mixing municipal waste before it is fed into the furnace. The production process is further affected by the **humidity** of municipal waste. In the supply stage, the humidity of municipal waste is higher in summer and lower in winter with differences of between 10 - 15%. The mean annual humidity of municipal waste is in the range of: $W_m = 30 - 40\%$ (35%).

Another disruptive factor in the process is **non-combustible substances** in the waste. By eliminating non-combustible substances and substances with high water content, the specific combustion heat of the waste is increased, which makes the combustion process more uniform and even.

The following are installations that can be used for the thermal conversion of waste:

- energy installations in which the thermal energy of waste is not recovered (incineration plants);
- energy installations in which the intrinsic energy of waste is used for energy generation:
  - combined waste-fired heat and power plants for the production of heat and electricity;
  - waste-fired thermal power plants for the production of electricity alone;
  - waste-fired heating plans for the production of heat alone.

The incineration of waste has become a well-proven technology and is a waste management procedure increasingly used around the globe.

Figure 1 below shows the transforming process "from waste to energy" (Tuma, Sekavčnik, 2004).

Figure 1: Waste to energy process

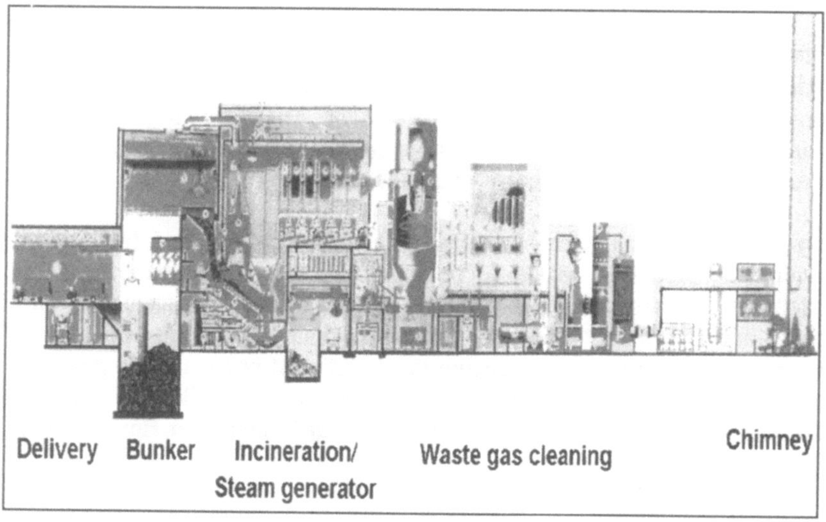

The process is divided into three phases:

- waste conveying to a place,
- burning and producing energy,

- flue gas cleaning and deposite – residue (ash and sludge) treatment.

Waste is mostly burnt by using the following technologies:
- special boilers with water-cooled grids,
- circulating fluidized bed boilers (CFB),
- pyrolysis unit – synthetic gas.

Each technology has some advantages and the final choice of an appropriate technology should be based on the pre-treatment of the waste.

Through the efforts of ecological movements and the raised ecological awareness of the population, public attention has turned to energy installations of all types. Consequently, regulations for the protection of the environment have become more stringent. Due to state-of-the-art incineration technologies, however, even the emission levels permitted under these strict regulations can be met.

2. Conclusion

The raised consciousness of the population, together with the desire for a safe present and friendly future life, has resulted in concern for the protection of the environment. As noted at the start of this paper, waste is here, we have produced it, and it is our responsibility to not "turn a blind eye" to the problem or "sweep it under the carpet".

By becoming a member of international organizations, and by signing ecological protocols (Kyoto), Slovenia has also committed itself to adopting standards and protocols concerning waste management. This paper is therefore just one link in the long chain of activities devoted to waste management – from reducing the quantity of waste and the possible recovery of energy from waste to the treatment of pollutants and the disposal of non-combustible residues (National Program for Environment Protection, 1999).

In a continuation of these efforts, and in the subsequent chapters of Marko Agrež's Master degree thesis, we will further carry out sorting, screening and thermal analyses of a waste sample (a briquette) in the calorimeter of an authorized laboratory. We will further prepare a precise analysis of the possible application of various incineration techniques, and analyze activated sludge from the water treatment plant in Ljubljana. We will also review the purification of gaseous and solid pollutants and combustion products. In all these analyses, the legislation and standards applicable in these fields will be taken into account.

The final aim set within the framework of this Master degree thesis, however, is to contribute to the "thermal solution" of municipal waste in terms of technology, ecology, economy and organization.

Bibliography and References

Agrež, M., Vuk, D. (2006): The Feasibility of Using the Combustible Fraction of Municipal Waste as a Primary Source for Generating Thermal and Electric Energy, Master Degree Thesis, Kranj.

Decree on Emissions of Flue Gases from Waste Incinerators (2000): Official Gazette of the Republic of Slovenia, No. 28/00.

Decree on Management of Separately Collected Wastes by Public Utilities Services (2001): Official Gazette of the Republic of Slovenia, No. 21/01.

National program for Environment Protection (1999): Official Gazette of the Republic of Slovenia, No. 83/99.

Operational Program for Waste Disposal Aiming to Reduce the Disposing of Biologically Disintegrating Waste (2003): Agency for the Environment of the Republic of Slovenia, Ljubljana.

Rules for Waste Disposal (2000): Official Gazette of the Republic of Slovenia, No. 5/00.

Rules for Waste Incineration (2000): Official Gazette of the Republic of Slovenia, No. 32/00.

Rules for Waste Management in the Republic Slovenia (2001): Official Gazette of the Republic of Slovenia, No. 84/98, 45/00, 20/01

The Report on Collected and Disposed Waste in Ljubljana – Barje Landfill in the years of 2001, 2002, 2003 (2001-2003), Public Utility Company, Snaga, Ljubljana,
online: http://holdingljubljana.si/b_snaga_odpadki

Tuma, M., Sekavčnik, M. (2004): Energy Systems, Faculty of Mechanical Engineering, Ljubljana.

Vuk, D. (1997): Ravnanje z odpadki (Waste Management – in Slovene), Publishing House Moderna Organizacija, Kranj.

Vuk, D., Koželj, B., Mele, M. (1996): Projekt poskusa uvedbe ločenega zbiranja komunalnih odpadkov Ljubljana – 2. faza – zaključno poročilo (Project of the Trial Implementation of the Separate Collection of Municipal Waste in Ljubljana – Phase 2 – Final Report in Slovene) University of Maribor, Faculty of Organizational Sciences, Kranj.

About the Authors

Marko Agrež graduated in mechanical engineering at the University of Ljubljana and achieved the degree of Master of Science from the University of Maribor, Faculty of Organizational Sciences. He is the general manager of the Thermal Power Plant Trbovlje (Termoelektrarna Trbovlje). His professional and research work are concerned with the fields of dynamic analysis of machine operation and maintaining concept, engineering of maintenance, energetics and thermal treatment of waste.

Drago Vuk is a professor at the University of Maribor, Faculty of Organizational Sciences. His main research field is environmental aspects of production processes. He is the author of a number of scientific papers which have 12 citations in the journals indexed by the SCI and SSCI bases.

The Using of Drinking Water as an Ecological Factor

Manca Jesenko

manca.jesenko@fov.uni-mb.si

Jože Jesenko

joze.jesenko@fov.uni-mb.si

Abstract

The development of contemporary society and its participation on Earth is a cause of the increase in the use of drinking water as well as the increase in environmental pollution. Thus, the pressures of using natural goods are on a constant increase, while resources and their regeneration are limited. A question that remains open is "how do we conceive this disharmony, in what way do we (contemporary users) respond to it and how could we measure and define the described relation?" In this contribution, we will deal with whether it is possible to isolate those factors that would help to describe the basic characteristics of the contemporary drinking water user (i.e. his or her profile) using the responses gathered from questionnaires that relate to various drinking water issues and the notion of water as a part of our environment. This will be followed by the consideration of the different uses of such information.

We have focused on three views that can link the user's characteristics into a more complex whole, i.e. a selection of his or her general characteristics: his or her perception of the water issue, his or her attitude to the water issue, drinking water and the environment and his or her actual behaviour (i.e. everyday habits in the use of drinking water). The results were interpreted from two aspects. Firstly, we interpreted the observed level of general awareness, i.e. in what ways can it be noticed and to what extent and in what way is the user adjustable to the contemporary environmental and water supply challenges? Secondly, we tried to ascertain how such information can lead to a more wholesome understanding of a concrete time and space- defined community, i.e. the inhabitants of south-west Slovenia. We started from the presumption that, if we know more about the profile of the average drinking water user, it will be easier to socially educate a conscious user.

Keywords: drinking water user profile, analysis of contemporary user characteristics, cluster analysis, water protection consciousness, ecological consciousness, water supply, south-west Slovenia.

1. Introduction

The concept of moderate consumption of water is, in the first place, dependent on the customs and behaviour that are performed by water users. Different, although linked, categories such as the relation between the supplied quantity and the consumed quantity of water, and the consciousness of the user may be involved. However, contemporary studies indicate that end-users perceive water primarily as a commodity, and further, their viewpoints concerning water issues are directly allied with their own, daily way of life (Connolly, Prothero, 2003, p. 280; Spaargaren, 2003, p. 680). Similar outline specifics were obtained through our study of drinking water end-users (see also Veljanovski, Ravbar, 2005, p. 502; Veljanovski, Ravbar, 2004, p. 35ff). Thereafter, we were mainly concerned with finding a way of highlighting certain appointed (and more conceptual) associations concerned with water issues, and simultaneously taking into account end-users' perceptions and behaviour towards water as a commodity in our modern way of life.

In this contribution, we were especially interested as to whether we could extract from the entire list of various variables those that may act as factors which would prove to be of assistance in describing the fundamental characteristics of the contemporary drinking water user in a concrete space and time frame, or whether we could create a typical profile.

We tried to evaluate and establish the inducements that influenced the bearings of an individual's answers (to the questions we posed to our respondents). Our main presumption was that such inducements could take place as the actual reflection of those circumstances that are the most trustworthy indicators of the users' position and behaviour towards drinking water in the household. We tried to understand the users' behaviour as a combination of social, economic, technological, natural and cultural factors in a concrete time and space frame. Our next presumption was that an individual's attitude towards drinking water is defined by social and demographic factors (gender, age, type of household, financial authority of household, education, location and similar factors). That is why we studied the connection between the responses of the individuals and their social and demographic characteristics, and thus the relation of the individual towards water as a commodity, and his or her living conditions.

Our aim therefore, was to form representative groups of contemporary drinking water users that could reflect the typical attitude towards water and the use of it in south-western Slovenia. Such groups reveal more complex relations than those that could be obtained from a simple descriptive statistical analysis. The main potential and aim of forming a representative profile of contemporary drinking water users was therefore:

- Establishing a profile of contemporary drinking water users with regard to the present water supply and other water issues on a more complex level (i.e. linkage of relations). According to our presumption, the profile depends on a person's individual understanding of the outer and inner world, and mirrors their responses.
- On this base, we could draw conclusions regarding his or her possible dimension of individual adaptation. In fact, we wished to discover the flexibility of contemporary users in the event that new technological and environmental challenges would emerge.

We are of the opinion that such research on public opinion (i.e. end-users) could offer a greater contribution to a more integral understanding of the problems related to water in a society defined by concrete space and time. When discussing water problems within the water supply issue, we consider the problems of providing sufficient quantities of suitable water and the protection of water resources. Water resources management has to be a part of the long-term planning and should be discussed on an international level. At the same time, we should not ignore the individual, his or her role in this process and his or her responsibility towards the natural balance. When the conclusions obtained from the analysis of contemporary users have been imbedded into the context of society as a union of users, we will be able to obtain the pattern of social behaviour. This pattern gives us the possibility to presume and co-ordinate the water supply needs of society, while at the same time keeping us prepared to take new measures for (un)expected water, supply challenges. Enhanced knowledge of water users' characteristics may further enable a better social education of a more conscious user.

This task proved to be rather complex, due to the nature of the questions that the users were asked. On the one hand, various clusters of questions allow us to perform more detailed queries and achieve more exact definition of characteristics and character linkage of a certain profile. However, on the other hand, they may increase the relation's complexity and decrease its comprehension. Due to this, we decided to begin with the structuring of characteristic user profiles by taking into account the selected users' perspectives. On such a base, we can draw conclusions about the most asserted linkage of relations for providing completely reliable representatives or determinants reflecting social characteristics, perception, attitude and behaviour for forming a common, representational users' profile.

Firstly, we classified the data by using cluster analysis for categorical data:

- the perception of the respondents in relation to the water issue (what they think of it),
- their attitude towards water problems (how they would actually react),
- their actual behaviour with water (how they actually treat drinking water).

It was believed that these three viewpoints (ranks) could lead towards more reliable conclusions as regards the dominating motives and reactions of the socio-demographic structures in south-west Slovenia. With regard to these three rankings of data classifications, the explanation of user responses, reactions to the global and local social processes, and the manners that are reflected through an individual' daily habits, could turn out to be of greater importance. At times, even the less sharp feature of separation between the perception of the water issue on one side and the attitude towards it on the other confirms the assumption that these three rankings have to be mutually complemented. Therefore, the main output of the results of these three contemporary water user rankings is the answer to the following question: How many different levels of separation can be anticipated from the responses, and in which users viewpoints are these differences the most obvious? Through the entire procedure and the main characteristics of the "isolated user profiles" we were able to depict the main factors that constitute the key characteristics of the obtained profiles and keep it on a statistically significant level. At the same time, we were able to select those questions (variables) that most evidently create the differences between users (i.e. their perceptions, attitudes and behaviour towards water).

Our last step was to form typical profiles of drinking water users, a profile that can be understood as representative groups regarding the particular pattern of people from south-west Slovenia. Four typical (and statistically significant) profiles of contemporary drinking water users in households were obtained. The users can be classified into four groups: "non-constructive critics", "inactive environmentalists", "active environmentalists", and "environmentally non-aware" individuals. The formed aforementioned profiles are connected to several social and demographic factors: age, family status, gender, as well as factors relating to location and type of household. The type of water supply (public, local, own water supply) did not significantly influence these profiles. A more in-depth view of the characteristics of contemporary representative drinking water users and the procedure used for forming the profiles will follow in the next sections.

2. Methodology for Determining the Characteristics of Contemporary Drinking Water Users

We used the cluster analysis method to form the previously described profiles relating to the selected levels of the drinking water user's view (perception, attitude, behaviour). The chosen method enables clustering in such a way that the units within the groups are as similar as possible with regard to the studied characteristics and as different as possible when individual groups are compared.

The selection of variables (questions) used to describe the selected level of the water user's view was predominantly based on the content judgement of the sensibility of the chosen variables. The homogeneity (i.e. the sufficient variability of variables) was decided upon the basis of the previously performed frequency distribution of variables.

Taking into account the nature of the studied variables (the variables are of a nominal and partially ordinal type) and the complexity of the measured occurrences, we can expect a higher level of measurement error. Due to this, it would be wise to presume that the structures obtained through clustering will not be distinctive (certain groups will cover each other). On the basis of this presumption, we have opted for Ward's classification method to form the profiles. This method joins the groups in such a way that it minimizes the sum of squares within the groups (maximizes the homogeneity of the groups). For the measure of variability, we have chosen χ^2–distance (square of the Euclidian distance), taking into account the type of variables (dichotomous, nominal) in the individual clustering.

Ward's method is a hierarchical technique of sorting units into groups, for which the effect of "greed" is typical (units or groups on the lower levels of merging are clustered into groups in a sub-optimal way as regards the higher levels of clustering) – especially in the case of covering groups. In the case of ratio and interval variables this effect can be partially reduced by the K-means method (non-hierarchical clustering methods), while in the concrete case of categorical variables this is not possible (Jesenko, Jesenko, 2007, p. 175).

Apart from the formed profiles related to the selected level of a water user's view, we also wished to come up with a common water user's profile. In forming the common profile, we did not use all of the variables on individual levels, because while forming the profiles we noticed that some variables were poorer at differentiating the typical user profile. Apart from this, the interpretation of the results with a larger number of variables is much more complex. With regard to the selection of appropriate variables for describing the common profile, we have taken into account not only the logic of the selected variables but also the statistical importance of the variables in the differentiation of the profiles on the individual as well as on the common level. At this point, we have used the aid of correspondence analysis.

A relatively complex choice of appropriate variables, which also includes a subjective approach, demands a certain degree of caution when interpreting the results. As regards the reliability of the results that are obtained on the basis of the research, we can conclude on the basis of their logic (content), while the confirmation of the results would demand a new measurement of the studied occurrences.

Apart from this, we also have to take into account the limitation of the research with a concrete time and space frame. The studied part of Slovenia differs slightly from the typical Slovenia, which can also be seen from the socio-demographic structure of the sample. Especially the information as regards the average age within the sample (47 years) shows a great deviation from the average age of the Slovene population (39 years). In relation to this, it is worthwhile pointing out that the mentioned demographic deviation is also a factor of a respondent's comprehension of the studied issue (one of the factors of forming his or her viewpoint). To a great extent, this is linked to the studied occurrence, especially as we can enter the field of "non-typical" social-cultural, political, economic and information-technology environment. When we transfer the research into a field with a different typical environment, we can thus expect a (slight) deviation in the results. Regardless of the fact that we are always limited when gathering data through questionnaires, we believe that large enough samples and properly composed questions offer a sufficient insight into the complex picture of the measured occurrences, or at least into the dominating opinion of the respondents with regard to the studied variables (McGarigal et al., 2000, p. 150).

3. Presentation of User Profiles

3.1 Perception of the Water Issue

The typology of the respondents' perception towards water issues is based on variables determining whether the water resource management in the local area needs to be addressed, the overall quality of the water environment in the surrounding area, their trust in the quality of tap water supplied to their home, adequate information on tap water quality, opinion on tap water quality, opinion on water price and the perception of the respondents regarding the water issue in the near future.

Based upon the analysed characteristics of variables that have been chosen, we identified four significant user groups, regarding their view (standpoint) and perception of the water issue. Typical characteristics and the size of each group can be described as the following:

(i) users that are not aware of the water issue (38 %),
(ii) users that are aware of the water issue, but are not sensitive towards it in their environment or in their home (13 %),
(iii) users that are aware of the water issue; they are sensitive towards it in the environment, but not at home (23 %), and
(iv) users that are aware of the water issue, are sensitive to it in the environment as well as in their household (26 %).

For a better understanding of how each group is structured, a short outline of their characteristics is given below.

The first group (i) is not aware of a water issue. It differs from other groups in the fact that it includes the highest share amongst all groups of respondents (25 %) that are of the opinion that it is not necessary to address the water resources management. At the same time, this group holds the lowest share of those who are of the opinion (3 %) that the quality of water has not deteriorated during the last period, 30 % of them even believe that the water quality has improved. The predominant part (98 %) has confidence in the daily water supply, although it cannot said that they are well informed about its quality. A large share (76 %) also believes that tap water is of good quality (only 2 % are of the opinion that it is of poor quality), and at the same time, they find (69 %) water to be expensive. It can be noticed that 7 % of the respondents from this group believe that we will run out of drinking water during the next 20 years and 61 % of them see this as a possibility (in total 68 % believe in a pessimistic outcome).

For the second group (ii) of respondents, it is significant that the great majority (95 %) is of the opinion that water resources management is necessary, if not today, then certainly in the near future. We can observe that the respondents in this group are much more divided with regard to their perception of the water quality in their milieu. 47 % are of the opinion that the water quality has deteriorated during the last decade, 37 % are of the opinion that it has not changed, while 16 % believe it has improved. The majority (79 %) has confidence in the drinking water supply. Of all the groups, this group has the highest share of those (30 %) who believe that they are well informed about the quality of tap water. Compared to the other groups, this group also contains the highest share of respondents (93 %) that believe their tap water is cheap, while 70 % of them find it to be good quality. This group also leads by the percentage of respondents (21 %) who believe we will not run out of drinking water in the next 20 years, or believe that this is impossible (28 %). In total, 49 % are convinced of an optimistic outcome.

The third group (iii) is well aware of the water issue and they are also sensitive towards this in their environment, although they fail to notice a problem within their household. Similarly to the second group, this one is also well aware of the importance of water management (100 %). We could say that the respondents in this group have noticed that a water issue exists in their milieu, since 91 % are of the opinion that the water quality has deteriorated. In spite of this, 82 % remain confident in the water supply, however, it could not be said that they feel well informed about its quality. Most of the respondents find the tap water, to be good quality (97 %), but expensive (67 %) or at least moderately priced (33 %). This group includes the largest share of respondents who believe that the water resources will run dry during the next 20 years (15 %) and a further 55 % are of the opinion that this is a possibility (70 % believe in a pessimistic outcome).

For the fourth group (iv), it might be said that they are well aware of the water issue in their environment, as well as in their households. The majority (98 %) believe that water management is an urgent matter or will prove to be in the near future. It is interesting that all of them are of the opinion that the water quality has deteriorated during the last period and the lowest share here of them have confidence in the water supply (69 %). This group also heads the rankings for the share of respondents who feel that they are inadequately informed (38 %) or even uninformed (39 %) about the quality of drinking water. The group also has the highest share of completely dissatisfied users with the quality of tap water. We can find the largest share of those who think that their tap water is of poor quality (29 %) or at least not of good quality (71 %), while at the same time holding the opinion that it is expensive (77 %). 6 % of the respondents from this group believe that water resources will run short during the next 20 years, while 69 % consider this to be a possibility (in total, 75 % believe in a pessimistic outcome).

The analysis of the socio-demographic structure for each individual group did not reveal any significant differences amongst these four user groups. From the viewpoint of regional representation, it seems that the inhabitants from the Slovene coast and the Pivka basin are those most aware of the water issues (groups iii and iv). They are followed by the inhabitants from the Vipava valley (groups ii and iii), and inhabitants from the Brkini hills and the River Reka area. It is interesting that the inhabitants from the Kras region are the most non-homogeneously divided, for they have the largest share of respondents who are not sensitive towards water issues (group i), while at the same time a large share consider themselves sensitive to water use in the environment as well as at home, (see Table 1).

3.2 Attitude towards Water Issues

The attitude towards water issues was determined through questions that dealt with the respondents´ willingness to be involved in discussions on the present and future management of water resources in the nearby environment and on their willingness to pay an additional charge within the household water bill, which would directly support the protection of water in the environment. It was also determined on the basis of their willingness to accept water of lower quality for their toilets with no effect on the normal household water bills, but with the knowledge that this would help the environment, and their willingness to install a grey water system which would be used to flush their toilets and water the garden.

Based upon the chosen variables regarding the water issue attitude, we found two characteristic groups of an approximately similar size. It might be said, that:

(i) environmentally conscious users form the first group (49 %), and the second group is characterized by

(ii) the rest of the users (51 %).

For the first group (environmentally conscious or sensitive), it is significant that over 50 % of the respondents asked in the poll would be prepared to co-operate in a discussion dealing with the management of water resources, while some of them (7 %) are already involved in this process. 88 % of the respondents in this group are even willing to pay a higher price for water, if this would help to improve the water conditions in nature. At the same time, all respondents classified into this group are (in principle) prepared to use water of a lower quality for flushing their toilets, and 82 % would be willing to install a grey water device and use it in their toilets and for watering their gardens.

In the second group (others), there are only 10 % who are willing to co-operate in a public discussion that would deal with the management of water resources and, currently, nobody is involved in this process. Only 47 % would be willing to pay more for water, if this would improve the water conditions in the environment. Similarly, a rather small share (48 %) of these users would accept water of lower quality to be used for flushing toilets and only 21 % would be willing to install and use a grey water device.

The demography of the groups reveals that, among the environmentally concerned, there is a slightly higher share of younger respondents (18–24 years) than one would expect and a slightly under-represented share of the oldest population (over 64), when compared to the average age classes.

3.3 Actual Behaviour and Treatment of Water

The actual behaviour and treatment of water was determined through questions on water consumption within the household, the willingness to switch on the largest water consumers during cheap intervals if a pricing system based on peak use were to be introduced, the willingness to take measures in order to reduce the consumption, and on the actual behaviour when running the largest water consumers.

Based upon the chosen variables regarding the actual behaviour of the respondents towards water, we identified two equally represented groups of respondents. We denoted them:
(i) economical users (49 %), and
(ii) others (51 %).

For the "economical users" group, it is significant that all of the respondents would be prepared to use cheap time intervals for substantial water consumers if this would reduce their expenses by 25 %. Compared to the other group, a noticeably higher share (38 % vs. 22 %) also claimed that they would reduce their water consumption if the price were to rise by 25 %. 99 % stated that they always took care that the dishwasher or the washing machine was fully loaded before they started using it.

On the other hand, the group "others" is significant due to the fact that over 50 % of the respondents would not be willing to use large water consumers in cheap time intervals, while 42 % are not convinced. 78 % of the respondents in this group claimed that their consumption would not be any lower if the price of water rose. There is also a smaller share of respondents who make sure that their dishwashers or washing machines are full before they start using them. However, the variable of the opinion how much water is used in their home did not play a significant role in classifying users in either of these two groups.

According to the socio-demographic characteristics, there is a small difference only in the age structure. Economically behaving respondents include a slightly higher share of people aged between 46 and 64 years, and only a small share of people aged between 25 and 44. This might indicate a pattern of younger families and a part of the most active inhabitants, who find it the hardest to keep up a principle stand for economic reasons.

Table 1: The relations of regional distribution of the inhabitants as regards the groups of selected levels of user views (attitude, behaviour, perception) towards the water issue

REGION	ATTITUDE			BEHAVIOUR			PERCEPTION
	environmentally conscious (1)		others (2)	Economical (1)		others (2)	(1) Not aware of the water issue. (WI) (2) Aware of the WI, are not sensitive towards it environment nor in their home. (3) Aware of the WI; they are sensitive towards in the environment, but not at home. (4) Aware of the WI, are sensitive towards in the environment as well as in their household.
Slovene coast	1	~	2	1	~	2	Aware of the WI, sensitive towards it in the environment and in their household (3,4,2,1).
Vipava valley	1	>>	2	1	>>	2	Aware of the WI, although not sensitive towards it (2,3,1,4).
Kras plateau	1	<	2	1	<	2	Not sensitive towards the WI or more sensitive towards at home than in the environment (1,4,2,3).
Pivka basin	1	<<	2	1	<<	2	Sensitive towards it in the environment and in household (4,3,1,2).
Reka/ Brkini and river Reka	1	<	2	1	~	2	Not sensitive towards the WI; more aware of it in the environment then at home.

We have noticed interesting relations in the regional distribution of respondents within the three typologies and their groups. A summary of these is given in Table 1.

The results of forming profiles according to the selected levels of water users´ views (perception, attitude, behaviour) point towards the fact that we can differentiate between those users who try to save while using water and those who do not (however, at this stage, we cannot assume the right reasons for this) and, further, those who are, on an environmentally friendly principle, prepared to act and those who are most likely to remain cold towards the issue. The greatest number of layers amongst the respondents can be noticed in their opinion and understanding of the water issue. This can range anywhere from no worries at all, to worries shown only in relation to the natural environment or the water supply to their households, or both. With the selection of those variables that most efficiently differentiate the described characteristics of the users, we have formed the common joint profile.

3.4 Joint Typology of Typical Drinking Water Users

Based upon the context/content and classifying power of the variables from all three previous sections (perception, attitude and behaviour), we have chosen a few, yet highly proving, variables to create a final joint typology of respondents. They deal with the following issues: opinion on the overall change in the quality of the water environment in the surrounding area, opinion on being adequately informed about the quality of tap water supplied to homes, opinion on the quality of tap water, willingness to be actively involved in the discussions on the present and future management of water resources, willingness to pay an additional charge in the household water bill, which would directly improve the water conditions in the environment, willingness to accept lower quality of water for flushing toilets with no effect on household water bills, but the knowledge that it would help the environment, willingness to install a grey water system in the house for toilets and watering the garden, willingness to switch on the largest water consumers during cheap intervals if a pricing system based on peak use were to be introduced (i.e. to consider using smaller amounts of water during peak hours), and willingness to take measures to reduce the consumption in the event that the water prices would increase.

We identified four groups of respondents through the classification procedure. We denoted them as:

(i) non-constructive critic users (13 %),

(ii) environmentally non-concerned users (33 %),

(iii) passive environmentally concerned users (30 %) and
(iv) active environmentally concerned users (24 %).

For the group (i) of "non-constructive critic users", it is significant that it has the highest share of respondents (72 %) who are of the opinion that the quality of water in their surroundings has deteriorated. This group also has the largest share of those who believe that the information they receive about the quality of water supplied to their households is poor (47 %) or even non-existent (42 %). At the same time, they have the lowest share of those (26 %), who believe that their tap water is of good quality. This group holds the absolutely highest share (56 %) of those who are prepared to co-operate in public discussions dealing with the management of water resources, while not a single respondent is willing to pay more for the water in his or her household, even if this would help to protect the water in its natural environment. The majority would find it acceptable to receive poorer quality water for flushing their toilets (86 %), but only half of them (49 %) would be willing to accept grey water for flushing their toilets and using it in their garden, while the rest are opposed to this idea. A fair share (61 %) would switch on the larger water consumers during a cheap time interval, which is similar to other groups, but most of them (77 %) stated that they would not reduce water consumption in the event of a hypothetical price rise.

In the "environmentally non-concerned" group (ii), 50 % of the respondents believe that the quality of water in their environment has deteriorated, 38 % are of the opinion that it has not changed, while 12 % think the water in their environment has improved. Similarly, this group is relatively disperse as regards the information on water quality, for half of them are of the opinion that they are insufficiently informed (not informed at all or badly informed). This group is also rather content with the quality of their drinking water, since most of them (74 %) are of the opinion that their tap water is of good quality (2nd place amongst all groups) and only 4 % considered it to be of a poor quality. 73 % of the respondents are not interested in public discussions dealing with the management of water resources, however 67 % would be willing to pay more for their water, if this would help to improve the water condition in the natural environment. The significance of this group lies in their carelessness in their answers to the following two issues. Only 50% would accept low quality water for flushing their toilets and as much as 89 % would not be prepared to install the grey water system and use it in their toilets and gardens. 66 % would switch on the larger water consumers during cheap time intervals (which placed them 2nd amongst all groups), but on the other hand, there is also a relatively high share of those who would not. Similarly, in the event of a price increase, 65 % would not take measures to use less water, and again, there is a non-negligible share of those (when compared to other groups) who would be triggered towards a more economic use of water when faced with such a financial threat.

In the "passive environmentally concerned" group (iii) 60 % believe (2nd place amongst all groups), that the quality of the water in their environment has deteriorated (35 % are of the opinion that it stayed the same). It should also be said that they took second place amongst the groups regarding their content with the received information on the quality of their tap water. This group is also not satisfied with the quality of their tap water, since only 55 % of the respondents find it to be of a good quality. 37 % of the respondents from this group are willing to co-operate in public discussions, yet this places them 2nd amongst all groups with regard to this point. This group has the highest share and an outstanding majority (94 %) of those who claim that they would be prepared to pay more if this would help to protect the water in its natural environment. A high share (81 %) would accept poorer quality water for flushing their toilets (3rd place amongst all groups). A lower share (68 %), but still holding 2nd place amongst all groups, would install the grey water system in their households. In this group we can find the lowest share of respondents (11 %) that would switch on larger water consumers during a cheap interval (distinctly last place among groups). Similarly to other groups, the majority (71 %) would not decrease consumption if the price of water increased; however, we can observe a remarkably indecisive share of respondents who are not convinced that they would be able to reduce their consumption.

In the "active environmentally concerned" group (iv), 51 % of the respondents are of the opinion that the quality of water in their environment has deteriorated, however, 22 % are of the opinion that it has improved. It appears that this group is the best informed as regards the quality of the supplied water, and likewise it has a high share of respondents who are of the opinion that their tap water is of a good quality (77 %). It is noticeable that this group has the lowest share (14 %) of those who are willing to co-operate in public discussions about the management of water resources. However, 70 % would be willing to pay more if this would help to improve the water conditions in the natural environment (2nd amongst all groups). Of all the groups, this group has shown the highest willingness to take measures towards a more economic use of drinking water. As a result,

99 % of them would accept low quality water for flushing their toilets and 90 % would install the grey water system and use it in their toilets and gardens. Furthermore, a convincing 81 % would switch on larger water consumers during cheap time intervals, but they would not use less water, if the price of water were to increase.

According to the socio-demographic characteristics, certain differences are noticeable between the four groups as regards age, gender, location, type of living accommodation and water supply type This analysis was made on the basis of assuming an even or random distribution of respondents in an individual group. Deviations from the average are thus perceived as idiomatic within the socio-demographic structure of the groups.

It can be seen that, in the "non-constructive critic" user group, which is the smallest of them all (13 % of the entire sample), males (63 %, i.e. 17 % above the hypothetical sample on the average - HSA) and middle-aged respondents (2nd and 3rd class; 84 % against 55 % HSA) dominate. No deviation from the sample average is observed in the living accommodation and only a subtle deviation can be noticed in the water supply system (households connected to the public supply system predominate slightly: 4 % above HSA). To a lesser degree (10 % below HSA), the respondents are from the Kras region and, to a greater degree, the respondents are from the Slovene coast (10 % above HSA).

The "environmentally non-concerned" user group, which holds the largest percentage (33 %) of all groups, is not gender influenced, however, it is rather predominated by the oldest people class (4th age class: 10 % above sample average). This group also entails the highest share of households with their own water capturing system and the lowest share of respondents connected to the local supply system. Other factors do not play a distinctive role in this user group. It includes a slightly higher number of respondents (3 %) than expected from the Brkini hills and river Reka valley region, and a slightly lower number then expected (4 %) from the Vipava valley.

The "passive environmentally concerned" user group, which includes 30 % of the entire sample, has the lowest number of males (but still 42 %), although it would be hard to claim that females dominate this group. The two younger age classes are above the sample average (10 % above the sample average). This group is also comprised of smaller households, which are more likely to be houses (82 %) then flats. The water supply system does not affect this user group. More distinctly represented are those from the Kras region (10 % above HSA) and Pivka region (6 % above HSA), while the respondents from the Slovene coast are represented distinctly below average (10 % below HSA).

The "active environmentally concerned" user group, which includes 24 % of the sample size, does not differ greatly in the gender or age classes. However, the respondents that fall into this user group are more likely to live in an apartment (almost 10 % above the sample average: 27 %) than in a house. This user group is also characterized by the highest share of those who have a local water supply system. In view of the regional classification, the deviations are mostly diverse. Significantly under represented are the respondents from the Pivka region (9 % below HSA) and the Kras region (7 % below HSA) while significantly over represented are the respondents from the Vipava valley (10 % above HSA) and the Slovene coast (7 % above HSA).

3.5 Overlapping Between the Selected Views of the User and the Common Profile

As already stated, we have formed the common profile on the basis of the behaviour of the variables, their informational value and their capability for efficient differentiation amongst the users. At this point, we would also like to state how the groups obtained with a chosen view of the user are placed within the groups formed in the common profile.

It is shown that the two groups from the typology of *attitude* are firmly nested in the expected groups from the common typology. Thus, both groups 'passive´ and ´active environmentally conscious users' mainly include those that were placed amongst the 'environmentally sensitive' in the attitude typology, and vice versa. Amongst the 'non-constructive critics', and even more amongst the 'non-environmentalists' the 'others' from the attitude typology prevail. In a similar way, a sensible scheme is also visible at the crossing of the *behaviour* typology and the common profile of users. Amongst the 'active environmentally aware users' the largest share of 'water saving users' can be found, while the 'passive' group hosts the smallest share. In the remaining two groups, i.e. 'non-constructive critics' and 'non-environmentally aware' the relation is less explicit. In general, both groups (water saving and less saving users) are similarly present. Cross-referenced relations between the groups from the typology *perception of the water issue* and the groups from the common typology are less linear. Because the transition between the four groups of perception is softer, a more explicit correlation is not visible. However, the typologies do not encounter direct content opposition.

The described comparison also makes us firmly believe the statement that, with a careful procedure over all available variables, we have managed to choose good and reliable determinants for consideration of a common profile. Of course, the nature of the monitored occurrences is so complex that we cannot explain the entire diversity of the operation and response of the contemporary drinking water users merely with the formation of typical profiles. As we are going to show, some relations are revealed. It is important that we have managed to merge three, in their nature not truly simple, postures of the individual, i.e. perception, attitude and behaviour towards the water issue into a whole that makes sense.

4. Discussion

The procedure of defining the profiles of water users, that we have presented in this contribution, is credible in its methodological frames as well as in the relation to the characteristics of the gathered data. The nature of the gathered data has predicted that there will be certain overlapping amongst the groups, and this took place. However, we have to be aware that this is also a general and non-alienable characteristic of all occurrences. Taking into account the universal caution at the general and special characteristics of the methodology and the content logic of the results, we are of the opinion that the groups can be understood as representative examples of water users in south-west Slovenia. We have ascertained that the formed groups reveal at least *three basic characteristics*, which define the otherwise complex relations and sufficiently single-sidedly point towards the ways they are intertwined within an individual group, while at the same time show the logic of the socio-demographic indicators, which can more typically determine the attitude and actions as regards the water issues. We can summarize these three user's characteristics as follows:

- capability of monitoring and critically observing the conditions in the environment (awareness),
- level and type of willingness to adjust to the contemporary technological and water protection solutions (taking measures), and

- level and type of willingness to change habits in the use of drinking water (behaviour).

We have primarily searched for the profiles of typical groups of contemporary water users in order to ascertain whether such a data analysis is useful for recognising the more complex relations within the concrete spatial and time community. In doing so, we encounter the question of why we should form groups (profiles) like this and what we can gain with such data. It is hard to offer a short answer, for it is a sensitive field, where the reliability of the information gathered through questionnaires and the semantic linking of this data in order to understand the viewpoints and the relations of the individuals are in constant opposition.

The European Union guidelines emphasise that, while searching for the solutions for the water supply in the future, it would be wise to take into account the local solutions, i.e. the local conditions. In this sense, the water end-users' profiles can offer an insight into the users and their values. Thus, we could establish what they are like according to their socio-demographic structure, how they behave, what we can expect from them with regard to the protection or endangerment of their own environment, how adjustable they are and how ready they are to take action to improve the conditions and, finally, how to approach them.

In this discussion, we wish to offer a possible useful value of the profiles on the basis of the expressed socio-demographic factors and those characteristics, which merge the respondents into an individual group. This means that we are going to try to reach a level further into the representative profiles and then interpret them:

- from the aspect of the possible adjustments or flexibility of the contemporary drinking water user, if we confronted him with a new challenge, as well as
- in which field more should be done in the future in order to strengthen the values of a chosen user's profile.

4.1 Typical Groups of Drinking Water Users: Common Characteristics – Level Of Consciousness – Flexibility

Once again, we are going to look at all four groups that represent the typical examples of drinking water users. They should be looked at from the three most recognisable characteristics: what is the level of their awareness, how are they willing to co-operate and under what terms and conditions would they change their habits as regards their use of drinking water – i.e. in what fields and to what extent are the users flexible?

For the first group of respondents (i), it is typical that it is rather homogenous in the fact that they express by far the greatest dissatisfaction with the water conditions (as regards the water conditions in the environment, their level of information about the quality of water and the quality of drinking water in their households) and that they want to actively co-operate in public discussions. However, they are not willing to adopt any measures to change their drinking water consumption. Interesting is also the fact that older men dominate and that the largest relative share is represented by the respondents from the Slovene coast, while the smallest is from the Kras region. Thus, we can say for the so-called **non-constructive critics** group that *their environmental awareness is more a show than reality and that this group is the least flexible towards any adaptations or changes.*

The respondents in the second group (ii) are rather non-homogenous regarding the information at their disposal as well as their observation. However, they are relatively satisfied with the quality of water in their households. This group is the most opposed to the introduction of contemporary use of poorer water in their households and in this respect shows the greatest unawareness of the water issue and the environment in general. They would change their behaviour with drinking water at home, but mainly due to financial pressures. This group has the most respondents from the Brkini hills and the river Reka valley and Pivka region, while the least come from the Vipava valley. We could not state that it is in the majority defined by those who are not aware of the water issue, however, we can conclude from the results that they would not be prepared to actively approach the problem. Due to the *poor and ecologically non-principled response to the introduction of changes to their homes,* we consider them to be **environmentally non-aware users**, who are *sensitive and will adopt changes only if those are related to the increase of costs.*

The third group (iii) has rather critical views on the condition of the water in the environment and they are also quite dissatisfied with the information at their disposal and the quality of drinking water in their households. They are relatively prepared to co-operate in public discussions and they would by all means financially support the effort for improving the water conditions. They would not mind using poorer quality water in their homes, but they would not be prepared to reduce the use of drinking water in their homes due to financial or other pressures. This group includes a large share of respondents from the Pivka region and a very small share of respondents from the Slovene coast. The female part of the population has a larger share in this group than the male or younger part of the population. For this group, it is thus typical that they are aware of water issues and they would be willing to help in order to protect the environment. However, they are honest about the fact that they would find it hard to change their habits in the use of drinking water in their homes. This is the group of the so-called **passive environmentally aware users**, who are, on the *principle level, satisfied with the level of information at their disposal as well as flexible towards the introduction of technological novelties*. However, they are honest enough to realise that *in order to implement the demanded adjustments in their actual habits of water consumption, they would need to be encouraged by some other incentives (e.g. financial) and not only by their conviction and their will.*

The fourth group (iv) includes respondents who notice the positive as well as negative differences in the environment, are of the opinion that they are well informed about the quality of drinking water and also think that tap water is of good quality. They do not think that they would improve the situation by participating in public discussions. However, they are willing to contribute their share in any other way (financial support, measures for the introduction of saving technologies and willingness to act more carefully with water). This group includes a large share of respondents from the Vipava valley and the Slovene coastal, while the smallest share of respondents comes from the Pivka region. Because the group shows a *fair level of self-initiative and environmental awareness*, the so-called **active environmentally aware users** are most probably the *most flexible group towards numerous contemporary water supply challenges and solutions.*

4.2 Differences between the Profiles of Water Users between the Regions in the Light Of Turning Them into More Environmentally Aware Users

If we trust the characteristics of the profiles and accept them as the main advantages and/or disadvantages of the contemporary drinking water users, we recognise them as a sample of social behaviour. As we have mentioned already in the introduction, we could use this in order to foresee a long-term harmonization of the water supply demands brought forth by the society and the preparation of measures for an appropriate response to the (un)expected water supply challenges. In doing so, we start from the presupposition that, if we had a better insight into the drinking water user, it would be easier to plan the social education of a conscious user. It is not our intention to offer proposals for concrete actions, but after a comparison (and in accordance with the other contributions of the section on contemporary water supply),we could have a look in which regions, something should be done in order to improve and direct the inhabitants towards changing into more environmentally conscious users and in what regions we can be satisfied with the attitude of the respondents.

The regional structure of representation in individual groups (i.e. shares within individual groups) shows that the situation is the best in the *Vipava valley*. Of all regions, this was the one that had the largest share of respondents belonging to the 'active environmentally aware user' and the lowest share of 'environmentally non-aware users'. They are followed by the respondents from the *Slovene coast,* who also have a large share of 'active environmentally aware users'. From the data that shows that the largest share of 'non-constructive critics' comes from this region, it can also be noticed that they are deeply involved in the water issue. Typical for this region, which, amongst other things, also has the lowest share of 'passive environmentally aware users', is that it tries to solve the problems in one way or another, but most certainly in an active way.

We can be less satisfied with the conditions in the *Kras region*. Most respondents from the *Kras region* could be found in the 'passive environmentally aware users' and the least amongst the 'non-constructive critics'. The results show that, a certain awareness is present. However, it can be seen that this region has the most passive approach to solving water supply issues out of all regions. The latter is especially worrying if we consider that this area is the most ecologically vulnerable. A poorer state in the field of environmental consciousness as well as the individual's attitude can be seen with the respondents from the *Pivka region*. Amongst them, there is the largest share of those who overlap in the categories 'environmentally non-aware' and 'passive environmentally aware users', and of all the regions, this is the region with the lowest share of respondents in the 'actively environmentally aware' group. For the respondents from this region, it is thus typical that they have a lack of will and conviction. The poorest state from the viewpoint of environmentally friendly users can be noticed in the *Brkini hills and* the *river Reka valley*.

Out of all the regions, this is the one with the greatest share of respondents that belong to the 'environmentally non-aware users' group. On the other hand, it is true that this region has so far had the least problems with drinking water supply and the consequences of environment pollution.

The world is getting increasingly worried about the consequences of pollution. However, we are interested in those conclusions that can be sufficiently analysed, understood and explained, so they can be used in practice. To conclude, we thus shed some light on the possibility of using the profiles as indicators for planning the values of the selected user profiles in a concrete spatial and time society, i.e. inhabitants of south-west Slovenia.

The comparison of the ascertained condition as regards the water and environmental protection awareness of the so-called typical profiles is confirmed by the results of the remaining analysis of the respondents' samples (see also Černigoj, 2005, p. 40; Veljanovski, Ravbar, 2005, str. 502). A relatively complicated procedure for defining the profiles (which also includes a subjective approach) certainly also demands a fair share of caution at the interpretation of the results. As regards the reliability of the results obtained from this research, we can at this point in time conclude only on the basis of their awareness as regards the contents and the knowledge of the conditions in the treated environment, while the conformation of the results would demand a new measurement of the studied occurrences in new conditions. Here it should be taken into account that the research is limited mainly by the fact that it derives from a concrete time, space and methodology frame. Nevertheless, it has been confirmed that also in Slovenia, attitudes towards water are most significantly triggered in the light of the properties of water as an assured commodity that belongs to the modern societal life. It is down to the broader field of scientists to determine the actual usability and implementation of such conceptual approaches, keeping in mind how to ensure a joint future for all of us.

Bibliography and References

Connolly, J., Prothero, A. (2003): Sustainable consumption: consumption, consumers and the commodity discourse. *Consumption, Markets and Culture* Volume 6, Number 4, Routledge.

Černigoj, T. (2005): Problematika sodobne vodooskrbe v očeh anketirancev petih izbranih regij jugozahodne Slovenije (The issue of contemporary water supply as seen by the interviewees from five selected regions in south-west Slovenia). In: Mihevc, A., Stančič, Z., Babij, V. Horvat, J. Stanonik, M., Veljanovski, T. (eds.), *Voda in življenje v kraški pokrajini (Water and life in karst landscape)*. Založba ZRC SAZU, Ljubljana.

Jesenko, J., Jesenko, M. (2007): Multivariatne statistične metode (Multivariate Statistical Methods), Moderna organizacija, Kranj.

Spaargaren, G. (2003): Sustainable Consumption: A Theoretical and Environmental Policy Perspective. *Society & Natural Resources* Vol. 16, No. 8, 687-701. Taylor & Francis.

McGarigal, K., Cushman, S. Stafford, S. (2000): Multivariate Statistics for Wildlife and Ecology Research; Springer-Verlag, New York.

Veljanovski, T., Ravbar, N. (2005): Družbeno kulturne značilnosti porabe pitne vode in odnosa do nje v gospodinjstvih na območju jugozahodne Slovenije – Socio-cultural determinants of drinking water consumption and relation to it in south-westwrn Slovene households. In: Mihevc, A. (ed.) Kras: voda in življenje v kamniti pokrajini = water and life in a rocky landscape, (Projekt Aquadapt), Založba ZRC SAZU, Ljubljana.

Veljanovski, T., Ravbar, N. (2004): Socio-cultural determinants of water utilisation in the SW part of Slovenia: Aquadapt wp 2 final report for the Slovenian case study, Založba ZRC SAZU, Ljubljana.

About the Authors

Manca Jesenko is a research assistant at the University of Maribor, Faculty of Organizational Sciences. Her research field is statistics.

Jože Jesenko is a professor at the University of Maribor, Faculty of Organizational Sciences. His research fields are quantitative methods and quality management.

Current Business – IT Alignment Issues

Jindrich Kaluza

jindrich.kaluza@vsb.cz

Ludmila Kaluzova

ludmila.kaluzova@vsb.cz

Abstract

Alignment between the business (users, executives) and information technologies in various organizations is one of the top management concerns today. The discussion is based on the MIS Triad model analysis and its extension reflecting the strategic issues of IT implementations today. The understanding of ITs nature and perspectives should be an attribute of all three Triad's nodes representatives: users, executives and, of course, the IT staff. In such a case, the key question is to what degree IT expertise should be shared by each player. Corresponding knowledge profiles and responsibilities for the users and the executives are defined. Specific attention is given to the IS development (planning) process structure. The system analysis approach and the strategic management one, both offering the information system development process structure, are critically compared from the perspective of what new the strategic conception (which is younger, of course) brings. The comparison is summarized in conclusion that both structures complement each other well where the system analysis approach is more focused on procedural aspects of the IS development, while the strategic management view underlines the "strategic" circumstances. Improved methodologies being utilized within the information system development life cycle do not bring only a higher productivity of system analytical work but also contribute to a higher quality of mutual communication with users. They practically represent another dimension of business-IT alignment effort. Two of them are discussed further: CASE methodologies and data modelling utilizing the object-oriented approach.

Keywords: information systems, management information systems, information systems planning, business-IT alignment, MIS Triad, system analysis, CASE tools, data modelling, object-oriented approach

1. The Importance of IS – a Strategic Function

Information technologies are becoming critical to many businesses and government operations. Today, without computing, bodies like credit card companies, retail banks, airlines and certainly a number of other businesses would very likely break down. Information technologies offer new business and management opportunities. They have the potential to be a strategic weapon according to (Earl, 1989, p. 8) in at least four different ways:

- To gain competitive advantage
- To improve productivity and performance
- To enable new ways of managing and organizing
- To develop new businesses.

New information technologies have dramatically changed the nature of information management and management information systems. New products, computer value-added products, flexible manufacturing and delivery, just-in-time, inter-organizational information systems, electronic commerce etc. are documenting the current development.

We have been talking about Management Information Systems for more than fifty years. Originally, those were not based on computers, then the era of mainframes and batch processing came, and nowadays MIS are penetrated by information and communication technologies. The adjective "strategic" for today's information systems is more feasible in strengthening the aspect of their strategic importance. Armies of system analysts, programmers, database administrators and technical staff take care of the running of information systems. Eighteen years ago (Jones, 1986, p. 122), estimated that 4 million programmers in new development and 6 million in maintenance would be in action worldwide in 2000. Today, we could likely estimate that these figures were rather pessimistic. It is beyond dispute that current information systems in most implementations are of strategic importance. This is the reason why, besides researchers dealing with the process of system analysis and design, the methodology of IS development and implementation is also drawing the attention of many authors who represent the theoretical approach of strategic management.

2. Top Information Management Concerns Today

A survey of nearly 300 firms conducted by the Society for Information Management published in (CIO Magazine, 2005, p. 1) came up with 10 top information management concerns of today:

- IT and business alignment
- Retaining IT professionals
- Security and privacy
- IT strategic planning
- Speed and agility
- Government regulation
- Complexity reduction
- IT governance
- Information architecture (a tie with above)
- Business process reengineering.

Similar results were presented by the "State of the CIO around the World" survey (Varon, Cosgrove, 2005, p. 1), where the most frequently defined information management priorities are:

- Aligning IT and business goals
- Increasing business efficiency through IT
- Increasing usage of IT.

The first priority will be discussed further on, focussing on three key entities (stakeholders) that could be identified, and on their mutual relations: users, IT staff and executives. Relations between business and IT and between users and IT still play a key role in current information management.

Other research (Pastore, Cosgrove, 2005, p. 1) signalizes that only 50% of companies perceive IT's value as positive (44% see it as neutral and 6% as poor). At the same time, the survey brings up five alignment practices that were most effective in improving businesses' perception of IT:

1. business sponsor shares ownership and accountability with IT for IT-business initiatives

2. employment of internal relationship managers/account executives to work with the business
3. positioning of the CIO as a member of the corporate board or executive committee
4. CIO reporting to the CEO
5. business sponsor owns and is accountable for IT-business initiatives.

The most effective practices for IT-business alignment are found where the CIO has a place and a voice where strategic decisions are made and where practices involve prominent responsibility and accountability for IT value by the business. This sort of positioning provides the CIO with an opportunity to influence how the CEO and other executives view IT's role and, ultimately, its value to the business. This acknowledges that IT is not the sole creator or recipient of IT value, but that IT shares responsibility and rewards with the business unit sponsors. Perception will be greatly influenced by the degree of ownership the business takes in IT value. But in fact, most companies struggle to make business sponsors accountable for IT value. A "shared" responsibility with IT is somewhat more effective than having the business sponsor solely responsible.

CIOs believe that the greatest risks they face by failing to turn IT doubters into believers in the strategic value of IT are missed opportunities for innovation and growth, continued inefficiency and cuts to the IT budget.

We could summarize the findings by citing Michael Gerrard, vice president of the Gartner Group, who said: "If a business doesn't believe in IT and doesn't believe that investing in IT is a choice that will produce results, they can put themselves at a competitive disadvantage to companies that believe in IT and do invest".

There are three main groups of stakeholders here: senior management, users and IT staff. The interactions among them from the perspective of understanding, support and co-operation will be discussed below.

3. The Extended Model of MIS Triad

More than 20 years ago, Brookes, Grouse, Jeffery and Lawrence (Brookes et al., 1982, p. 89) presented the following model called the MIS Triad.

Figure 1: The MIS Triad Model

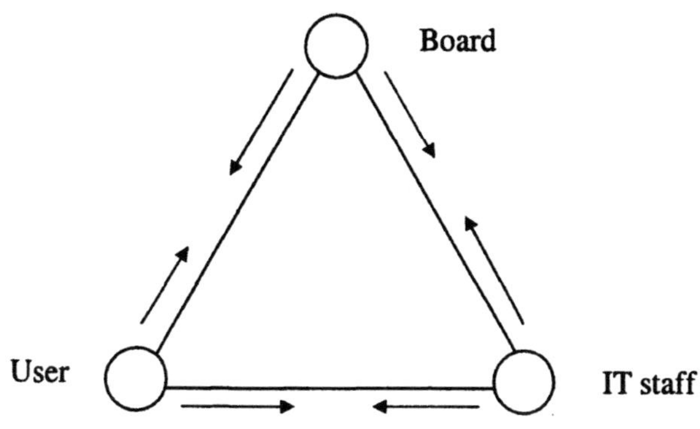

The two-way arrows along each side represent the necessary flow of information. The Board-IT flow means budget policies, MIS needs, master plans, the Board-User flow contains policy on priorities, objective setting, monitoring, the User-Board flow is new service needs and nomination of project benefits, the User-IT flow means needs, system problems, choice of design and project control, the IT-User flow is options of project designs, cost and benefits of proposals and the IT-Board flow represents budget advice and equipment options for MIS needs.

The authors did not take into account the "distances" leading to potential "deformations" between the Triad's nodes. They very likely issue from the fact of the low perception of the "strategic role" of information technologies realised today. When considering the distances in terms of representation of "mutual alignment", we could distinguish three extreme situations:

1. "Tall Triad" representing executives who are too far from ITs and from users
2. "Left-Developed Triad" representing users similarly
3. "Right-Developed Triad" representing same for IT staff.

These considerations are based, of course, on fulfilment of geometrical rules for the triangle definition. The distances are not understood as exactly measurable, but rather as representative ones.

The first situation is typical for organizations where information technologies could be sufficiently implemented but rather on operational and/or tactical levels of management, while the executives are not appropriately concerned. In the previous chapter, such circumstances were adequately addressed: the business – IT alignment is to be a primary issue for the strategic information system analysis and design in an organization.

Figure 2: The "Tall Triad"

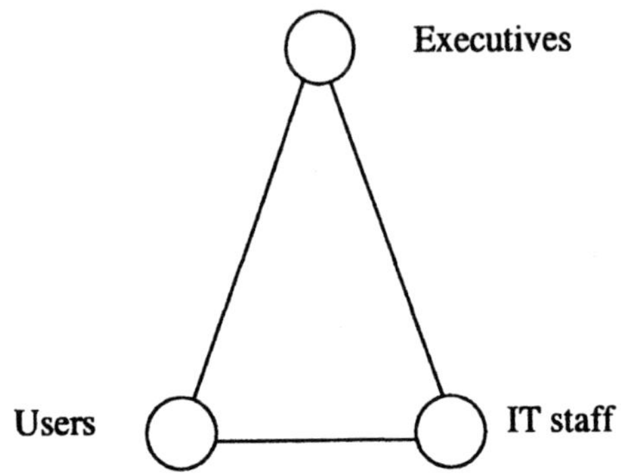

The second possibility is, in terms of practical occurrence, rather rare. Some institutions of public administration possibly could tend towards a similar constellation (decentralized users each responsible for a very specific area have a weak coherence towards system integration) although one could argue that the previous situation is more realistic here.

Figure 3: The "Left-Developed Triad"

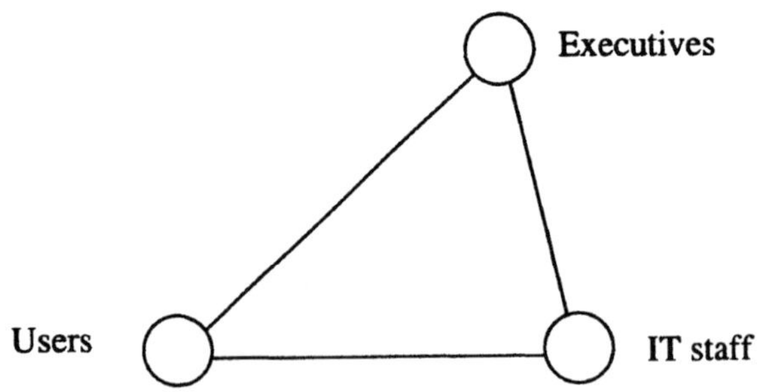

The third situation depicts a typical situation where Its' are not aligned with the business, or users or executives. This was "typical" in the early stages of information systems development when their strategic importance was not sufficiently known and valued. Despite this, even today, some rather small organisations could correspond to such a situation.

Figure 4: The "Right-Developed Triad"

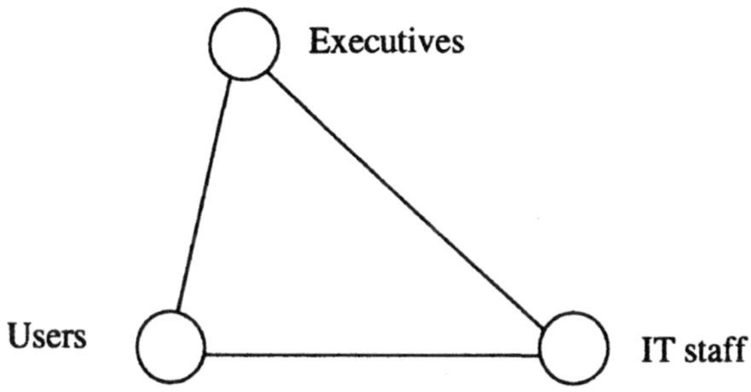

When turning back to the five most effective "alignment practices" discussed in the previous section, in the words of the Triad model, the second recommendation practically leads to the shortening of the "distances" between nodes in the Triad, while the remaining ones contribute specifically to shortening the distance between IT staff and the executives. Some further research dealing with the "measurement methods" development in terms of the Triad's distances should be inspiring.

One of the key issues here is to what degree each player other than IT staff should know the nature of computer information technologies, and what the division is of the relevant knowledge within the Triad, i.e. in other words, "how to get closer" between the Triad's nodes - key players.

Some older views emphasized the needs of "IT understanding" from the side of the users. Users' lack of computer literacy was seen as a key problem for the successful implementation of information technologies. This is not the case today; practically all users are familiar with basic information technologies represented by relevant application software and standard Microsoft Office packages. People have adopted computers as a "normal" part of their lives.

Most of the recent research confirms that a lot of information systems have problems just due to the lack of attention given by executives to ITs (or due to the lack of realization of their strategic opportunities and necessity). How to get the business closer to Its' is a key problem now. Some findings have been presented in the previous sections. The five most effective practices established there could be grouped into three principal ones:

1. *strategic planning* of information system and technologies implementation
2. *shared accountability* of executives and managers with IT staff for IT-business initiatives
3. *organizational viewpoint* expressed by the increasing importance of the CIO as a member of the executive committee.

Strategic planning seems to be of key importance. Each organization should have the strategic objectives of their information system defined and aligned with the business objectives. IS development and implementation is a time- and resources-consuming process that has to be planned according to the methodology selected from existing methodological approaches. These reflect various views, from which the one that best addresses the organization's needs should be applied.

Any IT initiative requires shared responsibility of IT staff and executives, although the latter are fully responsible for the final decision. The executives should understand the IT in terms of business and competitive advantage. Formally, the shared accountability is anchored organizationally as a relevant position of CIO in the executive structure.

4. What Users and Board Should Know about Information Technologies

It is indisputable that IT knowledge and experience have become an issue not only for IT professionals. Both non-IT nodes of the Triad also have to be familiar with IT and IS expertise. The only question is *to what degree* they should absorb IT expertise to meet the above formulated requirements. There are two extremes here – users and executives as IT professionals, and the opposite: both parties rejecting computer and systems learning. The truth is (not surprisingly) somewhere in the middle.

The following recommendations are based on the authors' long-term practical experience with implementations of information systems and also on a number of discussions with executives and managers during various educational and training activities. There was no problem finding a consensus here; however, the problems are with the practical application. Nevertheless, clearly defined IT responsibilities could minimally help in the education and training of managers and decrease the size of problems mentioned in previous paragraphs.

Users

Users should play a key role when forming and implementing an information system. They are consumers of technology. Users' involvement in ITs could be specified as follows:

- capability of requirements determination – what should be developed, improved or changed
- understanding the nature of the utilized IT (passively, at least)
- capability to work with system analysts and other IT staff:
    - during identification, selection and planning activities of IS development
    - in conceptual modelling of the system
    - at the end of implementation when installing and documenting the system
    - during the training and system maintenance.

Executives

The role of executives linked to ITs should be as follows:

- understanding the strategic opportunities offered by concrete information technologies disposable in the market
- understanding which information technologies could effectively support the business strategy
- having a knowledge of existing ITs implementation within the organization, what the strong and weak points are, what threats and opportunities through ITs installation are.

All three node representatives should absorb a common communication language that enables them to communicate mutually and with the systems. The language involves also a number of formal means belonging to current CASE tools and workbenches.

Finally, both groups should eliminate the resistance to changes – surprisingly this "old" aspect is still indicated by many researches and reports. The executives must play a key role here and appropriately motivate users to co-operate.

5. Information Systems Development Process Structure – Two Approaches and Their Comparison

Systems analysts see the whole process as the *information system development life cycle* consisting usually of the following phases (Hoffer et al. 2002, p. 136):

1. Project identification and selection
2. Project initiation and planning
3. Analysis
4. Design
5. Implementation
6. Maintenance

The term *project* means here part or all of an information system, depending on the concrete situation of the extent of the system.

Each phase is, of course, further specified in detailed steps and it is carried out dynamically through an iterative approach. This structure reflects *the experience with practical system development work.* Every software producer and most of the medium-sized and large corporations have their own specific life cycles or systems development methodology in place. Some authors consider the life cycle to be a spiral, in which we constantly cycle through the phases at different levels of detail. The iterative approach plays a key role within the so-called *rapid application development methods* (prototyping e. g.) – see (Bourne, 1994, p. 25).

In fact, all such methodologies lead to the structure specified above; the differences are caused either by the generalization of some phases or their specialization (expressed in data modelling terminology) or by the degree to which the iteration process is emphasized. The life cycle structure here reflects the logical set of steps that has to be practically completed before the new system is successfully implemented.

The *strategic management view* talks about the *(strategic) information systems planning (SISP)* – see (Remenyi, 1991, p.196). The whole process is defined in the following set of steps:

1. Obtain authorization
2. Establish a team and arrange accommodation tools
3. Allocate responsibilities and create timetable
4. Determine the corporate goals, objective, mission
5. Establish the firm's corporate strategy
6. Define the critical success factors
7. Establish the key performance indicators
8. Define the critical data set
9. Incorporate the firm's IT architecture
10. Conduct a systems audit
11. Rank current systems conditions and prioritize current systems proposals
12. Brainstorm for new systems and create an IT opportunities list
13. Perform cost benefit and risk analysis
14. Conduct filtering workshops
15. Produce an Action Plan
16. Communicate the Action Plan to all appropriate staff
17. Identify and appoint Project Champions
18. Arrange for top management to publicly commit to the SISP
19. Create feedback mechanisms
20. Updating the SISP

SISP here is presented as an ongoing activity, becoming a regular and continuous process in the organization.

At a glance, when trying *to compare both structures*, the latter seems to be more detailed, but in fact, each of the IS development life cycle phases could be relevantly decomposed into corresponding sub-phases (Hoffer et al., 2002, p. 136, p. 165ff). However, such considerations, although interesting, could lead us away from the main topic of this paper.

Nevertheless, let us look at both structures and try to find the substantial differences. The first step of the SISP – *Obtain authorization* corresponds partly (the authorization itself) to the life cycle phase 1 (*Project identification and selection*) and partly (budget and team leader specification) to the phase 2 (*Project initiation and planning*). SISP steps 2 to 5 belong fully to the life cycle phase 2. Steps 6 to 8, which are very closely related to each other, do not have a relevant action within the life cycle phases.

SISP step 9 – *Incorporate the firm's Information Technology (IT) architecture* needs more analysis. Curiously, the term "information technology" is not interpreted in the relevant literature in the same way.

In older books – e.g. in (Earl, 1989, p. 21) - the definition of *IT* that "… comprises all the supply, development and use activities in which an organization has to be involved if it wishes to exploit these technologies to its advantage" is very broad, naming practically all components as one "big" organization's information technology. In other words, this term is understood here as something like "new era data processing" (Earl talks of the 1990s decade as a "new era").

Later on, (Remenyi, 1991, p. 43) adds a new term – *IT architecture* as a "firm's long-term requirements for hardware, software and communications". In fact, Earl's definition of IT is here enriched by the aspect of long-term objective planning.

Robson (1997, p. 82) presents a slightly different definition of *IT* as "… all the machinery and software that, at one time, was seen as belonging to individual technology disciplines". IT is used here in the plural i.e. in one organization we could recognise a number of specific information technologies in various phases of implementation (e.g. "traditional" software packages for payroll, accounting etc., software and hardware for e-business, portable computers for salesmen etc.) and the *Information System* could be seen as a *set of ITs directly assisting the organization in achieving the business strategy.* These meanings of both terms currently prevail. The word "architecture" could then be more usefully linked to the "information system" – *Information System Architecture* – meaning the structure of all ITs implemented in a particular IS in a particular time. Possibly, the requirement "*Incorporate the firm's Information System Architecture*" reflects better the contents of the action.

Anyway, back to the previous discussion comparing the two structures: IS development life cycle and Strategic IS planning. The SISP step 9 represents a part of the first phase of the life cycle – *the Information System Plan* – see (Hoffer et al., 2002, p. 151). The whole process of information system planning is concentrated purely on that phase here. It is a narrower interpretation of the word "planning" corresponding only to the planning (not executive) life cycle phases.

SISP steps 10 to 14 – *System audit, Current system conditions ranking, Brainstorming for new system, Cost Benefit & Risk Analysis, Filtering Workshop* - are fully covered by the analytical phase of the life cycle, i.e. requirements determination and structuring, alternatives generation and selection. Moreover, the system analysis approach, besides the alternative selection activity as a part of the analytical phase, deals with the project feasibility assessment. It is carried out at the end of project planning for the whole project before the analysis. Practically, it means that the project selection decision-making process is split into two parts: at the end of the planning phase the most feasible project is selected and at the end of the analysis, the best alternative is chosen.

The following steps (15 to 16) represent clearly a part of the design phase, the expression "a part of" means that the most important part of the design phase – detailed data and processes modelling is not specifically touched on here.

Steps 17 and 18 are of an implementation nature; step 18 *Top management public commitment to the SISP* brings a very benefiting aspect to the life cycle structure, the experience from many IS implementations witnesses the importance of top management public commitment, announced in advance, for the IS success.

Steps 19 *Feedback mechanisms* and 20 *Updating the SISP* finalize the SISP structure, the presence of the former is slightly problematic. Feedback simply must be respected, but permanently during the whole life cycle, the latter belonging to the maintenance phase.

All in all, the difference between both approaches is that the system analytical one is more focused on procedural aspects of the IS construction (data flows analysis, data modelling, process hierarchy, algorithms modelling etc.) while the strategic management one enriches the structure of key "strategic" features (critical success factors and performance indicators, corporate strategy, top management involvement etc.). There is no contradiction between the approaches - one enriches the other.

6. Methodologies and Tools Supporting the Developmental Process

This section is focused on two areas where the latest progress has occurred most visibly: *CASE methodologies* and *object features in data modelling.*

At present, a relatively wide offer of CASE tools is available, supporting the information system analysis and design process. According to a particular functionality towards a final programme solution, they are usually divided into the Upper, Middle and Lower CASE. From the original simple tools improving the system analyst's work, complex systems for analysis and design have been created today, forming various CASE workbenches and, eventually, the I-CASEs (integrated CASEs).

A pilot work (Yourdon, 1989) influencing the particular form of a lot of CASE products was the methodology based on *structured analysis and design.* This methodology rather freely interconnects a set of methodological tools trying to express a model of an analysed system in a graphic form in as complete a way as possible.

In the part of the *structured analysis,* a so-called *essential model* comprises the *context diagram* covering the substance, determination of an analysed system and a *behaviour model* created by:

- an information model (modelling the data structure)
- data transformation model (i.e. the functional structure)
- model of dynamics (mapping the system behaviour).

The *structured design* is then expressed in three mutually complementary models:

- model of the processor environment (hardware part of a design)
- model of the software environment (software part of a design)
- model of a program structure (solution of the respective program modules).

The methodology itself didn't bring a completely new system analysis method. However, its merit is the integrated conception of the methodology associated with an applicable whole, the tools having been used in a separate and system-free way. Some criticism towards the methodology could be expressed due to the fact that data and functional models are created during the analytical phase separately or, moreover, at the very beginning, mutually independently. The models are then (during the phase of design) worked out in more detail and extended by further models, so a relatively good number of weakly related models occur.

A lot of particular CASE products are based on Yourdon's structured analysis and design, such as CASE/4/0 of the microTool company, System Architect of the Popkin Software (Telelogic AB now), PowerDesigner of Sybase Inc., Oracle Designer 2000 and a number of others.

The *object-oriented approach* was originally utilized in the area of computer programming and its success led to the implementation within the information systems design later on. This approach is based on the theory of a data and process model: it works with *objects* that describe both data and process (algorithmic) aspects of the problem being solved. Mutual insulation of data and functional aspects of the system does not exist here. Within the analytical phase, the models express the problem being solved and then, within the phase of design, they are worked out into the shape needed by the computer implementation.

A number of various methodologies for object analysis and design have been developed in the past, and the effort has led to the unified development of object-oriented approach theories in the frame of so called Unified Modelling Language (UML). This prevailingly graphical set of tools has been continuously under development since 1994 and many software solutions follow such a methodological paradigm, e. g., Rational Rose of IBM, AllFusion of Computer Associates International, Inc., Corporate Modeller of Casewise Ltd. and others.

CASE methodologies reflected in various concrete software solutions could not replace the human activity linked to the reality perception meaning the necessary process of abstraction. The CASE tools make further steps of system analysis and design easier. Their effectiveness has to be assessed for the process as a whole.

Data modelling is a process leading to the definition of database structures in the frame of information system design. It represents a part of the system design. A lot of attention has been given to the methodological development of that in theory. The hierarchical, network, relational and object conceptions were theoretically and practically worked out. The starting point of all of these conceptions was the definition of hierarchies or sets or entities or classes with no explanation of how to reach them. That is why we have concentrated our research on this aspect and tried to present more complex and also more detailed methodology based on both general and also more focused (object) approach – see (Kaluza, Kaluzova, 2001, p. 322). Undoubtedly, the *object approach* brings the most advanced features into the data modelling through the fundamental principles which the conception is based on (abstraction, inheritance, encapsulation, persistence and polymorphism).

The methodology is then defined in three levels expressing the top-down gradual procedure of data modelling:

- semantic
- conceptual
- logical

Semantic modelling forms a starting level of the process identifying the user's input requirements and a set of data elements that reflect a part of the real world mapped into the data model. At this level, data is modelled in the prescribed verbal form. The process is completed then by the structure of data elements and their recognized characteristics.

Conceptual modelling using a graphical interpretation further elaborates the semantic model. It is based on either E-R philosophy or on the UML Class Diagram and gradually converts the semantic elements into the structure of entities or classes and relationships including their cardinality and optionality specification. A full set of attributes as well as methods is basically specified. A conceptual data model is not tightly linked to the concrete database system and modelling conception. It could be implemented in various modelling environments (relational, object-relational, object). Such implementation is a subject of the following (final) level.

Logical modelling transforms the conceptual model into the set of elements defined by a particular data modelling conception, e.g. relational, object-relational or object oriented (historically previous conceptions are not taken into account here due to their practical uselessness). Data types and tables are specified, as are also the references depicting data relationships. After the domain's definition, the data model is ready to be rewritten into the concrete data definition language.

More detailed specification of the methodology is presented in (Kaluza, Kaluzova, 2001, p. 323).

Improved methodologies being utilized within the information system development life cycle do not only bring a higher productivity of system analytical work but also contribute to a higher quality of mutual communication with users. This practically represents another dimension of business-IT alignment effort.

7. Conclusions

The business-IT alignment is one of the key problems of current information systems implementation. There are three principal recommendations for how to contribute to a successful solution to that: users' education, strategic planning and methodological development.

The analysis based on the MIS Triad leads to a recommendation to shorten the distances between the nodes. All three key players, i.e. users, executives and IT staff should work in closer co-operation. Education and training of users and executives should issue from clearly defined responsibilities and the necessary IT knowledge. Some language of communication involving basic CASE formal tools among all three nodes representatives is needed. Attention should permanently be given to overbridging the resistance to changes on the users' and on the executives' side.

Information systems planning could be seen from two perspectives: strategic management and systems analysis & design. Both approaches bring specific features enriching the overall structure of the planning process. Information systems planning has a strategic importance for business today.

Methodological development leads not only to an analysis and design productivity increase, but also to closer co-operation and better communication with users.

8. Bibliography and References

Bourne, K. C. (1994): Putting Rigor Back in RAD, Database Programming&Design, No. 7.

Brookes. C. H. P., Grouse, P. J., Jeffery, D. R., Lawrence; M. J. (1982): *Information Systems Design*, Prentice-Hall.

CIO Magazine (2005): Top 10 Information Management Concerns, CIO Magazine, No. 2.

Earl. M. J. (1989): *Management Strategies for Information Technology*, Prentice Hall Int. Ltd., Cambridge.

Jones, C. (1986): *Programming Productivity*, New York, NY: McGraw-Hill.

Hoffer, J. A., George, J. F., Valacich, J. S. (2002): Modern Systems Analysis & Design, Prentice-Hall International, Inc.

Kaluza. J., Kaluzova, L. (2001): *New Approach in Data Modelling Based on UML Methodology*, Int. Conf. Strategic Management and its Support by Information Systems, Horni Becva, TU Ostrava.

Pastore, R., Cosgrove, L. (2005): Turning IT Doubters into True Believers, CIO Magazine, No.6.

Remenyi, D. (1991): *Introducing Strategic information Systems Planning*, NCC Blackwell, Oxford.

Robson, W. (1997): *Strategic Management & Information Systems*, Pitman Publishing, London.

Varon, E., Cosgrove, L. (2005): The State of CIO Around the World, CIO Magazine, No. 4.

Yourdon, E. (1989): *Modern Structured Analysis*, Prentice Hall, Englewood Cliffs

About the Authors

Jindrich Kaluza has a Master's degree in systems engineering (TU Ostrava) and PhD from the Prague School of Economics. Currently, he works at the Technical University of Ostrava as a professor. His specialist area is information systems analysis and design, the strategic role of IS, data modelling and databases.

Ludmila Kaluzova is a reader at the Department of Systems Engineering of the Technical University of Ostrava. She has a Master's degree and a PhD from the same university. Her specialist area is data modelling, database structures and database management systems.

Rewarding of Project Work

Janez Mayer

janez.mayer@fov.uni-mb.si

Jože Ban

ban.raj@siol.net

Tomaž Kern

tomaz.kern@fov.uni-mb.si

Abstract

In contrast to project management methodologies, whose procedures are clearly defined, there are not many motivational methods for defining rewards to project group members that directly depend on the success of a project. Only by defining a suitable reward method that focuses on rewarding the successful realisation of each individual result (product or service) in the project (excluding rewarding by invested time), preparing an adequate budget in advance for rewarding all members of the project group (either as a percentage of salary or a percentage based on total project value), and implementing rewards in line with the agreement between sponsor, project manager and project team members is it possible to expect greater possibilities for the successful management and completion of a project. Only after the members of a project group have been rewarded may a project be considered completed.

Keywords: criteria for assessing project work efficiency, reward method for project group members

1. Introduction

Successful projects are important for further development and for improving the performance of any company, but, regretfully, inefficient projects are (too) common in practice.

A survey by Roberts (1992) of corporate R&D projects found that less than half met their time-to-market and budget objectives (Lyneis et al., 2001, p. 237).

A study conducted by the Standish Group in 1995 uncovered a striking record of failure in IT projects. Of the more than eight thousand systems projects Standish examined, only 16 percent were considered successes – completed on time and on budget and fulfilling the original specifications (Carr, 2004, p. 110).

There are various reasons for project inefficiency. The most frequent are:

- undefined roles of project participants,
- undefined project goals, resources and activities,
- inadequate planning, management, supervision and reporting on project progress,
- non-specific methods for managing changes in a project,
- insufficient motivation of project (work) group members, and
- others.

The consequences of inefficient projects are the higher costs of project implementation and the distrust from sponsors (project clients) and other project participants. In the worst-case scenario, inefficient projects result in a company losing its customers, market share, or even jeopardising its further operations.

Due to project complexity, the number of participants, and limitations arising from the environment, dynamic and intangible advantages are particularly important for project work. They are translated into innovations, improvements and development of new knowledge.

All employees have to be involved in this, and their diverse knowledge, experience and skills applied. Therefore, once employees are included in project work, their direct responsibility for performed work (Treven, 1998, p. 22) increases, and so do their expectations of appropriate incentives and rewards.

2. Factors of Project Work Efficiency

The basic efficiency factors of a project are:

- application of teamwork principles,
- efficient promotion of the advantages of project work,
- definition and introduction of project management methodology, and
- constant motivation and raising the level of employee culture and knowledge,

which can be translated into four key areas of comprehensive quality control:

- team organisation in the company,
- focus on the customer,
- ongoing process improvement, and
- improvement of corporate culture and employee knowledge.

A comprehensive quality management system advocates the approximation of the long-term interests of the employees, owners/shareholders and customers based on the constant improvement of processes. This results in a broader benefit for society.

In the case of project management, this entails approximation of the interests of the project client (owners, shareholders, management, key users, etc.), project group and working group members (internal and external resources), and of the users of project results (end-users, customers, etc.).

2.1 Application of Teamwork Principles

A precondition for the successful introduction of project work is the consideration of general principles which apply to efficient and successful teamwork (Gabrijelčič, 1995, p. 136):

- the goals and the paths leading to these goals must be clear to all group members,
- the goals should be defined in co-operation with the colleagues working on subsequent realisation of the goals,
- when structuring activities and goals, the probability of these goals being realised should be high,
- the goals should be set with utmost comprehensiveness, meaning that all group members must be acquainted not only with individual problems, but with the entire picture,

- the activities should be designed so that all members are maximally engaged in all their integrity, and with consideration for their wishes, needs, feelings and opinions,
- an atmosphere of mutual co-operation must be established, so that colleagues feel like partners in an important assignment,
- group philosophy must be promoted to ensure the understanding of the needs and wishes of all group members,
- activities and tasks should contain a development component,
- certain connections and a chronological order must be established between individual goals and activities, and
- theory and practice should complement each other.

2.2 Promotion of the Advantages of Project Work

Project work covers a series of activities that are crucial for project implementation and also refers to business accomplishments realised through projects (Žurga, 2003, p. 13).

The opinions and evaluations of the importance and advantages of project work by project managers and sponsors differ considerably. Project managers stress the technical advantages of project management (tools, planning, reporting, etc.), whereas sponsors think more strategically, focusing on the connection between the project strategy and business strategy (impact on company growth, attainment of business objectives).

Unfortunately, the (in)efficiency of project work too often stems from the fact that a project is launched because of identified operating crises (Project Management Institute, 2007, p. 1), instead of a proactive, previously adopted approach to change management.

It is therefore important that project managers consider the sponsors as customers and promote project management according to the principles which apply to the marketing of services (Potočnik, 2000, p. 46) by:

- applying marketing philosophy, both in the company and in individual project groups,
- planning activities on the level of individual projects,
- setting up a support information system providing for faster and more efficient performance of operational and administrative activities within the scope of project work,

- measuring user satisfaction,
- establishing a base of knowledge and experience as the basis for defining the necessary changes in the quality of project implementation,
- segmenting of the project work market, enabling the selection of projects consistent with the company's business objectives,
- differentiating and positioning the service range within the framework of project management, and
- internal marketing, encompassing the promotion and motivation of project group members to constantly improve the culture of work and the required expertise.

2.3 Definition and Introduction of Project Management Methodology

Every improvement of the process or product in fact represents the solving of problems, which is more successful if the following preconditions are taken into account (PDCA, SDCA principles):
- improved supervision over the process,
- reactive process enhancement (in the initial period), and
- proactive improvement of the process, enabling taking of actions before problems and related costs arise.

If the principles of constant improvement of processes and teamwork are followed, this alone leads to the defining of procedures that will ensure successful achievement of the set goals.

Several methodologies have been developed for project management (PRINCE (PRINCE2, 2002), PMBOK (PMBOK, 2004), IPMA (IPMA, 2006)). They all aim to provide the parties ordering the project and the parties conducting the project with supervised, well-planned, organised and managed activities to yield desired results.

The successful implementation of methodology in a company – irrespective of the selected methodology – requires:
- support and active co-operation of the company's top management,
- definition of methodology as the applicable standard for project work implementation,
- personnel and information support of project work,

- acquisition of the necessary knowledge about project management by all persons participating in the project work (sponsor, working-group members and end-users), and
- continuous integration of new knowledge and experience gained from completed projects.

2.4 Constant Motivation and Raising of the Level of the Employees' Culture and Knowledge

Project work is one of the mechanisms used for improving the performance of a company. In addition, it can function as an efficient method for the company's management to obtain maximum knowledge and experience from its employees, as it is a known fact that employees' performance is poor to average if they perform work they are obligated to do, and excellent if they perform work they wish to do (Rozman et al., 1993, p. 66).

Motivation in project work can be achieved by providing adequate conditions for project work and through the rewarding of project work, both in material and non-material forms.

3. Rewarding of Project Work

In contrast to project management methodologies, whose procedures are clearly defined, there are not many motivational methods for defining rewards to project group members that directly depend on the efficiency of a project.

A project group often assumes individual activities that are otherwise carried out by the company's management, the selection of project group members, the planning of project activities, the co-ordinating of activities with the sponsor, and other activities either related to the project or within the company's operations.

At the same time, they cannot do without the »telemetry data« of their business process if they wish to use process efficiency to improve the company success (Scheer et al., 2002, p. 41), so it is highly recommended to implement efficient and operative project office support (Kern et al., 2007, p. 197).

Moreover, quality control is carried out as an important factor for achieving comprehensive project work quality (Žurga, 2003, p. 13). This provides for a much higher quality of implemented tasks and greater satisfaction of the project sponsor due to:

- reliable performance of agreed activities,
- responsiveness in the provision of project outputs (products) or problem solving,
- the feeling of trust created by the knowledge and reliability of project group members,
- attention focused on the sponsor, and
- palpable (tangible) elements – physical evidence, for example the neat appearance of project group members, reliability and availability of the necessary equipment, an efficient information system providing project work support, and transparent and well-organised documentary material.

3.1 Problems in Motivation and the Rewarding of Project Work

Problems in motivating and rewarding project group members, particularly in the case of project groups in a company which employs the members of the group, stem mainly from the nature of project work and the interaction of the following:

- a complex, yet unique task and the existing work organisation in the company,
- standard organisation and project organisation, which intertwine and hence change the roles of project implementers according to the formal distribution of employees,
- internal labour markets (ILMs) and external labour markets (ELMs) should be viewed as integrated entities (Rutheford, 2006, p. 200),
- the subjective assessment of project efficiency and the predefined criteria for determining the efficiency of a particular project (before and after the project is completed),
- the existing reward system in the company and the character of a unique, for the most part, increased work load,

- the legal bases prescribed in the Employment Relationship Act and the particularities of project work not dealt with by the Act, and
- the employees' desire to be rewarded based on invested time (overtime) and the tendency of the client/sponsor and project management towards performance-related rewarding.

It seems that in order to improve organisational performance, firms should develop capabilities that focus around personnel issues. Specifically, firms may wish to employ individuals with an internally oriented focus of control and reward them not on the basis of pre-defined responsibilities, but rather on the basis of their value-added to the firm (Newbert et al., 2008, p.14)

3.2 Principles of Rewarding Project Efficiency

Several approaches may be applied when choosing the method of rewarding project work efficiency, but it is important that the following principles are considered in all cases:

- the criteria for measuring project work efficiency must be defined and approved before the project is launched (they are a constituent part of the project implementation agreement and of the approval of the project order) and can be different regarding type of the project and skills needed (Swink et al., 2005, p. 554; Hoegl, Parboteeah, 2006, p. 116),
- rewarding must be based on the efficiency of achievement of individual project goals (excluding rewarding on the basis of time invested), as the introduction of project work may result in higher costs (Treven, 1998, p. 23) if not directly related to project results,
- budgeting in advance for rewarding members of the project group (either as a percentage of salary or based on the project value), and
- implementation/realisation of rewarding in accordance with the agreement (rewards must be paid out).

When rewarding the efficiency of project work, it is necessary to foresee the possibility of project inefficiency and non-payment of rewards as well as the possibility of sanctioning project group members.

The sanctions for unsuccessful management or work on a project depend on the applicable human resources policy and payroll system of a company. The following possibilities may be employed:

- discharge of the project manager or dismissal from the function of project manager,
- non-payment of the performance-related bonus (within the project and/or the company's reward system),
- 'negative' bonus (the limit must be set, usually prescribed by legal provisions), and
- exercising of performance warranties/guarantees (if the contractor has signed an agreement or was outsourced).

3.3 Assessment of Efficiency by Means of Score Cards

Assessment of efficiency by means of score cards includes:

- defining of criteria,
- determining the weights for an individual criterion,
- target and limit values of an individual criterion, and
- calculation of project efficiency at the end of the project.

The method is deficient for failing to specify the following:

- the possibility and method of integrating the assessment into individual project management methodologies,
- connections with the existing methods of payroll accounting,
- managing of changes in the project, and
- above all, insufficient hands-on experience in project management.

3.4 Expanded Method for Assessing Efficiency by Means of Score Cards

The expanded method for assessing efficiency by means of score cards takes into account all elements of recommendations of the basic method, and is upgraded by the following:

- the procedure for preparing and documenting adequate and necessary data and documents,
- preliminary agreement on the criteria used in the assessment of project results,
- budgeting of rewards for project work efficiency,

- defined procedure for managing changes in a project and criteria related thereto,
- calculation of project efficiency at its completion, and
- calculation of reward to project group members for their work on the project.

3.4.1 Preparation and Documenting Procedure

The preparation and documenting procedure provides for the consideration of at least the following:

- business goals of the project (short- and long-term),
- planned results (description of services and/or products),
- list of all participants in the project (organisational structure),
- detailed schedule,
- detailed plan of all project resources and expenses,
- definition of project complexity, and
- definition of support to the project (information system, project office, project secretary, etc.).

3.4.2 Previous Agreement on Assessment Criteria

The project sponsor and management must agree on the number, type and value (range) of any criterion which is applied in the assessment of a particular project. For reasons of control, it is reasonable to select from five to maximally ten criteria.

It is recommended that the definition of applied criteria also include constant and variable assessment criteria. Constant assessment criteria can include the project completion deadline, expenses (budget) of the project, satisfaction of the client (buyer!), documentation organisation, and the use of other tools determined by the agreed project management standard in a company.

Table 1: Agreement upon introduction

1. Agreement on indicators for assessing project results upon introduction

Project name: **EXAMPLE**

							Goal					
Indicators	**Weight**	**50**	**60**	**70**	**80**	**90**	**100**	**110**	**120**	**130**	**140**	**Score**
a. Results	40%	50	55	60	65	70	**75**	80	85	90	100	**40**
b. Project complexity	10%	20	30	40	**50**	60	70	80	90	95	100	**8**
c. Costs (in '000)	15%	/	/	/	/	/	**11 million**	/	/	/	/	**15**
d. Deadline	15%	/	/	/	/	/	**26.1.2004**	/	/	/	/	**15**
e. Client's assessment	10%	50	60	70	80	90	**100**	110	120	130	140	**10**
f. Evaluation of the application of project management standards	10%	1.5	2	2.5	3	3.5	**4**	4.5	5	5.5	6	**10**
											Total:	**98**

Project Manager: *First name and surname* Sponsor: *First name and surname*
Date: *DD.MM.YY* Date: *DD.MM.YY*

Variable criteria depend on the type of the project (organisational, methodological, etc.), the size of the project, and the project's importance for the project sponsor (connection with the implementation of the business policy).

3.4.3 Budgeting of Rewards for Efficiency of Project Work

The budgeting of rewards for project participants depends on the quality and confirmation of the previous two phases of assessment of project work efficiency.

The budget is important since the calculation of project costs often overlooks the costs of employees' salaries (internal resources) and the realisation of risks in the project. Frequently, the budget for rewarding the employees participating in a successful project is not drawn up at all.

The amount of the reward budget must be added to the total planned project costs before the project is launched and the range of the cost criterion defined.

3.4.4 Definition of the Procedure for Managing Changes in a Project

Changes in projects are very frequent, which is why an adequate procedure must be formulated to ensure that the changes are considered when setting project efficiency assessment criteria.

Usually, the procedure for managing changes in a project is defined in the applied project management methodology. The intertwining of the latter and the project efficiency assessment procedure calls for subsequent agreement between the sponsor and the project manager, if the scope of the changes could affect the range of a particular criterion.

Every change must be properly documented and recorded in the project management information system, if available.

3.4.5 Calculation of Project Efficiency at Project Completion

At the completion of the project, the project manager must prepare a suitable report according to the project management methodology as well as a proposal for payment of rewards to project participants.

Since the amount of rewards can be relatively high or sanctions may be imposed on the project group because of project inefficiency, the calculation of efficiency – together with the proposed rewards (sanctions) – must be submitted to the sponsor and in some cases to the company's management (if other than the client). In the case of major discrepancies, the top management must adopt a substantiated decision to approve or reject the proposed payment of rewards (sanctions) to project participants.

Table 2: Aggregate efficiency report

I. Overview of project group and scope of work on the project:

	Hours in project IS by month: Entire project		
Project group members	Plan	**Realised**	Difference
First name and surname	52	33,5	18.5
First name and surname	142	179	-37
First name and surname	108	129	-21
First name and surname	0	24	-24
First name and surname	14	0	14
Organisational unit	34	40	-6
Total:	350	405,5	-55.5

Comments:	

II. Summary of project indicators:

Indicators	**Actual Indicator value**	**Score**	**Note**
a. Results	75	40	All results achieved
b. Project complexity	46	8	Less demanding
c. Costs (in mio)	10.6	15	Within the plan
d. Deadline	27.2.2004	15	According to plan
e. Client's assessment	100	10	As expected
f. Evaluation of the application of project management standards	6	14	Very satisfactory

Total score - project efficiency:	**102**	

III. Coefficient for calculating the portion of salary arising from project efficiency

% for calculation:	**30%**

Project Manager:	*First name and surname*	Sponsor:	*First name and surname*
Date:	*DD.MM.YY*	Date:	*DD.MM.YY*

3.4.6 Calculation of Reward to Project Group Members for Their Work on the Project

The reward to project group members can be calculated in different ways, depending on:

- previous verification of project efficiency and the related payment of rewards,

Table 3: Agreement upon completion

3. Agreement on indicators for assessing project results upon completion

Project name: **EXAMPLE**

Indicators	**Weight**	**50**	**60**	**70**	**80**	**90**	**100**	**110**	**120**	**130**	**140**	**Score**
a. Results	40%	50	55	60	65	70	**75**	80	85	90	100	40
b. Project complexity	10%	20	30	40	**50**	60	70	80	90	95	100	8
c. Costs (in '000)	15%	/	/	/	/	/	**10.6 million**	/	/	/	/	15
d. Deadline	15%	/	/	/	/	/	**27.2.2004**	/	/	/	/	15
e. Client's assessment	10%	50	60	70	80	90	**100**	110	120	130	140	10
f. Evaluation of the application of project management standards	10%	1.5	2	2.5	3	3.5	**4**	4.5	5	5.5	6	14
											Total:	102

Project efficiency	% for calculation	
0-69	-40%	Inefficient
70-74	-30%	
75-79	-20%	
80-84	-10%	
85-89	0%	
90-94	10%	**Efficient**
95-99	20%	
100-104	**30%**	
105-109	40%	
110-114	50%	
115-119	60%	Very efficient
120-124	70%	
125-129	80%	
130-134	90%	
135-140	100%	

Project Manager:	*First name and surname*
Date:	*DD.MM.YY*

- the availability of information support for calculating the efficiency of a project and the pertaining rewards according to project efficiency,
- the basis used for the calculation of efficiency of an individual project, which may be:
- base employee salary (net, or preferably gross),

- agreed percentage of project value, or
- agreed percentage of expected project results or savings,
- the diversity and size of the project group, and
- the organisational structure and existing standards of the company.

Rewards must be paid as soon as the project completion is confirmed by the sponsor or after the expiry of a warranty period (if applicable) stipulated for the project results.

4. Experience in Using the Reward Method

The reward method was used for managing information projects in the subsidiary of the Intereuropa Group, Intereuropa IT d.o.o., which in 2002 introduced the principles of project management, including formal documents, suitable training, establishment of a project office and a project IT system.

At the start of 2003, the project work methodology was complemented by an expanded method for assessing project efficiency and the calculation of salary percentage depending on efficiency. By means of the reward method, the efficiency of 14 projects was calculated, with the scores ranging between 102 (out of 140 maximum), which represented a 30% coefficient for calculating the performance-related salary portion, and 120, which accounted for a 70% coefficient for calculating the salary portion depending on efficiency.
Project costs equalled between EUR 20,000 and EUR 510,000, exclusive of rewards.

The number of project participants was between 3 and 15.

The amount of reward which depended on the project efficiency coefficient, the basis for reward calculation (the employee's salary in this particular case), and the scope of the employee's work on the project was between 11% and 96% of the basis. The highest reward paid accounted for 400% of the basis.

Table 4: Summary – proposal for payments

4. Proposal for payment of a portion of salary based on project efficiency

PROJECT: **EXAMPLE**

Duration in months	6
Total number of project days	42
hours	332
Coefficient for calculating efficiency	**30%**

Company ID number	Participants	Total participation in hours	Total participation in days	Total participation in %	Planned payment without advance payment (gross)	Paid out so far as ADVANCE PAYMENT	Payment including advance (gross)	Salary considered in calculation	% of considered salary	% acc. to resolution
7777	First name and surname 1	179	22,4	16,95%	121.101,61	50.000,00	**71.101,61**	396.475,50	17,93%	**18,00%**
8888	First name and surname 2	129	16,1	12,22%	86.731,81	25.000,00	**61.731,81**	396.475,50	15,57%	**16,00%**
9999	First name and surname 3	24	3,0	2,27%	18.652,37	11.000,00	**7.652,37**	455.946,83	1,68%	**2,00%**
	Total	332	41,5		**226.485,79**	**86.000,00**	**140.485,79**	1.248.897,83	**18,13%**	**18,00%**

Payment can also be NEGATIVE if project results differ from expectations. In such a case, the base salary may be reduced (if the base salary is used as the basis) up to the amount defined by law or the company's internal rules.

Enter notes, particularities or explanations, if any, that explain the calculation. Not obligatory!

BASES:

1) Company's Rules on Salaries (Article XX, item Y, Article QQ, item W)

2) Organisational Regulations on Project Management

3) Method for calculating the portion of salary arising from project efficiency

4) Aggregate report on project efficiency

5) Final project report

ATTACHMENTS:

1) Overview of monthly portions of salary arising from project efficiency and employee's participation in the project

2) Monthly data about the employee's gross salary

At present, the method for rewarding project work results is being introduced in Tosama d.d., one of the most successful corporate groups in Slovenia. However, the content of the projects at Tosama d.d. differs from those conducted at Intereuropa IT d.o.o. and is related to marketing and development projects. Therefore, the importance of rewarding project results is even more important for the successful performance of the group. Consequently, the systematic and transparent method of rewarding project participants is gaining importance.

5. Conclusion

Only when project group members are rewarded may a project be considered completed and the appointment of a project group for an individual project terminated. This accomplished, the monitoring of all of the project's financial events may be terminated, including the costs of rewards.
Therefore, a dynamic company that aims to increase the number of successful projects and, indirectly through these projects, to alter its operations and business strategy implementation, must place in the centre a person (Kotler, P., 1998, p.47) as the project leader and provide them with all of the necessary levers in the form of motivation and reward to enable them to carry out their task as expected.

In any case, even if the reward system provides for project work rewarding, it is reasonable for the company's management to base the rewarding on the rationale which Drucker decades ago defined as the precondition for successful management of operations (Tekavčič M., 1998, p.60): "Even though the operations seem different in each company, they are always accompanied by a single fundamental truth: each product, each task and each activity must be tested every two to three years. They must be treated by equal criteria applied to any new products, new tasks and new activities."

Bibliography and References

Carr, N. G. (2004): Does IT matter? Information Technology and the Corrosion of Competitive Advantage, Harvard Business School Press, Boston.

Gabrijelčič, J. (1995): Od kakovosti k odličnosti (From Quality to Excellence), Dolenjska založba.

Hoegl, M., Parboteeah, K. P. (2006): Team reflexivity in innovative projects, R&D Management 36. 2, © 2006 The Authors Journal compilation © 2006 Blackwell Publishing Ltd.

IPMA (2006): International Project Management Association, The proceedings of 20th IPMA World Congress on Project Management, Shanghai, China, 15-17 October 2006.

Kern, T., Roblek, M., Urh, B. (2007): Prosis - Project Management Support System. V: Projektni menadžer - profesija budućnosti. Beograd: Udruženje za upravljanje projektima Srbije – YUPMA.

Kotler, P. (1998): Marketing management, Trženjsko upravljanje, Slovenska knjiga.

Newbert, S. L., Gopalakrishnan, S., Kirchoff, B. A. (2008): Looking beyond resources: Exploring the importance of entrepreneurship to firm-level competitive advantage in technologically intensive industries, Technovation 28 (2008).

PMBOK (2004): A Guide to the Project Management Body of Knowledge, Project management Institute.

Potočnik, V. (2000): Trženje storitev (Marketing of Services), Gospodarski vestnik, Ljubljana.

PRINCE2 (2002): A practical Handbook, 2nd ed. Oxford, Boston: Butterworth-Heinemann.

Project Management Institute (2007): Selling Project Management in Your Organisation, Knowledge & Wisdom Center Knowledgebase, http://knowledgebase.pmi.org.

Roberts, E. B. (1992): Strategic Management of Technology: Global Benchmarking, 10 December, 1992 (Results of a survey sponsored by the Massachusetts Institute of Technology, Cambridge, Mass and PA Consulting Group, London, England).

Rozman, R., Kovač, J., Koletnik, F. (1993): Management, Gospodarski vestnik, Ljubljana.

Rutheford, T. D. (2006): Requiem or rebirth? Internal labour markets and labour market restructuring in the Kitchener and Sault Ste. Marie regions, The Canadian Geographer / Le Geographe canadien 50. no 2 197-216.

Scheer, A. W., Abolhassan, F., Jost, W., Kirchmer, M. (2002): Business Process Excellence: ARIS in Practice, Springer.

Swink, M., Talluri, S., Pandejpong, T. (2005): Faster, better, cheaper: A study of NPD project efficiency and performance tradeoffs, Journal of Operations Management 24 (2006) 542 – 562.

Tekavčič, M. (1998): Obvladovanje stroškov (Costs Management), Gospodarski vestnik, Ljubljana.

Treven, S. (1998): Management človeških virov (Human Resources Management), Gospodarski vestnik, Ljubljana.

Žurga, G. (2003): Projektni menedžment, Izzivi so tu – izkoristimo jih (Project Management, Challenges Are Here - Let's Overcome Them), Delo, Znanost supplement.

Lyneis, J. M., Cooper, K. G., Els, S. A. (2001): Strategic management of complex projects: a case study using system dynamics, System Dynamics Review, Volume 17, Number 3, 237 – 260, Fall 2001.

About the Authors

Janez Mayer, PhD, assistant professor at the University of Maribor, Faculty of Organizational Sciences, is a doctor of psychology. He is the author of a special assessment procedure for measurements of intellectual potential of the most promising people in organizations.

Jože Ban earned a master's degree for his thesis "Rewarding of Project Work". He is the author and co-author of several professional publications, project tasks, papers and methods related to the organisation, business process optimisation and rewarding principles.

Tomaž Kern is an associate professor at the University of Maribor, Faculty of Organizational Sciences, and lectures on business processes and project management. He leads a team of experts. His bibliography includes over 200 scientific and technical papers and articles.

Requirement Specification: Resource Scheduling Definition Language

Alenka Baggia

alenka.baggia@fov.uni-mb.si

Robert Leskovar

robert.leskovar@fov.uni-mb.si

Abstract

Resource scheduling methods are becoming more effective and refined. Different constraints and the importance of criteria are being considered. Usually, scheduling methods cannot be used for different resource scheduling problems. Some scheduling problem researches discuss a problem description. Several languages for the definition of specific scheduling problems are also proposed in the literature. With a general scheduling problem definition language, a comparison of different scheduling algorithms is enabled and the most appropriate scheduling algorithm for specific problem can be chosen. The resource scheduling problem description language development procedure, including the syntax and semantic scheme of the language, is presented here. An object-oriented methodology is used for the presentation of the resource scheduling model.

Keywords: requirement specification, scheduling, resource, definition language

1. Introduction

The problem of resource scheduling is only one of many problems that are likely to be described with a unified model. As shown in Brucker (2001), the theory of scheduling is characterized by a virtually unlimited number of problem types. Scheduling is the allocation of activities/actions over time to resources according to certain performance criteria (Spyropoulos, 2000,

p. 102). Different types of resources can be scheduled, and for each type, diverse solutions or scheduling algorithms exist. In some examples, one solution can be used to schedule different types of resources. The management of the organization must choose the most appropriate scheduling system, keeping in mind the importance of the scheduling and prior experiences of experts in scheduling. As presented in Papler et al. (2003, p. 329ff), the importance of the scheduling system is in better usage of capacities, better understanding of the problem, centralized information, keeping the knowledge in the organization and more efficient scheduling.

The difference between scheduling algorithms in the production scheduling problem and the personnel scheduling problem was presented in Baggia (2005, p. 469f). When scheduling production orders, the most appropriate activity for a specific resource in the time horizon is to be found under consideration of the constraints. In the case of personnel scheduling, the most appropriate resource for a specific activity in the time horizon is to be found. Constraints are also considered in the case of personnel scheduling. The result of both algorithms is the same; the difference is in the approach.

Scheduling problems are described in different ways. When deciding to buy or develop the scheduling system, an organization cannot compare different methods or scheduling algorithms. Because of the different input and output data, it is also not possible to use a general user interface. Cesta et al. (2001, p. 369ff) proposed a symbolic language to describe the domain and the rules. There is a need to develop a universal language to describe a resource scheduling problem.

The aim of this paper is to present our approach to the development of the resource scheduling definition language. The language is based on a general resource scheduling model, with which different types of resource scheduling problems can be described. Section 2 presents some relevant prior researches. The resource scheduling is explained in section 3. We introduce the general resource scheduling problem, its description and the development of the resource scheduling definition language in section 4. In section 5 the validation process is presented. Some concluding remarks are presented in section 6.

2. Prior Research

Diverse languages are proposed for the process description. Andrews et al. (2003) presents the BPEL (Business Process Execution Language), a programming language based on XML (eXtensible Markup Language). BPEL enables programming, which can involve larger groups of people or smaller groups over longer time periods. Similar languages can be used for the description of the resource scheduling problem.

Colindres (1992, p. 45ff) presented a high-level specific purpose language called RCSL (Resource-Constrained Scheduling Language), based on the concepts of heuristic scheduling. The functionality of RCSL was not established, since the testing was not performed on real scheduling problems. Beck et al. (1993) introduced DDL (Domain Description Language) which aims to represent a detailed description of a generic factory production model. The structure of the language is based on entities, explained via tables of components similar to standard relational database.

The language, called REDOM, can be applied to different scheduling application domains with a minimum degree of effort, because it is based on a generic meta-model of the resource scheduling problem (Thrampoulidis et al., 1997, p. 1135) REDOM was tested on a real-world example of airline scheduling. Thrampoulidis and Tranoris (1999) later presented a revised plan of the REDOM metamodel using the Unified Modelling Language (UML).

A language for describing process scheduling problems is presented by Zentner at al. (1998, p. 125ff). The goal of the language is to provide a compact, intuitive and context-independent means of representing the wide variety of process scheduling problems that arise in the chemical/pharmaceutical industry. Planning Domain Definition Language (PDDL) presented by Ghallab et al. (1998, p. 1ff) is intended to express what actions are possible, what the structure of compound actions is and what the effects of actions are in the domain.

The research by Bartak and Rudova (2001, p. 19ff) presents a generic model for the covering scheduling and timetabling problems as well as some problems from planning under time and resource constraints. Formal language is not presented in this stage of the model development.

Language for specific domains is also presented by Golden (2002, p. 59ff) and Garagnani (2004, p. 389ff). Rodríguez-Moreno et al. (2004) tried to combine workflow tools with scheduling tools. In some cases, eXtensible Markup Language (XML) is used for process description (Ishimaru et al., 2000; Savva and Drescher, 2005; Choi et al., 2003, p. 85ff).

Based on presented prior researches, we established that no tested and useful model or language for the definition of the general resource scheduling problem is available. A set of benchmark instances was introduced and used for an "International Timetabling Competition" to which 24 algorithms were submitted by various research groups active in the field of timetabling (Chiarandini et al., 2006, p. 403). As we would like to enable future comparison of different scheduling algorithms, we will present a model and definition language requirement specification. The resource scheduling problem will be presented in the following section.

3. The Resource Scheduling

A scheduling problem may be defined as a set of parameters which define the set of machines, set of resources, set of tasks or operations, set of optimality criteria and the type of schedule. Not all of these parameters must have a value, but the class of schedule must always be defined. Thus, a scheduling problem is in fact a set of instances obtained by assigning values to all the problem parameters (Colindres, 1992, p. 25).

Scheduling algorithms have been an important area of research in the last few decades. Different approaches are used to schedule resources, including mathematical models, heuristic methods and artificial intelligence. Methods are efficient and refined, different constraints can be considered and the importance of criteria can be added. The problems are often restricted to the development of efficient scheduling algorithms. As presented in Baggia and Leskovar (2004, p. 379ff), research in the field of production scheduling and personnel scheduling has shown the importance of the definition or the model of the problem.

A general model of the resource scheduling problem is based on prior experiences from the area of production scheduling and personnel scheduling. In the beginning, the most important element of scheduling, a resource has to be defined. Resource is, in the literature, sometimes defined as one of the constraint types. Research by Chua et al. (2003, p. 295ff) defines the constraint resource that represents the availability of key physical resources, e.g., materials, manpower, equipment and space etc. Since the aim of this research is to develop a general resource scheduling problem model, resource has to be defined in a wider scope. Resource is not only just one of the constraints. Resource can represent the key object of the scheduling process that is the resource that needs to be scheduled. Resource has, similar to constraint, defined attributes, which are not only ability and availability, but also a hierarchical structure, the location of the resource, incompatibility with other resources, the group that it belongs to, etc. Based on a detailed description of a resource scheduling problem and its most important element, the resource, the requirement specification for a general resource scheduling definition language is presented.

4. The General Resource Scheduling Problem

The review of prior research showed a wide spectrum of demands included in resource scheduling. It may be of interest in the future to study more specific models that combine machine scheduling with personnel scheduling (Pinedo, 2002, p. 507).

A metalanguage for the description of personnel scheduling problem was developed on the basis of research, presented in Baggia and Leskovar (2004, p. 379ff), which was focused on the development of reusable software for scheduling hospital personnel. A precise model is a preliminary condition for a successful usage of scheduling algorithms. Baggia (2004, p. 23ff) presented the metalanguage, used in the case of a Slovenian hospital. It was presumed that a personnel scheduling model can be described as a set of attributes belonging to this object. A common set of an object's attributes regardless of whether it is a person, process or constraint, is:

O { ts, v, i, te}, where

O ⇒ Object
ts ⇒ Start time
v ⇒ Value
i ⇒ Interval
te ⇒ End time

As mentioned above, all other classes can be described using the same set of objects in the problem of personnel scheduling. The detailed descriptions of some classes (person, process etc.) were described as entities in a relational database. Only scheduling rules were described using the presented metalanguage, so separated descriptions of objects are still an issue.

The scheduling problem was expanded to the production environment in Baggia (2005, p. 77ff). The personnel scheduling problem in health care and the problem of production scheduling differ only in their scheduling algorithms. It was assumed that every resource scheduling model can be described with general elements. The XML was used for the description of the model.

In this research, the following hypothesis is examined:

The definition of resource in scheduling problems is independent of scheduling type. Therefore, a definition of a specific resource is stated with common set of attributes.

Diverse research methods will be used to examine the hypothesis. After data gathering from different resources in two scheduling problems, the structure and object analysis is performed. The synthesis of conclusions includes the implementation of an UML-based model. Object-oriented programming languages are suitable for the transformation of the model into a resource scheduling definition language. Testing methods include the testing of a logical structure, dynamic testing and verification of the language via application to other scheduling problems.

4.1 The Description of the Resource Scheduling Problem

Object-oriented technology is very useful for modeling real problems. The Unified Modeling Language (UML) is used to show the functionality of the scheduling process. The use case diagram allows for the specification of high-level user goals that the system must carry out. More formally, a use case is made up of a set of scenarios. Each scenario is a sequence of steps that encompass an interaction between a user and a system. The use case brings scenarios together that accomplish a specific goal of the user.

The use case, presented in Figure 1, shows the resource scheduling process flow independent from the type of resource that is to be scheduled. The *Data Entry* use case includes three specific use cases. Some data about resources and requirements are partly collected in the *Information System.* Not all attributes are available from the *Information System,* so the *Scheduler* must enter some of the data. The process of *Scheduling* can start when all the data are collected. The *Schedule Feasibility* has to be established, and at the end, the schedule is *Published* and made available to the *Executant* of the schedule. The actor *Executant* plays an important role in the scheduling process, as this is usually the person that gets the first feedback about the schedule efficiency.

The process of resource scheduling was presented with a use case diagram. The model for the description of the presented process was developed. The model is presented with a specific language.

Figure 1: Resource scheduling use case diagram

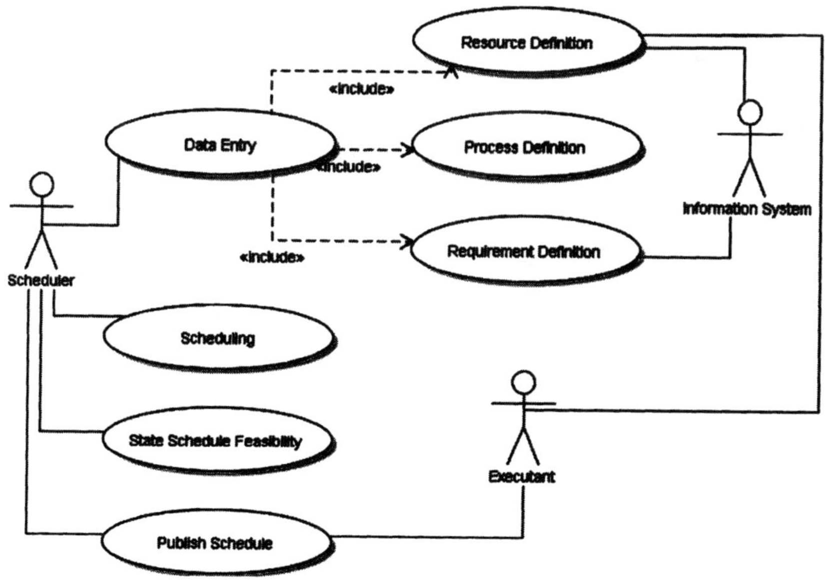

4.2 The Development of the Language

As stated by Šuster (2000, p. 57ff), the study of symbol systems comprises of three fields: pragmatics, semantics and syntax. Pragmatics is a theory about relations between symbols and the subjects that use the symbols. Syntax deals with relations between symbols, and the semantics are involved in the relation between the symbols and the referred objects. The syntax and the semantics of the language will be discussed in the following sections.

A metalanguage is described as a language (about another language), a description language, which is used by linguists and logicians to analyze and describe the sentences of the researched subject language. As a metalanguage for presenting the resource scheduling problem definition language, UML class diagrams will be used.

4.3 The Formal Definition Of Syntax

The class diagram does not represent dynamic information, only a static structure of the model. The basic unit of the object-oriented technique is an object, which is an entity with attributes, behaviour and identity (Wampler, 2002, p. 7). Basic elements of the class diagram, used in this case, are presented in Figure 2.

Figure 2: Basic elements of the class diagram

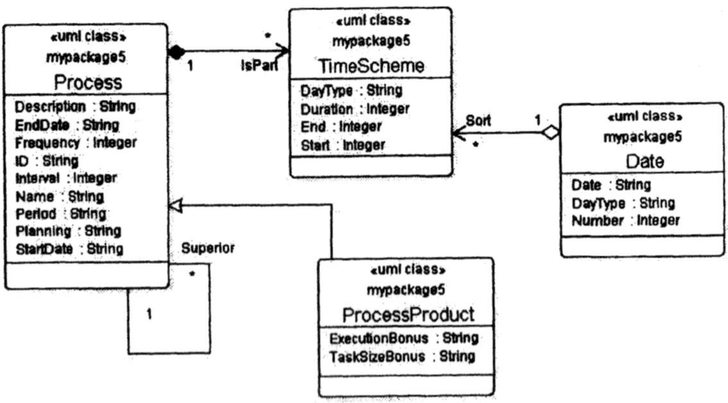

The diagram presented in Figure 2 constitutes three main elements in the system: ***Process***, ***TimeScheme*** and ***Date***. Each of these elements is a class, with its own attributes and methods. Each attribute has a defined data type and the option of visibility. Associations connect the objects. A directed association shows the path of querying. Associations with no arrows are bidirectional. Multiplicity can also be defined for associations. Composition, aggregation and generalization are special cases of association. Detailed descriptions of class diagrams will not be presented in the paper and are available from the Object Management Group (OMG, 2005) specification.

4.4 The Semantical Scheme of the Language

Logical semantics studies relationships between linguistic expressions of formal language and structures, with which these expressions can be interpreted, about which expressions talk. The structure used to interpret the symbols of the formal system is called a model (Šuster, 2000, p. 58). The UML framework for meta-modeling is based on architecture with four layers:

- Meta-metamodel
- Metamodel
- Model
- User objects

The functions of these layers are presented in Table 1:

Based on presented four-layer metamodel architecture we established our research is focused on the metamodel layer, since our aim is to develop a language for specifying a model. For this purpose we present classes and their attributes in the class diagram. We used real-world scheduling problems for the determination of general scheduling problem characteristics.

Five different cases of resource scheduling problems were used to define a model with which it is possible to capture any resource scheduling problem. A case of production scheduling (Papler, 2001, p. 25ff), personnel scheduling in a Slovenian hospital (Baggia, 2004, p. 23ff), the resource scheduling problem in the chemical/pharmaceutical industry (Zentner et al., 1998, 125ff), the nurse scheduling problem in a Belgian hospital (Vanden

Berghe, 2002) and the problem of personnel scheduling in the area of gambling (www.schedulerexpert.com) were included in the development of the model. It was established that all the attributes of the objects, used in the presentation of a generic model for scheduling and timetabling problems, presented in Bartak and Rudova (2001, p. 19ff), were also included in the collected scheduling problem characteristics, used to define the model of the resource scheduling problem.

Table 1: Four-layer Metamodel Architecture (OMG, 2003)

Layer	**Description**	**Example**
meta-metamodel	The infrastructure for a metamodeling architecture. Defines the language for specifying metamodels.	MetaClass, MetaAttribute, MetaOperation
metamodel	An instance of a meta-metamodel. Defines the language for specifying a model.	Class, Attribute, Operation, Component
model	An instance of a metamodel. Defines a language to describe an information domain.	StockShare, askPrice, sellLimitOrder, StockQuoteServer
user objects (user data)	An instance of a model. Defines a specific information domain.	<Acme_SW_Share_98789>, 654.56, sell_limit_order, <Stock_Quote_Svr_32123>

4.5 The Model of the Resource Scheduling Problem

A general model of the scheduling problem is presented as a class diagram. The advantage of object-oriented technology can be seen in the case of the *Resource* definition. A special type of association "generalization" was used for the description of the *Resource*. Attributes of the class *Resource* were defined on the basis of five different researches, as shown in Figure 3.

Figure 3: Resource class

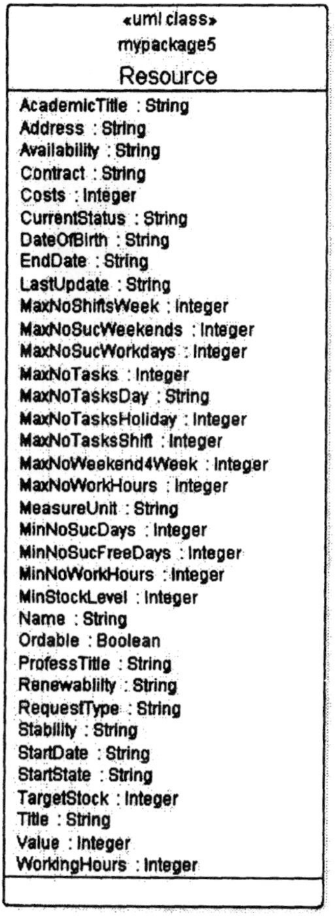

Some attributes of the *Resource* class, presented in Figure 3, cannot be used in all scheduling problems. When scheduling personnel, it is not reasonable to use the attribute *TargetStock*, and similarly in the case of production scheduling, there is no need to describe the *AcademicTitle* when describing a product. The association of generalization is used to resolve this kind of problem. Generalization describes a relationship inferior – superior. The class *Resource* can only be described with general attributes, new inferior classes are defined for special attributes, as presented in Figure 4.

Figure 4: Resource class with inferior classes Person and MaterialResource

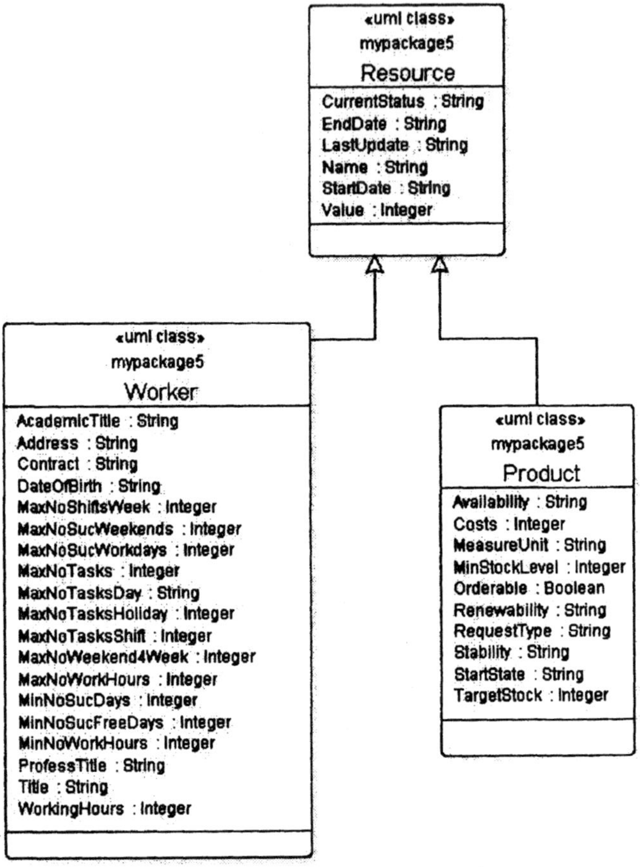

Classes *Person* and MaterialResource, presented in Figure 4, inherit all the attributes of the basic, inferior class *Resource*, and add their own attributes to the ones defined by the *Resource* class. The structure of the class *Resource* does not have to change when adding new attributes. If a new attribute appears, it is simply added to the *Person* or *MaterialResource* class. In case adding the new attribute is not logical for any of the existing classes, a new class is added to the diagram and connected to the *Resource* class with the relationship of generalization. The problem of extensibility is solved similarly in other objects in the model.

For resolving the problem of extensibility in the model, some inferior classes were added in the case of:

- Structure - quantity is not important when scheduling personnel
- Rule - some scheduling systems do not use penalty
- Process - quantity bonus is not usable in the case of personnel scheduling
- Unit - the reception unit is not defined in production scheduling
- ResourceProperty - a responsibility level can not be defined for a product
- Work
    - Shift rotations are typical for personnel scheduling, while
    - Quantity is typical for item scheduling.

The model has to be validated before use in real-world examples. The validation includes different real-world problems of scheduling, as presented in the next section.

5. Validation

The validation process provides supporting evidence that the software satisfies system, requirements allocated to software, and solves the right problem (IEEE, 1998, p. 2).

The purposed model has to be validated on different levels. The validation of the model starts with the UML notation. The model was developed with the Oracle JDeveloper 10g tool that only allows valid elements to be used in the development process. Further validation of the object-oriented notation will be performed with the translation of the UML model into the selected programming code.

The second level of model validation is related to the real problems of scheduling. Prior research was focused on production scheduling (Papler, 2001, p. 25ff) and personnel scheduling in a hospital (Baggia, 2004, p. 23ff). For both problems, all the data needed for scheduling were collected during the time of research.

It was established that all the data for production scheduling as well as the data for personnel scheduling in a Slovenian hospital could fit into the presented model. The model can handle all the exceptions, so the model is usable.

6. Conclusions

The problem of resource scheduling can be found in different areas of manufacturing and services. The decision on which algorithms or scheduling systems to use or even develop is always difficult. The comparison of different approaches is almost impossible, since different input data are used to start the scheduling algorithms. With a general model for the description of the resource scheduling problem decisions, would be easier. Since the basic input data would be the same for all problems, the output of the algorithms could be compared.

The presented model is the first step towards resolving the problem of the resource scheduling problem general description. The examined hypothesis is confirmed. The definition of resource in scheduling problems is independent of scheduling type, and therefore the definition of a specific resource is stated with a common set of attributes.

Further development will show which programming language to use for the description of the model. Since object-oriented technology is used for the representation of the model, XML and Java promise good results. XML was appropriate for the description of the problem state, but different types of relations between objects are difficult to describe. Java is not as widely used as XML, but it has some advantages when describing the extensibility of objects.

Further validation will be carried out for the UML notation when the model is translated to the selected metalanguage. The model will also be validated on the real-world example of the Faculty timetabling problem.

Bibliography and References

Andrews, T., Curbera, F., Dholakia, H., Goland, Y., Klein, J., Leymann, F. Liu, K., Roller, D., Smith, D., Thatte, S., Trickovic, I. & Weerawarana, S. (2003). *Business Process Execution Language for Web Services: Version 1.1*. Available from:

ftp://www6.software.ibm.com/software/developer/library/ws-bpel.pdf (Accessed 13 October 2005).

Baggia, A. (2004). Meta-Language Framework for Personnel Scheduling. In *ECON '04*. Edited by Jašková, M. (23-30). Ostrawa: Technical University of Ostrava.

Baggia, A. (2005). *Splošna definicija problema razporejanja virov (A general definiton of the resource scheduling problem)*. Synergy of methodologies: proceedings of the 24th International Conference on Organizational Science Development, Kranj: Moderna organizacija.

Baggia, A. & Leskovar, R. (2004). Design of Reusable Modules for Health Care Scheduling System. In *Informatics and Management: Selected Topics*. Edited by Florjančič, J. & Pütz, K. (379-390). Frankfurt am Main: Peter Lang.

Bartak, R. & Rudova, H. (2001). *Integrated Modeling for Planning, Scheduling, and Timetabling Problems*. Proceedings of the Twentieth Workshop of the UK Planning and Scheduling Special Interest Group. Edinburgh: University of Edinburgh.

Beck, H., Currie, K. & Tate, A. (1993). *A Domain Description Language for Job-Shop Scheduling*. Available from: http://www.aiai.ed.ac.uk/project/ftp/documents/1993/93-tosca-ddl.ps (Accessed 5 January 2005).

Brucker, P. (2001). *Scheduling Algorithms*. Berlin: Springer-Verlag.

Cesta, A., Cortellessa, G., Oddi, A., Policella, N. & Susi, A. (2001). *A Constraint-Based Architecture for Flexible Support to Activity Scheduling*. Proceedings of Advances in Artificial Intelligence (369-381), Berlin: Springer-Verlag.

Chiarandini, M., Birattari, M., Socha, K., Rossi-Doria, O. (2006). An effective hybrid algorithm for university course timetabling. *Journal of Scheduling*, 9: 403-432.

Choi, I., Minseok, S., Chulsoon, P. & Namkyu, P. (2003). An XML-based process definition language for integrated process management, *Computers in Industry*, 50: 85-102.

Chua, D.K.H., Shen, L.J. & Bok S.H. (2003). Constraint-Based Planning with Integrated Production Scheduler over Internet, *Journal of Construction Engineering and Management*, 129: 293-301.

Colindres, A. (1992). *RCSL: Resource-constrained scheduling language*. Doctoral dissertation, Houston: University of Houston.

Garagnani, M. (2004). *A Diagrammatic Meta-Language for Planning Domain Descriptions*. 16th European Conference on Artificial

Intelligence, Workshop Planning and Scheduling: Bridging Theory to Practice. Available from: http://galahad.plg.inf.uc3m.es/~dborrajo/ecai04-workshop/papers/Garagnani.pdf (Accessed 1 July 2004).

Ghallab, M., Howe, A., Knoblock, C., McDermott, D., Ram, A., Veloso, M., Weld, D. & Wilkins, D. (1998). *PDDL – The Planning Domain Definition Language*. Technical Report, Yale Center for Computational Vision and Control. Available from: http://www.informatik.uni-ulm.de/ki/Edu/Vorlesungen/GdKI/WS0203/pddl.pdf (Accessed 19 August 2005).

Golden, K. (2002). *A Domain Description Language for Data Processing*. International Conference on Planning and Scheduling, workshop on the future of PDDL.

IEEE (1998), IEEE Std 1012-1998, IEEE Standard for Software Verification and Validation.

Ishimaru, T. & Yosuke, T. (2000). Definition and Use of WPDL-XML. Available from: http://www3.toshiba.co.jp/ccc/page/img/wpdlxml.pdf (Accessed 29 June 2005).

OMG (2003). *OMG Unified Modelling Language Specification*. Available from: http://www.omg.org/docs/formal/03-03-01.pdf (Accessed 8 August 2005).

OMG (2005). Object Management Group home page. Available from: http://www.omg.org (Accessed 13 October 2005).

Papler, A. (2001). *Interaktivno večkriterijsko razporejanje proizvodnje (Interactive multicriteria production scheduling)*. Master thesis, Kranj: Univerza v Mariboru, Fakulteta za organizacijske vede.

Papler, A., Leskovar, R. & Kljajić, M. (2003). Design of Interactive Multicriteria Production Scheduling System. In *Organisation and Management: Selected Topics*. Edited by Florjančič, J. and Paape, B. (321-331). Frankfurt am Main: Peter Lang.

Pinedo, M. (2002). *Scheduling Theory, Algorithms, and Systems*. Upper Saddle River: Prentice Hall.

Rodríguez-Moreno, M.D., Borrajo, D., Oddi, A., Cesta, A. & Meziat, D. (2004). *Planning and Scheduling for workflow domains*. Available from: http://galahad.plg.inf.uc3m.es/~dborrajo/ecai04-workshop/papers/Moreno-et-al.pdf (Accessed 1 July 2005).

Savva, A. & Drescher, M. (2005). JSDL Introduction. Available from: https://forge.gridforum.org/projects/jsdl-wg/ (Accessed 15 May 2005).

Spyropoulos C.D. (2000). AI planning and scheduling in the medical hospital environment. *Artificial Intelligence in Medicine*, 20: 101-111.

Šuster, D. (2000). *Simbolna logika (Symbol logic)*. Maribor: Pedagoška fakulteta.

Vanden Berghe, G. (2002). *An Advanced Model and Novel Meta-heuristic Solution Methods to Personnel Scheduling in Healthcare,* Doctoral Dissertation, Gent: University of Gent.

Wampler, B.E. (2002). *The Essence of Object-Oriented Programming with Java and UML*, Boston: Addison-Wesley.

Trampoulidis, K., Diamantopoulos, N. & Housos, E. (1997a). REDOM: An OO Language to Define and On-line Manipulate Regulations in the Resource (Re)Scheduling Problem. Software – Practice and Experience, 27: 1135-1161.

Trampoulidis, K. & Tranoris, C. (1999). *Using UML For Stating And Handling Regulations In The Resource (Re)Scheduling Problem.* 5th International Conference of the Decision Science Institute, Athens, Greece.

Zentner, M.G., Elkamel, A., Penky, J.F. & Reklaitis, G.V. (1998). A language for describing process scheduling problems. *Computers and Chemical Engineering*, 22: 125-145.

About the Authors

Alenka Baggia is a teaching assistant at the University of Maribor, Faculty of Organizational Sciences. Her research fields are production scheduling and personnel scheduling.

Robert Leskovar is a professor at the University of Maribor, Faculty of Organizational Sciences. His research fields are multiple criteria decision making, software quality and modeling and simulation.

Measuring the Economic Effectiveness of a Manufacturing Process Using Stochastic Modelling

Alenka Brezavšček

alenka.brezavscek@fov.uni-mb.si

Alenka Hudoklin

alenka.hudoklin@fov.uni-mb.si

Abstract

In this paper, the economic effectiveness of a manufacturing process is studied, and a measure of the economic effectiveness is defined, which is expressed as a function of the direct cost involved in the manufacturing process. A mathematical model to calculate the value of this measure is developed. In order to obtain the model parameters, a manufacturing process is described by a homogeneous finite reducible Markov chain. It was found that the absorption characteristics of the Markov chain can be used for calculating the main parameters of the model. The usefulness of the model is shown by its application on an example of a particular manufacturing process, although it is applicable to different types of these. It can be also used for monitoring changes of the economic effectiveness of a manufacturing process due to technological or/and organizational modifications.

Keywords: manufacturing process, economic effectiveness, stochastic mathematical model, Markov chain

1. Introduction

The assessment of the economic effectiveness of manufacturing processes is an old problem that has attracted the attention of many researchers in different industrial branches (see, e.g. Zuev, 1969, p. 207ff.). The authors of numerous publications have tried to solve this problem using different approaches, but rarely mathematical ones (see, e.g. Tyre and Hauptman, 1992, p. 301ff.; Al-Najjar, 2000, p. 267ff.). In recent years, it has become widely known that economic processes can be successfully described by mathematical models. First, statistical methods (see, e.g. Magda, 1994, p. 47ff.; Antony, 2001, p. 812ff.) and later, stochastic models were used to describe manufacturing processes (see, e.g. Lu and Qiao, 2004, p. 1ff.; Loher et al., 2003, p. 531ff.; Goetz et al., 2006, p. 1ff.).

The aim of this paper is to examine the economic effectiveness of a manufacturing process, which is treated as a stochastic process. A mathematical stochastic model for measuring the manufacturing process's economic effectiveness is developed. We assume that the economic effectiveness of a manufacturing process is a function of the direct cost involved in the process. In order to calculate this cost, we model the manufacturing process as a homogeneous finite reducible Markov chain. The calculation is based on the absorption properties of the Markov chain, namely the probability of absorption from the transient states to the absorbing states, and the expected number of visits to the transient states. The usage of the model presented is demonstrated on a simple manufacturing process.

2. Stochastic Mathematical Model of a Manufacturing Process's Economic Effectiveness

2.1 Model Development

Consider a manufacturing process producing products of a given type. The process consists of k operations, including manufacturing operations and inspections. To fulfil a customer order or other requirements, a given number of products should be successfully completed. The effectiveness of a manufacturing process depends on the time needed to produce a requested quantity of good products, and on the number of defective items that are discarded during the process. As a measure of the economic effectiveness of a manufacturing process, we choose the ratio E given by the expression:

$$E = \frac{C_{id}}{C}, \tag{1}$$

where

C is the expected direct production cost per successfully completed product of an actual manufacturing process,
C_{id} is the direct production cost per product of the associated "*ideal*" manufacturing process.

We call a manufacturing process "*ideal*" if, input material being specified, no defective items are manufactured. The cost C_{id} can be calculated as follows:

$$C_{id} = C_M + \sum_{i=1}^{k} t_i c_i \,, \tag{2}$$

where

C_M is the cost of input material per product,
t_i is the number of labour hours needed to complete the i-th operation of the manufacturing process,
c_i is the cost of one labour hour of the i-th operation of the manufacturing process.

However, an actual manufacturing process always produces a certain number of defective items that are either sent to an earlier manufacturing operation for reworking or they are classified as scrap. Reworking results in a larger cumulative number of operations needed to produce the required number of successfully completed products. In practice, successfully completed products are frequently categorized into different classes according to their quality. Owing to scrap, the cumulative number of operations per unit of input material decreases. On the other hand, in order to manufacture the desired number of successfully completed products, a larger quantity of material entering the manufacturing process is needed. A larger quantity of entering material means that the cumulative number of operations increases.

Considering an actual manufacturing process, the cost C used in (1) can be written as follows:

$$C = \frac{1}{F}\left(C_M + \sum_{i=1}^{k} r_i t_i c_i \right), \tag{3}$$

where

- r_i is the expected number of executions of the i-th operation of a manufacturing process,
- F is the expected fraction of successfully completed products of any quality class.

For a given manufacturing process, the parameters C_M, t_i, c_i, i=1, 2, ..., k, used in (2) and (3) are constant and predetermined. The main problem in assessing the direct cost (3) is the assessment of the parameters F and r_i, i=1, 2, ..., k. In the following text, we shall present a method for the determination of these two variables.

2.2 Determination of Model Parameters

The fraction of successfully completed products as well as the cumulative number of executions of a given operation of a manufacturing process depends on a variety of factors and can be treated as random variables. To calculate the expected values of these two variables, we will describe a manufacturing process as a stochastic process.

Preliminaries

A stochastic process is a collection of random variables $\{X_n\}$ or $\{X(t)\}$ defined for all relevant values of n (*discrete time*) or t (*continuous time*). The set of possible values of X_n or $X(t)$ is the *state space* of the process. If the state space contains a finite number of states, the process is called *finite stochastic process*. The state space is *discrete* if it contains a finite number or enumerable infinity of points, otherwise it is *continuous*. The process has the *Markovian property* if, the present state of the process being known, we can determine the probability of any future state without reference to the past. Such processes are called *Markov processes* (see, e.g. Stroock, 2005, p. 23ff).

A large number of economic situations can be mathematically modelled by *Markov chains* (see Shamblin and Stevens, Jr., 1974, p. 53ff; Beichelt, 2006, p. 233ff). Markov chains are defined as Markov processes in discrete time with a discrete state space. A Markov chain is said to be *homogeneous* if a transition in unit time from one given state to another depends only on the two states and not on time. The probability of transition between the two states of a Markov chain in a given time interval is called transition probability. Of particular importance are the *one-step transition probabilities*. We denote the one-step transition probability between the states i and j by the symbol p_{ij}. If the state space is finite and equal to $S=\{1,2,\ldots,N\}$, then all one-step transition probabilities can be included in a *transition matrix* **P**:

$$\mathbf{P} = \begin{array}{c} \\ 1 \\ 2 \\ \vdots \\ N \end{array}\!\!\begin{array}{c} \begin{array}{cccc} 1 & 2 & \ldots & N \end{array} \\ \begin{bmatrix} p_{11} & p_{12} & \cdots & p_{1,N} \\ p_{21} & p_{22} & \cdots & p_{2,N} \\ \vdots & \vdots & \ddots & \vdots \\ p_{N,1} & p_{N,2} & \cdots & p_{N,N} \end{bmatrix} \end{array}.$$

The states of a Markov chain fall into distinct types according to their limiting behaviour. If the ultimate return to the initial state j is a certain event, the state is called *recurrent*. If the ultimate return to the initial state has a probability of less than 1, the state is called *transient*. The states of an arbitrary Markov chain can be divided into two sets (one of them may be empty): one set composed of all the recurrent states, and the other set composed of all the transient states. The recurrent states can be decomposed uniquely into *closed sets*, denoted by C. A closed set is a set of recurrent states from which there is no escape. Once a closed set is entered, it is never vacated. A state i is *absorbing* if $\{i\}$ is a closed set. A Markov chain consisting of both sets of states, recurrent and transient, is *reducible*. If all the states are of the same type, the Markov chain is *irreducible*. When a finite reducible Markov chain contains l closed sets, the transition matrix **P** can be written in the following form:

$$\mathbf{P} = \begin{bmatrix} \mathbf{Q} & \mathbf{R}_1 & \cdots & \mathbf{R}_l \\ \mathbf{0} & \mathbf{P}_1 & \cdots & \mathbf{0} \\ \vdots & \vdots & \ddots & \vdots \\ \mathbf{0} & \mathbf{0} & \cdots & \mathbf{P}_l \end{bmatrix}, \qquad (4)$$

where the matrix **Q** contains one-step transition probabilities between the transient states, the matrices $\mathbf{P}_i$, i=1, 2, ..., l, contain one-step transition probabilities within the i-th closed set, and the matrices $\mathbf{R}_i$ i=1, 2, ..., l, contain one-step transition probabilities from the transient states into the i-

th closed set of the recurrent states. All the elements in the matrices denoted by **0** are zeroes.

The matrices **Q**, $\mathbf{P}_i$, and $\mathbf{R}_i$, i=1, 2, ..., l, being known, one can calculate the probabilities that the chain leaves the transient states and is *absorbed* into one of the closed sets of the recurrent states. The probabilities of absorption from the transient states to a given closed set C_i, $i=1,2,\ldots,l$, are the elements of the column vector $\mathbf{f}_{C_i}$ calculated from the following equation (see, e.g. Hudoklin-Božič, 2003, p. 76):

$$\mathbf{f}_{C_i} = (\mathbf{I}-\mathbf{Q})^{-1}\mathbf{R}_i\mathbf{1} = \mathbf{N}\mathbf{R}_i\mathbf{1}, \qquad i=1,2,\ldots,l,$$

where **I** denotes the identity matrix and **1** is the column identity vector. The matrix $\mathbf{N}=(\mathbf{I}-\mathbf{Q})^{-1}$ is called the *fundamental matrix*. Its elements represent the expected number of visits to a given transient state.

If the state i is an absorbing state, the probability of absorption to $C=\{i\}$ is calculated as

$$\mathbf{f}_C = (\mathbf{I}-\mathbf{Q})^{-1}\mathbf{R}_C = \mathbf{N}\mathbf{R}_C, \tag{5}$$

where $\mathbf{R}_c$ is the column vector containing one-step transition probabilities from the transient states to the absorbing state i.

Calculation

In order to calculate the values of the parameters needed to determine the ratio (1), we choose a finite homogeneous reducible Markov chain for modelling the manufacturing process. Our choice is based on the following facts: The manufacturing process is a time sequence of stages. Therefore, the process can be observed in discrete time. Each stage of the manufacturing process represents a state of the chain. It is evident that the state space of the chain is finite. The states of the chain are of two types, transient and absorbing. The absorbing states are a "*successfully completed product of a given quality class*", and "*scrap*". The transient states represent k operations, including manufacturing operations and inspections. The one-step transition probabilities between the states of the chain can be estimated as the fractions of items at the entrance of a given state that enter one of the other possible states. We suppose that the manufacturing conditions are stable, so the manufacturing process can be modelled by a homogeneous chain. Since the fraction of items entering a given stage of the manufacturing process depends only on the fraction of items at the end of the operation performed immediately before, we can assume that the chain has the Markovian property.

The parameter F used in (3) can be determined as the sum of the probabilities of absorption from the state of the Markov chain that represents the first operation of the manufacturing process to one of the l-1 absorbing states representing the successfully completed product of a given quality class. The parameter r_i, i=1, 2, …, k, can be obtained as the expected number of visits to the i-th transient state of the Markov chain starting in the state representing the first operation of the manufacturing process.

To calculate the values of the parameters F and r_i, i=1, 2, … k, the transition matrix **P** is constructed. According to (4), the transition matrix of the manufacturing process under consideration can be written down as follows:

$$\mathbf{O}\ \ \mathbf{R}_1\ \ \mathbf{R}_2\ \ \mathbf{R}_{l-1}\ \ \mathbf{R}_l$$

$$\mathbf{P}=\begin{array}{c} \\ 1 \\ 2 \\ \vdots \\ k \\ k+1 \\ k+2 \\ \vdots \\ k+l-1 \\ k+l \end{array}\begin{array}{c} \begin{array}{cccc:c:c:c:c:c} 1 & 2 & \cdots & k & k+1 & k+2 & \cdots & k+l-1 & k+l \end{array} \\ \left[\begin{array}{cccc:c:c:c:c:c} p_{11} & p_{12} & \cdots & p_{1,k} & p_{1,k+1} & p_{1,k+2} & \cdots & p_{1,k+l-1} & p_{1,k+l} \\ p_{21} & p_{22} & \cdots & p_{2,k} & p_{2,k+1} & p_{2,k+2} & \cdots & p_{2,k+l-1} & p_{2,k+l} \\ \vdots & \vdots & \ddots & \vdots & \vdots & \vdots & \ddots & \vdots & \vdots \\ p_{k,1} & p_{k,2} & \cdots & p_{k,k} & p_{k,k+1} & p_{k,k+2} & \cdots & p_{k,k+l-1} & p_{k,k+l} \\ \hdashline 0 & 0 & \cdots & 0 & 1 & 0 & \cdots & 0 & 0 \\ 0 & 0 & \cdots & 0 & 0 & 1 & \cdots & 0 & 0 \\ \vdots & \vdots & \ddots & \vdots & \vdots & \vdots & \ddots & \vdots & \vdots \\ 0 & 0 & \cdots & 0 & 0 & 0 & \cdots & 1 & 0 \\ 0 & 0 & \cdots & 0 & 0 & 0 & \cdots & 0 & 1 \end{array}\right] \end{array}. \quad (6)$$

$$\mathbf{P}\ \ \mathbf{P}\ \ \mathbf{P}_{l-1}\ \ \mathbf{P}_l$$

In (6), the states denoted by 1, 2, …, k represent "*operations*" (including manufacturing operations and inspections), the states denoted by k+1, k+2, …, k+l-1 represent "*successfully completed product of a given quality class*", and the state k+l denotes "*scrap*". The states denoted by k+i, i=1, 2,

…, l, are absorbing states. Each absorbing state represents the closed set $C_i=\{k+i\}$, i=1, 2, …, l. In (6), the matrices $\mathbf{Q}$, $\mathbf{R}_1$, $\mathbf{R}_2$, …, $\mathbf{R}_l$, $\mathbf{P}_1$, $\mathbf{P}_2$, …, $\mathbf{P}_l$ are also marked.
Using the matrix $\mathbf{Q}$ from (6), we can calculate the fundamental matrix $\mathbf{N}$:

$$\mathbf{N}=(\mathbf{I}-\mathbf{Q})^{-1}=\left(\begin{array}{c} \\ 1\\ 2\\ \vdots\\ k\end{array}\!\!\begin{array}{c}\begin{array}{cccc}1&2&\cdots&k\end{array}\\ \begin{bmatrix}1&0&\cdots&0\\ 0&1&\cdots&0\\ \vdots&\vdots&\ddots&\vdots\\ 0&0&\cdots&1\end{bmatrix}\end{array}-\begin{array}{c} \\ 1\\ 2\\ \vdots\\ k\end{array}\!\!\begin{array}{c}\begin{array}{cccc}1&2&\cdots&k\end{array}\\ \begin{bmatrix}p_{11}&p_{12}&\cdots&p_{1,k}\\ p_{21}&p_{22}&\cdots&p_{2,k}\\ \vdots&\vdots&\ddots&\vdots\\ p_{k,1}&p_{k,2}&\cdots&p_{k,k}\end{bmatrix}\end{array}\right)^{-1}=\begin{array}{c} \\ 1\\ 2\\ \vdots\\ k\end{array}\!\!\begin{array}{c}\begin{array}{cccc}1&2&\cdots&k\end{array}\\ \begin{bmatrix}n_{11}&n_{12}&\cdots&n_{1,k}\\ n_{21}&n_{22}&\cdots&n_{2,k}\\ \vdots&\vdots&\ddots&\vdots\\ n_{k,1}&n_{k,2}&\cdots&n_{k,k}\end{bmatrix}\end{array}. \tag{7}$$

Since the elements of the fundamental matrix $\mathbf{N}$ represent the expected number of visits to a given transient state, the values r_i, i=1, 2, … k, can be obtained from (7) as follows:

$$r_i=n_{1,i} \qquad i=1,2,\ldots,k\,. \tag{8}$$

The probabilities of absorption to the closed sets C_i, i=1, 2, …, l-1, representing the successfully completed product of a given quality class, can be calculated according to (5) using the matrices $\mathbf{R}_1$, $\mathbf{R}_2$, …, $\mathbf{R}_{l-1}$ from (6). To simplify the calculation, these matrices are combined into one matrix denoted by $\mathbf{R}_{good}$. The probabilities of absorption to C_i, i=1, 2, …, l-1, are elements of the matrix $\mathbf{f}_{\{C_i\}}$ given by:

$$\mathbf{f}_{\{C_i\}}=\mathbf{N}\mathbf{R}_{good}=\begin{array}{c} \\ 1\\ 2\\ \vdots\\ k\end{array}\!\!\begin{array}{c}\begin{array}{cccc}1&2&\cdots&k\end{array}\\ \begin{bmatrix}n_{11}&n_{12}&\cdots&n_{1,k}\\ n_{21}&n_{22}&\cdots&n_{2,k}\\ \vdots&\vdots&\ddots&\vdots\\ n_{k,1}&n_{k,2}&\cdots&n_{k,k}\end{bmatrix}\end{array}\cdot\begin{array}{c} \\ 1\\ 2\\ \vdots\\ k\end{array}\!\!\begin{array}{c}\begin{array}{cccc}k+1&k+2&\cdots&k+l-1\end{array}\\ \begin{bmatrix}p_{1,k+1}&p_{1,k+2}&\cdots&p_{1,k+l-1}\\ p_{2,k+1}&p_{2,k+2}&\cdots&p_{2,k+l-1}\\ \vdots&\vdots&\ddots&\vdots\\ p_{k,k+1}&p_{k,k+2}&\cdots&p_{k,k+l-1}\end{bmatrix}\end{array}$$

$$=\begin{array}{c} \\ 1\\ 2\\ \vdots\\ k\end{array}\!\!\begin{array}{c}\begin{array}{cccc}k+1&k+2&\cdots&k+l-1\end{array}\\ \begin{bmatrix}f_{1C_1}&f_{1C_2}&\cdots&f_{1C_{l-1}}\\ f_{2C_1}&f_{2C_2}&\cdots&f_{2C_{l-1}}\\ \vdots&\vdots&\ddots&\vdots\\ f_{k,C_1}&f_{k,C_2}&\cdots&f_{k,C_{l-1}}\end{bmatrix}\end{array} \tag{9}$$

where $C_i=\{k+i\}$, i=1, 2, …, l-1.

The probabilities of absorption from the state of the Markov chain representing the first operation of the manufacturing process to the state representing the successfully completed product of the i-th quality class are obtained from (9) and are equal to f_{1C_i}, i=1, 2, …, l-1. We denote these probabilities with F_i. The values of F_i are the fractions of successfully completed products of the i-th quality class.

The value of the parameter F, corresponding to absorption from the state representing the first operation of the manufacturing process into any of the states representing l–1 quality classes of successfully completed product, can be obtained from (9) as follows:

$$F = \sum_{i=1}^{l-1} F_i = \sum_{i=1}^{l-1} f_{1C_i}. \qquad (10)$$

2.3 Numerical Example

Consider a manufacturing process producing products of a given type. It is a sequence of seven operations: four manufacturing operations and three inspections. Successfully completed products are divided into two classes according to their quality.

Defective items detected during the operations are either sent to an earlier manufacturing operation for reworking or they are classified as scrap. A schematic diagram of the manufacturing process is shown in Figure 1.

Data on the estimated number of labour hours needed to complete a particular operation of the manufacturing process as well as associated costs are shown in Table 1.

Figure 1: Schematic diagram of the manufacturing process

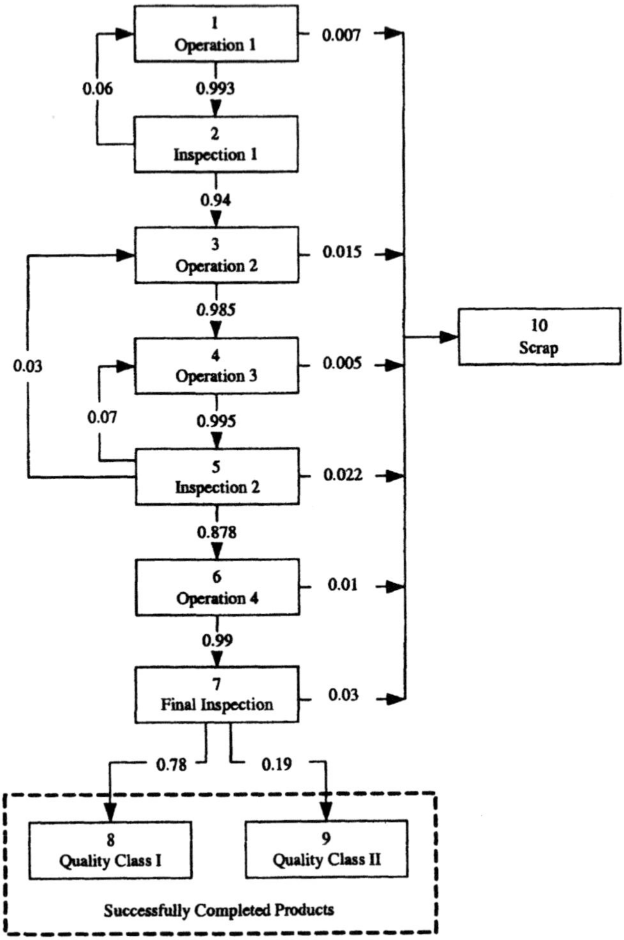

Table 1: Estimated values of t_i and c_i for the i-th operation of the manufacturing process

i	Operation	t_i [*hours*]	c_i [*units/hour*]
1	Operation 1	0.25	110
2	Inspection 1	0.03	50
3	Operation 2	0.33	150
4	Operation 3	0.30	130
5	Inspection 2	0.05	60
6	Operation 4	0.17	120
7	Final Inspection	0.08	80

Cost C_M of input material per product is estimated to be 15 *units*.

Using data from Table 1 and the value of the parameter $C_M = 15$ *units*, we can calculate the direct production cost C_{id} of an "*ideal*" manufacturing process according to (2):

$$C_{id} = 162.3 \; units. \tag{11}$$

In order to calculate the expected direct production cost C, the manufacturing process shown in Figure 1 is modelled by the reducible Markov chain. The chain contains ten states, seven states are transient and three states are absorbing states. Using the numbers given in Figure 1 as the one-step transition probabilities, we can write down the transition matrix **P** in the form of (6):

O (arrow to row 1, column 1) — **R**[illegible] (arrow to row 1, column 10)

$$\mathbf{P} = \begin{array}{c} \\ 1 \\ 2 \\ 3 \\ 4 \\ 5 \\ 6 \\ 7 \\ 8 \\ 9 \\ 10 \end{array} \begin{array}{c} \begin{array}{ccccccc:ccc} 1 & 2 & 3 & 4 & 5 & 6 & 7 & 8 & 9 & 10 \end{array} \\ \left[\begin{array}{ccccccc:cc:c} 0 & 0.993 & 0 & 0 & 0 & 0 & 0 & 0 & 0 & 0.007 \\ 0.06 & 0 & 0.94 & 0 & 0 & 0 & 0 & 0 & 0 & 0 \\ 0 & 0 & 0 & 0.985 & 0 & 0 & 0 & 0 & 0 & 0.015 \\ 0 & 0 & 0 & 0 & 0.995 & 0 & 0 & 0 & 0 & 0.005 \\ 0 & 0 & 0.03 & 0.07 & 0 & 0.878 & 0 & 0 & 0 & 0.022 \\ 0 & 0 & 0 & 0 & 0 & 0 & 0.99 & 0 & 0 & 0.01 \\ 0 & 0 & 0 & 0 & 0 & 0 & 0 & 0.78 & 0.19 & 0.03 \\ \hdashline 0 & 0 & 0 & 0 & 0 & 0 & 0 & 1 & 0 & 0 \\ 0 & 0 & 0 & 0 & 0 & 0 & 0 & 0 & 1 & 0 \\ 0 & 0 & 0 & 0 & 0 & 0 & 0 & 0 & 0 & 1 \end{array}\right] \end{array} . \tag{12}$$

Using the matrix **Q** from (12) the matrix **I–Q** is obtained:

$$\mathbf{I}-\mathbf{Q}=\begin{array}{c} \\ 1\\2\\3\\4\\5\\6\\7\end{array}\!\!\begin{array}{c}\begin{array}{ccccccc}1&2&3&4&5&6&7\end{array}\\ \begin{bmatrix}1&-0.993&0&0&0&0&0\\-0.06&1&-0.94&0&0&0&0\\0&0&1&-0.985&0&0&0\\0&0&0&1&-0.995&0&0\\0&0&-0.03&-0.07&1&-0.878&0\\0&0&0&0&0&1&-0.99\\0&0&0&0&0&0&1\end{bmatrix}\end{array}. \quad (13)$$

The fundamental matrix **N** is calculated by inversion of (13):

$$\mathbf{N}=(\mathbf{I}-\mathbf{Q})^{-1}=\begin{array}{c} \\ 1\\2\\3\\4\\5\\6\\7\end{array}\!\!\begin{array}{c}\begin{array}{ccccccc}1&2&3&4&5&6&7\end{array}\\ \begin{bmatrix}1.063&1.056&1.025&1.085&1.08&0.948&0.939\\0.064&1.063&1.032&1.093&1.087&0.955&0.945\\0&0&1.033&1.093&1.088&0.955&0.946\\0&0&0.033&1.11&1.104&0.97&0.96\\0&0&0.033&0.11&1.11&0.975&0.965\\0&0&0&0&0&1&0.99\\0&0&0&0&0&0&1\end{bmatrix}\end{array}. \quad (14)$$

From (14), the following values of the parameter r_i, i=1, 2, …, 7, are obtained:

$$r_1=1.063,\ r_2=1.056,\ r_3=1.025,\ r_4=1.085,\ r_5=1.08,\ r_6=0.948,\ r_7=0.939. \quad (15)$$

The probabilities of absorption to the states representing successfully completed products of the first and the second quality class are obtained from the matrix $\mathbf{f}_{\{C_1,C_2\}}$. It is calculated according to (9) using (14) and the matrix $\mathbf{R}_{good}$ from (12):

$$\mathbf{f}_{\{C_1,C_2\}} = \mathbf{N}\cdot\mathbf{R}_{good} = \begin{matrix} \\ 1 \\ 2 \\ 3 \\ 4 \\ 5 \\ 6 \\ 7 \end{matrix}\begin{matrix} 8 & 9 \\ \begin{bmatrix} 0.732 & 0.178 \\ 0.737 & 0.18 \\ 0.738 & 0.18 \\ 0.749 & 0.182 \\ 0.753 & 0.183 \\ 0.772 & 0.188 \\ 0.78 & 0.19 \end{bmatrix} \end{matrix} \qquad (16)$$

One can see from (16) that the fraction of successfully completed products of the first quality class is $F_1 = f_{C_1} = 0.732$, and the fraction of successfully completed products of the second quality class is $F_2 = f_{C_2} = 0.178$. The value of the parameter F is then calculated as the sum of F_1 an F_2:

$$F = 0.91. \qquad (17)$$

Using data from Table 1, the value $C_M = 15$ *units*, the values of the parameter r_i, i=1, 2, ..., 7, from (15), and the values of F from (17), we calculate the expected direct production cost C according to (3):

$$C = 184.02\ units. \qquad (18)$$

Finally, we calculate the ratio E according to (1) using (11) and (18):

$$E = 0.882. \qquad (19)$$

This result presents a measure of the economic effectiveness of the manufacturing process observed.

The model described is relatively simple and therefore suitable for monitoring changes of the process economic effectiveness due to technological or/and organizational modifications. As an example, we shall calculate the change of the value of E given by (19) under modified manufacturing conditions. We assume that technological and organizational improvements cause a 10% decrease in the number of labour hours needed to complete a given operation. The cost parameters remain unchanged. The new value of C_{id}^{*} is $C_{id}^{*} = 147.57\ units$. Besides, we suppose that the process improvements affect the one-step transition probabilities. The new transition matrix $\mathbf{P}^{*}$is

$$P^* = \begin{array}{c} 1 \\ 2 \\ 3 \\ 4 \\ 5 \\ 6 \\ 7 \\ 8 \\ 9 \\ 10 \end{array} \begin{bmatrix} 0 & 0.994 & 0 & 0 & 0 & 0 & 0 & 0 & 0 & 0.006 \\ 0.048 & 0 & 0.952 & 0 & 0 & 0 & 0 & 0 & 0 & 0 \\ 0 & 0 & 0 & 0.988 & 0 & 0 & 0 & 0 & 0 & 0.012 \\ 0 & 0 & 0 & 0 & 0.996 & 0 & 0 & 0 & 0 & 0.004 \\ 0 & 0 & 0.024 & 0.056 & 0 & 0.902 & 0 & 0 & 0 & 0.018 \\ 0 & 0 & 0 & 0 & 0 & 0 & 0.992 & 0 & 0 & 0.008 \\ 0 & 0 & 0 & 0 & 0 & 0 & 0 & 0.781 & 0.195 & 0.024 \\ 0 & 0 & 0 & 0 & 0 & 0 & 0 & 1 & 0 & 0 \\ 0 & 0 & 0 & 0 & 0 & 0 & 0 & 0 & 1 & 0 \\ 0 & 0 & 0 & 0 & 0 & 0 & 0 & 0 & 0 & 1 \end{bmatrix}.$$

The new value of C^* is $C^* = 163.04\ units$. Finally, we calculate the new ratio E^*=0.905. One can see that technological and organizational improvements cause a 2.61 % increase of the economic effectiveness of the manufacturing process observed.

3. Conclusion

In this paper, the economic effectiveness of a manufacturing process has been studied. The ratio between the direct production cost per product of an "*ideal*" manufacturing process, and the expected direct production cost per successfully completed product of an actual manufacturing process has been proposed as a measure of the economic effectiveness. We found that the direct cost involved in our model of the economic effectiveness of a manufacturing process depends on two random variables: the number of executions of a given operation of the manufacturing process, and the fraction of successfully completed products. In order to calculate the expected values of these variables, we have modelled a manufacturing process by a homogeneous finite reducible Markov chain. The random variables mentioned have been expressed by the two absorption characteristics of the Markov chain: the absorption probability and the number of visits to a given transient state. We have described a method for determination of the expected values of these characteristics representing the parameters of the model. The model has been tested on an example of a simple manufacturing process.

The model presented is applicable to different types of manufacturing processes, such as mass customized manufacturing, continuous flow productions or job shops. Because the model is relatively simple, it is suitable for monitoring the changes of the process economic effectiveness due to technological or/and organizational modifications.

Bibliography and References

Al-Najjar, B., Alsyouf, I. (2000): Improving effectiveness of manufacturing systems using total quality maintenance, Integrated Manufacturing Systems, **11**(4): 267-276. [Accessed 4 June 2007]. Available from World Wide Web: <http://www.emeraldinsight.com/Insight/ViewContentServlet?Filename=/published/emeraldfulltextarticle/pdf/0680110405.pdf>.

Antony, J. (2001): Improving the manufacturing process quality using design of experiments: a case study, *International journal of operations & production management*, **21**(5/6): 812-822.

Beichelt, F. (2006): *Stochastic Processes in Science, Engineering and Finance*, Chapman & Hall/CRC, Boca Raton.

Goetz, T. *et al.* (2006): A Stochastic Model for the Fiber Lay-down Process in the Nonwoven Production, Berichte des Fraunhofer ITWM, Nr. 102, *Fraunhofer-Institut für Techno- und Wirtschafts-mathematik ITWM*. [Accessed 4 June 2007]. Available from World Wide Web: <http://www.itwm.fraunhofer.de/zentral/download/berichte/bericht102.pdf>.

Hudoklin-Božič, A. (2003): *Stohastični procesi*, 6th Edition, Založba Moderna organizacija, Kranj.

Loher, M. *et al* (2003): Model-based optimisation of a virtual manufacturing process with neural networks, *The 36th CIRP-International Seminar on Manufacturing Systems*, 03-05 June 2003, Saarbruecken, Germany. [Accessed 4 June 2007]. Available from World Wide Web: <http://www.fhsg.ch/FHSHome/fhs_homepage.nsf/docUniqueID/0F9DE592CB3B4CC5C1256EEE004CE019/$FILE/weidig.pdf>

Lu, F. R., Qiao, G. (2004): Simulation modeling to optimize stochastic manufacturing processes and resources by a dynamic Monte Carlo method, Presented in the *Institute of Industrial Engineers (IIE) Annual Conference*, May 15-19, 2004. [Accessed 16 November 2006]. Available from World Wide Web: <http://www.decisioneering.com/articles/lu-qiao.html>.

Magda, R. (1994): Mathematical model for estimating the economic effectiveness of production process in coal panels and an example of its practical application, *International Journal of Production Economics*, **34**(1): 47-55. [Accessed 4 June 2007]. Available from World Wide Web: <http://www.sciencedirect.com/science/article/B6VF8-45JT1NC-2C/2/2e52804748303e65131719a5eb6bf32f>.

Shamblin, J. E., Stevens, Jr., G. T. (1974): *Operations research, A fundamental approach*, McGraw-Hill, New York.

Stroock, D. W. (2005). *An introduction to Markov processes*, Springer, Berlin.

Tyre, M. J., Hauptman, O. (1992): Effectiveness of organizational responses to technological change in the production process, *Organization science*, **3**(3): 301-320.

Zuev, V. N. *et al.* (1969) : The economic effectiveness of the continuous production of polyester fibre, *Fibre chemistry*, **1**(2).

About the Authors

Alenka Brezavšček is an assistant professor at the University of Maribor, Faculty of Organizational Sciences. Her research fields are stochastic processes, system reliability and availability, and information system security.

Alenka Hudoklin is an emeritus professor at the University of Maribor, Faculty of Organizational Sciences. Her research fields are stochastic processes, system reliability and availability, and information system security.

Applied Information Management[1]
How to Apply Organization Reference Models in the Real World

Petr Doucek

doucek@vse.cz

Ota Novotný

novotnyo@vse.cz

Abstract

This contribution contains characteristics of information management as a term and a scientific and research area together with selected practical possibilities for its implementation in organizations. Organization reference models (a new addition to the information management toolset) are described. Business reference models are business models representing a generally accepted way of managing, controlling, and executing activities specific to a certain industry or specific to certain business processes. They contain generalized knowledge ("best practices") of model developers in the model subject area. They are not only theoretical tools supporting information management competencies, but are also used in real business practice. In this text, we have provided real experience gained from the reference model implementation in the area of IS/ICT management (the KIT reference model).

Keywords: information management, IS/ICT management, IS/ICT management reference model, management.

---

1 This text was prepared with the support of the Czech Science Foundation GACR – research project 201/07/0455 Causality model between corporate performance, process efficiency and ICT effectiveness and research project 201/06/0175 Informatics management model modification.

1. Introduction

As Kotelnikov puts it: "For a long time, the conventional wisdom in business was that managers should do little else but keep a close eye on what their subordinates were doing: monitor, supervise, control - making sure that things below are proceeding properly…" (Kotelnikov, 2006, p. 3). Deficiencies of the above foreshadowed approach started to appear at the end of the last century, when organizations were confronted with new requirements for rapid adaptation to emerging business models and political, regulatory, societal and environmental conditions. The need for an instant response (usually provided by a flexible redesign of the organization business and process models) became the key criterion of managerial work.

New management theories and approaches were created in order to respond to the above listed issues. As an example, we can provide ideas from Hammer and Champy (2001, p. 23), who state that an organization: „Has to be changed thoroughly, radically and dramatically, if we are to progress in critical spheres of activities, such as: expenses, quality, services and swiftness." These approaches were often based on business process reengineering e.g. (El Sawy, 2001, p. 45), (Davenport, 1993, p. 24).

The general goal of information management as one of the above described management approaches is to assure data for satisfying a manager's information needs as well as to realize so-called data logistics – to transport relevant data to relevant persons at the right time. But what does "to assure data for information logistics" in fact mean? There is no single worldwide respected and accepted definition for the term "information management". Different definitions could be found e.g. in (Oesterle et al., 1993, p. 56), (Taylor, 1996, p. 84), (Earl, 1989, p. 17), (Best, 1996, p. 3), (Martin, 1995, p. 171), (Galiers, 2003, p. 91). It seems to be the main weak spot of this new part of social science, which has a multidisciplinary and interdisciplinary character and is positioned on the border of management, system science, theoretical informatics, business informatics, IS/ICT management, philosophy etc. (Doucek, 2005, p. 372).

The information management discipline gives a big accent to the implementation of its principles in a real environment by using specific tools (e.g. organization reference models described further on in this text). Principles used in these tools allow the fast reconfiguration of the enterprise organization and processes based on the changing business conditions and, therefore, form a bridge between theory and practice.

2. The Information Management Discipline

Actual interpretation of the term "information management" underlines the importance of managerial work. Experts in all different types of science have almost the same opinion - managerial work is the key activity for each organization. Primarily, it should be based on processes management, therefore the transition from a functional to a process approach in an enterprise must be completed first by managers (Kern, 2001, p. 56). A process approach to managerial work is significantly supported by information processes which support managerial work in order to supply required information to managers (Oesterle et al., 1993, p. 73). The time scale is also important. The above listed requirements are fulfilled by data logistics. A definition of data logistics is: "to deliver right and relevant data to the right person/place at the right time" (Doucek, 2005, p. 372). Effectiveness of information management application in practice is deeply related to data logistics quality (Best, 1996, p. 3).

Information processes are understood by experts as supporting processes. They are not included in core-business processes of organizations that are not IS/ICT services suppliers. Nevertheless, their significance for an organization is fundamental (Galiers, 2003, p. 101). Through their performance, information services are provided. Information manager have to manage IS/ICT as a complex of (Leibold et al., 2002, p. 42), (Earl, 1989, p. 22):

- sources – data, employees, finance,
- processes – identification, description and optimization (Ministr et al., 2003, p.4),
- organization structures – competencies, responsibilities, style of management (Scott Morton, 1991, p. 54),
- knowledge management – management of the knowledge life cycle – collect data, production, distribution and remove of knowledge (Porat, 1978, p. 26),
- strategic visions for further IS/ICT development in an organization in co-ordination with strategic goals of the core business (Scott Morton, 1991, p. 3).

Information management therefore penetrates into IS/ICT management, and it could also become a tool for the measurement of IS/ICT benefits and effects. The comparison of costs invested in the IS/ICT and final benefits gained from its improvement form the base of the economic dimension of information management – investment effectiveness measurement (IT Governance Institute, Cobit 4.0, 2006).

Information management competencies (Oesterle et al., 1993, p. 35), (Galiers, 2003, p. 18, p. 64, p. 95) in different areas are shown in Figure. 1. They could be separated into the three following levels of management:

- strategic,
- tactical,
- operational.

The first category of information management could be described as a tool for the **managing of top managers** – metamanagement on a **strategic level**. The main service and mission of information management on this level is to manage, plan, forecast, and teach top management to use related managerial tools. These tools such as, for example, mathematical models, business intelligence elements and applications, decision support systems, are regularly incorporated into decision making process (Kern, 2005, p. 36). They also evolve into the new methodologies describing the use of data, information and knowledge.

Figure 1 Area of potential synergic effects in information management

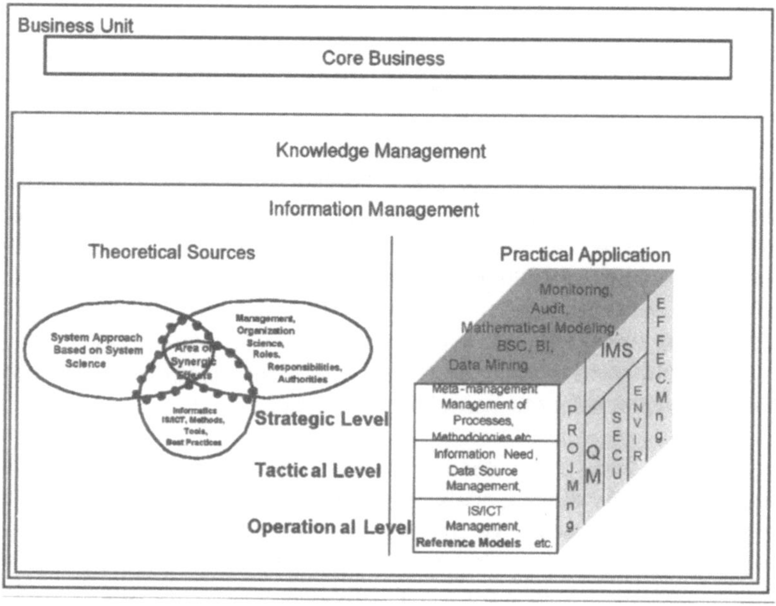

The second category, we could say "classical **tactical category"**, is the area of **planning and information need management** with special accent on managerial information needs fulfilment. The planning process of information needs coverage is deeply related to other aspects of managerial work such as organizational structures definition and authorities and responsibilities assignment for each employee in an organization. Information management is slowly becoming an irreplaceable part of organization science. The most important role of information management at this level is to interconnect the management of the organization to the IS/ICT management on the basis of a process and service approach.

The **operation management** category of information management is focused on data collection from real operations of the IS/ICT in an organization with the final goal of preparing data for effectiveness measurement and the IS/ICT effectiveness evaluation. It is characterized by significant interconnection with informatics management. In practice, it is represented mainly by IS/ICT reference models (Novotný, 2005b, p. 378), process descriptions (Ministr et al., 2003, p. 4), competencies and responsibilities descriptions.

3. Organization Reference Models in Information Management

3.1 Organization Reference Models

While we are modelling the organization and its activities from the different perspectives, we can use a number of different modelling and categorization techniques (e.g. business process modelling, functional modelling, data, object or business object modelling, service and product catalogues.). Such modelling work has to be usually started from scratch and always consumes a lot of resources. Therefore, since the beginnings of organization modelling, researchers and practitioners have been thinking about the reutilization (reuse) of models which had already been developed in one organization for other similar, organizations.

In order to keep the potential of reutilization, in many cases the construction of the above models has to be able to abstract from enterprise-specific characteristics. We therefore distinguish between enterprise-specific information models and reference models. While enterprise-specific models refer to a particular enterprise context, reference models pose target recommendations for a class of businesses (Thomas, Scheer, 2006, p. 10a).

Reference models are usually developed by consultancy companies, software developers, standardization institutions and academia. As an example, we can list the SAP R/3-reference models (Ladd et al., 1997, p. 22) and BAAN IV reference models (Baan, 1998) (note: Baan and Baan products were acquired by SSA Global in 2003), arising from the commercial practice or (Weber et al., 1999, p. 9) and (ISO/IEC 12207, 2002) primarily arising from the cooperation of academia with standardization institutions.

The term "reference model" is still not very well defined in the theory and we can find many variants of its definition. One of the reasons for such a situation is that this area could cover a wide range of model types used for different purposes e.g. business process models (Ladd et al., 1997, p. 253), (Baan, 1998) or quality models (Kim, Fox, 2002, p. 73). For our purposes, we will use the following definition (Novotný, 2005a, p. 374):

> "A reference model contains relevant structures and relationships among the model elements (process structures, levels, document structures.) and also the predefined knowledge (best practice examples) already included in these structures."

Reference models usually combine strengths of mathematical and data modelling techniques in their structure and knowledge management principles in their content. The biggest advantage of the reference models is that they allow extracting of the best practices and knowledge from the "heads" of their developers and provide them in the formalized model structure. It allows easier knowledge replication.

Figure 3: Three labelled transition systems: (a) the initial model (e.g., the reference model), (b) a particular configuration hiding and blocking specific edges/labels, and (c) the resulting model (Van der Aalst et al., 2006, p. 517)

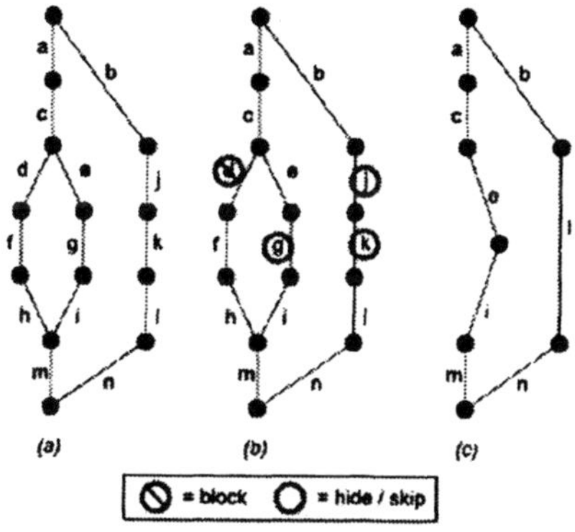

Reference modelling differs from traditional modelling. While we are modelling the organization "traditionally", we are building its models from scratch. While we are using the reference modelling principles, we select the relevant reference model(s) and later adapt them for the specific organization purposes. As stated in (Thomas, 2006, p. 10a), reference modelling promises, on the one hand, savings in time and costs to those carrying out business engineering projects and on the other hand, an increase in the quality of the model to be constructed, because reference models represent general recommendations for the subject area being studied.

The principle of the reference modelling is described in the example (Van der Aalst et al., 2006, p. 517) shown in Figure 3.

The most advanced area of reference model implementation can be found in business (or business process) modelling. Business reference models are business models representing a generally accepted way to manage, control, and execute activities specific to a certain industry or specific to certain business processes. They contain generalized knowledge ("best practices") of model developers in the model subject area. Best practices are not described in the form of plain text, but they are structured and formalized into reference model components (e.g. business processes, business functions, and roles) and their relationships. Reference models therefore enable modelling of processes, business functions and other model components, training, re-use of best practices and assessment of actual practices.

In this area, we can find the following types of reference models (Baan, 1998):

- production reference models (e.g. assembly to order, make to stock),
- industry processes reference models (e.g. automotive, wholesale),
- function domain reference models (e.g. finance, human resources management).

3.2 Information Management Toolset

Information management uses tools such as, e.g. mathematical models, business intelligence elements and applications, decision support systems. Reference models have recently become the new member of this set (see Figure 4).

Figure 4: Information management competencies and toolset

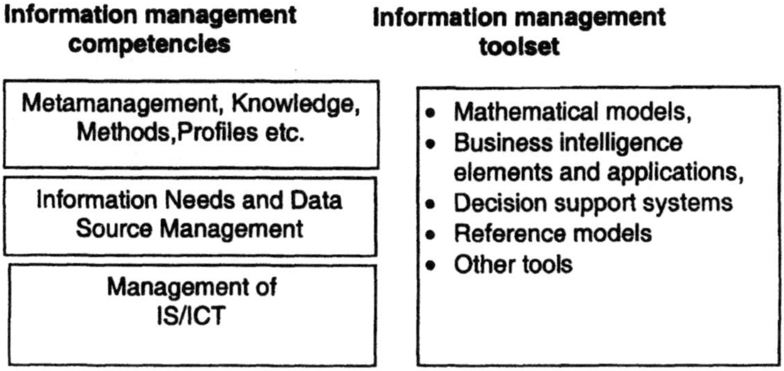

Reference models are used in all competencies of Information Management. They contain relevant structures and relationships among the model elements (process structures, levels, document structures etc.) and also the predefined knowledge (best practice examples) already included in these structures.

Common application of reference models as part of information management can be found in the area of business process management and IS/ICT management. In this paper, we will discuss their application in the latter.

4. Bridging the Gap between Theory and Practice - KIT IS/ICT Management Reference Model

As described in the previous chapter, reference models are not only theoretical tools supporting information management competencies, but they are also used in real business practice. In this text, we will provide an example of reference model implementation in the area of IS/ICT management.

Management of IS/ICT in an enterprise is becoming increasingly important and nowadays it is one of the critical success factors of any type of business. Application functionality overlap, technology and knowledge heterogeneity and constantly changing business pressures make this task very difficult. There is a strong need for methodologies and recommended best practices in this area.

Using the reference models principles (formalized structure and predefined content) in the area of IS/ICT management would help to address the above listed needs. If we expect the IS/ICT management to conform to the same principles as the management of e.g. logistics or production, there is no reason for not applying reference models also in this area.

There are two major sources of knowledge on which the IS/ICT management reference model could be elaborated:

- IS/ICT management methodologies,
- IS/ICT management tool.

Their roles in the reference model elaboration could be explained as:

IS/ICT management methodologies

IS/ICT management processes and some of the best practices are already described in several IS/ICT management methodologies, e.g. ITIL (The Stationery Office, Service Support, 2000), COBIT (IT Governance Institute,Cobit 4.0, 2006) or ISO/IEC 20000 (ISO/IEC 20000, 2005). The problem is that they are described in a form of plain text. Implementation of such a methodology in a real environment still needs a lot of implementation effort for it to be effectively used as a structured management system (IT Governance Institute, IT Governance Global Status Report, 2006).

An IS/ICT management reference model should contain the above listed best practices (mapping to relevant IS/ICT methodologies should be provided), but these have to be expressed and managed as formalized procedures, forms, relationship tables and other structured content, which could be instantly used while implementing the IS/ICT management. This suggestion is based on the empirical experience gained while implementing the IS/ICT management principles in real projects.

IS/ICT management tools

IS/ICT management tools (Pink Elephant, 2006), formerly also called meta-models, are used mainly for tracking information about IS/ICT assets structure (e.g. SW and HW location and configuration) and about events occurring in IS/ICT (e.g. incidents, problems). They contain predefined, partially customizable structures for each asset and event. Their disadvantage is that they come without reference content, so it is necessary to fill all the structures with data from scratch. They also usually do not track information about all the IS/ICT objects required for the IS/ICT management (e.g. documents or procedures, processes).

An IS/ICT management reference model should contain these structures for all the IS/ICT assets, but it should also include their predefined content (where it is appropriate).

Combination of the above listed sources into the IS/ICT management reference model can provide an IS/ICT manager with a powerful tool for supporting his or her tactical and strategic tasks. As examples (based on our empirical experience), we can list:

- cost of application upgrade (impact analysis) – application upgrade (e.g. new version of the SAP R/3 software package) usually comes with higher desktop hardware requirements (e.g. larger screen, more memory). With data stored in the IS/ICT management system, one can easily identify all the desktops where the SAP client software is installed, and their configuration. Then, it is easy to calculate the real cost of upgrading including the replacement of relevant desktops,
- Service Level Agreement (SLA) chargeback calculation – SLA are usually calculated in a "per user" or "per computer" mode. With the real data in the model structure it is easy to calculate how many users are using the specific service or on how many computers it is installed. Such data are then used for precise internal or external billing of IS/ICT services provided to enterprise organizational units,
- process catalogue – a predefined (reference) process catalogue is usually used as a basis for IS/ICT management implementation. In this case, it is not necessary to build everything (model all the processes) from scratch, but only update those processes which will be managed differently to common practice,
- document examples – document examples are used in the same way – if there is a need for any IS/ICT management document, its structure and outline could be found in the reference model and it could be instantly used.

4.1 KIT Reference Model

The aim of our research is to formulate process, data and organization models for efficient management and innovative development of IS/ICT and at the same time ensure that IS/ICT correspond to new complex tasks in the area of business, management, state and public authorities, supports processes not only inside organization and social subjects but also among themselves, and takes into account the changing user requirements for information and knowledge handling.
Therefore, we decided to elaborate a reference model for IS/ICT management (the KIT reference model) using the same principles which were already successful in the "traditional" business reference models subject areas described above. The aim of our IS/ICT management reference model was to:

- support service oriented IS/ICT management implementation,
- provide a structured (formalized) overview of the enterprise informatics structure and a base for its planning and management,
- support the operational IS/ICT management tasks,
- support the long-term IS/ICT management tasks.

The core of the KIT model is based on the service oriented approach to IS/ICT management (Voříšek, Dunn, 2001, p. 666). It means that IS/ICT provides for the organization (for business processes) defined IS/ICT services. These services are provided by specific IS/ICT processes using specific IS/ICT resources.

The KIT reference model is actually used for information strategy document elaboration (initial collection of data in the enterprise), for IS/ICT management processes and tasks definition (basis for definition of IS/ICT management system in the enterprise) and for IS/ICT management support (tool for everyday IS/ICT management support). This model has, in the last two years, been implemented in five organizations.

The KIT reference model is provided as a standalone MS Access database application. It therefore allows easy and fast implementation in any organization. In case the model is later used for regular IS/ICT management support, it is usually, after initial analysis, replaced by a more robust database application.

4.2 KIT Reference Model Structure

The KIT reference model contains (and tracks the structured information about) the following key components:

- Enterprise processes – information about business processes in the enterprise,
- IS/ICT processes – information about processes in IS/ICT
- IS/ICT activities – information about IS/ICT activities (parts of process flows),
- Services - information about IS/ICT services provided to enterprise,
- Applications (SW) – information about IS/ICT applications,
- Computer (HW) – information about the hardware,
- Users – information about users of IS/ICT services,
- Organization Units – information about organization units in the enterprise.

The KIT reference model also tracks the key relationships among the components (Figure 5). The structure of relationships allows an IS/ICT manager to identify e.g. which organization unit is using the IS/ICT service and how many users (or computers) from the unit are using it.

Figure 5: KIT reference model – key relationships tracked among model components

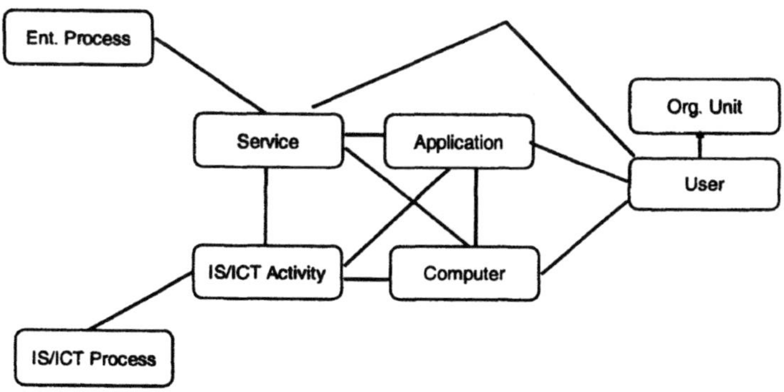

4.3 KIT Reference Model Content

It is obvious that, for some components of the reference model (e.g. list of users or organization units), it is not possible to prepare a common content because they are different in each model implementation. Some components could be only partially filled by the generic categorization (e.g. services catalogue).

Following key components in the KIT Reference Model contain the predefined "best-practices" structure:

Fully predefined content (could be adopted without any amendments):

- IS/ICT processes – IS/ICT process catalogue,
- IS/ICT activities – IS/ICT activities catalogue,
- IS/ICT services – IS/ICT service catalogue.

Partially predefined content (only generic content which has to be amended by real content from the enterprise)

- Applications (SW) – information about IS/ICT applications,
- Computer (HW) – information about the hardware.

Examples of the KIT Reference Model content are provided in Figure 6 (process description) and in Figure 7 (process flow).

Figure 6: KIT reference model predefined content – process description (Note: the KIT model is available in the Czech language version only)

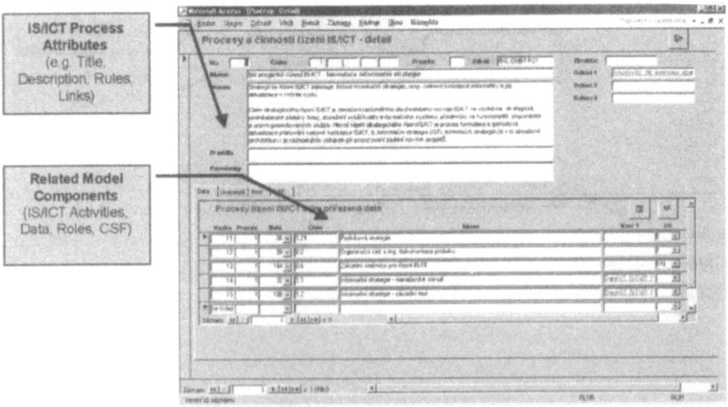

Figure 7: KIT reference model predefined content – process flow (Note: Simplified process notation is used in order to enable faster initial KIT model implementation)

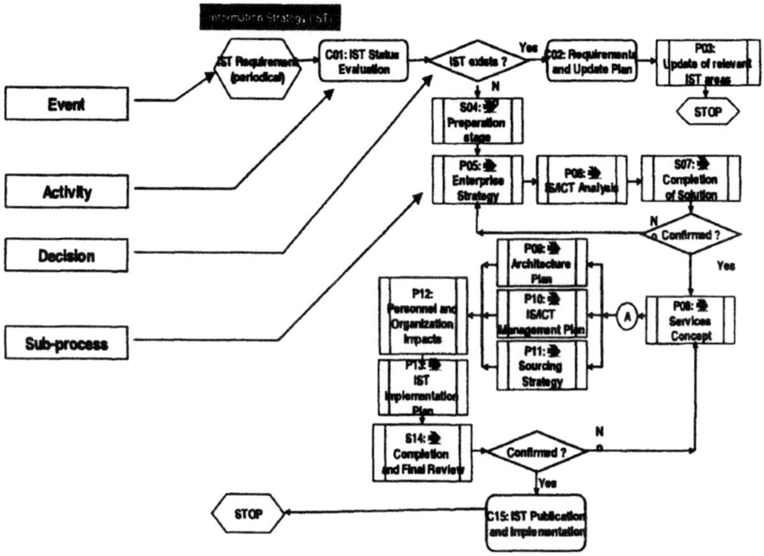

4.4 Implementation of the KIT Reference Model

Structured IS/ICT management has to be carefully planned and implemented. The "traditional" way of implementing of IS/ICT management processes in a company consists of the following steps:

a. analysis of the status and needs of IS/ICT and its management. It is based on business needs, SWOT (Analysis of the Strengths and Weaknesses of an organization and the Opportunities and Threats facing it), information strategy and other strategic documents. The core of this phase is in most cases based on a SWOT analysis of IS/ICT, which defines the core problems and project requirements,
b. formulation of the IS/ICT management concept respecting the conclusions of the previous phase,
c. detail analysis and design of the IS/ICT management components (functions, processes, documentations, roles, measures),

d. implementation of the designed solution (organizational and technological),
e. ongoing monitoring and support.

For all above listed phases (especially phases a, b and c), it is usually necessary to hire a consultant (either external or internal) and let him or her prepare the solution. A major problem of this approach is the significantly longer timeframe and limited participation of the internal IS/ICT specialists – they usually only review the results of the consultancy work. It could result in their refusing the proposed solution or, in different ways, in their sabotaging the proposed actions.

On the contrary – implementation of the IS/ICT management using the reference model is based on the assumption that most of the work is done by users of the model and not by consultants. Users are only coached when selecting appropriate model components and updating the model content.

When implementing the KIT reference model in a real environment, we use the following procedure:

a. analysis of the status and needs of IS/ICT and its management. It is based on business needs, company SWOT analysis, information strategy and other strategic documents. The core of this phase is in most cases based on a SWOT analysis of IS/ICT, which defines the core problems and project requirements,
b. kick-off workshop – the purpose and principle of the reference models is described to users,
c. model components selection – users by themselves select the model components they will be using in the IS/ICT management,
d. model relationships selection - users by themselves select the relationships among model components they will be using in the IS/ICT management,
e. model database and front-end customization – a model database application is customized based on user requirements (list of components and relationships),
f. model front-end training – users are trained how to work with the model database application,
g. component and relations editing (coached) – users are editing, updating and amending the model content,

h. integrity reports generation – number of integrity reports is generated. It allows the identification of editing mistakes and problematic spots in the management system,
i. implementation of the designed solution (organizational and technological),
j. ongoing monitoring and support.

The advantage of this approach is the engagement of the internal IS/ICT specialists in the IS/ICT management processes formulation and the shortening of the time necessary for the transfer of knowledge included in the reference model into the target environment.

4.5 Lessons Learned and Open Issues

During the model implementation in a real environment, we have found several interesting issues, presented here as "lessons learned".

The IS/ICT management team was usually very motivated by the fact that they were building "their own" IS/ICT management system "by themselves" and that they would not get it externally delivered. The selection of the MS Access database application as a core model environment is best suited to customization needs and is intuitive when used in a real environment – moreover the initial cost of the model implementation and customization is far lower than when using other robust tools (e.g. Aris Toolset). We also got positive feedback for the structured approach (using the templates for documents and structures for component records). It assures far better integrity of management information (compared to plain text descriptions used in methodologies). Last but not least, one positive lesson learned was connected with the fact that users understood the advantages of sharing the information in the management systems – and knowledge was moved from "their heads" to become a shared and structured resource.

We have - contrary to our expectations - found that the KIT reference model could not be distributed like other "package software". In reality, it still cannot be distributed and implemented without some coaching and customization.

We were quite surprised by the variety of the model implementations, especially on the emphasis which was given to different parts of the model by different IS/ICT managers in the different organizations. This might be explained by the fact that IS/ICT managers have different personalities and, therefore, that each implementation has to be different. Each manager needs different information for the successful management of his or her tasks, so each customization addresses different areas of the model.

There are still some open issues connected with the KIT reference model. As stated above, during the implementation, companies still have to rely on experienced consultants helping the managers with the component selection. We are planning to replace the consultant role (at least partially) by content and structure profiling and by including the expert system tool for the selection of appropriate content and relationships. We are now working on a pilot project which will provide such functionality for the selection of relevant IS/ICT measures.

5. Conclusions

The transition process from a traditional, old-fashioned type of organization to an innovative, knowledge oriented one is a great opportunity for every organization that wants to save its competitive advantage in our turbulent world. A possibility of realizing this vision is to apply an information management approach in the home organization.

Information management methods are applied at all levels of management in an organization. It is not only a sum of methods, but it represents a useful combination of philosophy, sociology (system science), information technology tools and methods (informatics) and management and organizational science (management) with the final aim of supporting effective achievement of strategic goals in an organization. Synergy effects caused by the use of an information management approach are presented in this contribution by the application of reference model principles to it.

Organization reference models form a new addition to the information management toolset. The most advanced area of reference model implementation can be found in business (or business process) modelling. Business reference models are business models representing a generally accepted way of managing, controlling, and executing activities specific to a certain industry or specific to certain business processes. They contain and concentrate generalized knowledge ("best practices") of model developers in the model subject area. Best practices are not described in a form of plain text, but they are structured and formalized into reference model components (e.g. business processes, business functions, and roles) and their relationships.

Reference models are not only theoretical tools for supporting information management competencies, but they are also used in real business practice. In this text, we have provided an example of reference model implementation in the area of IS/ICT management, which shows that, when implementing a structured IS/ICT management system in an enterprise, it is worth exploiting the "best practices" included in the KIT reference model.

The duration of implementation of the IS/ICT management system using the KIT reference model is much shorter then building it from scratch.

Bibliography and References

Baan IVc Reference Models (1998). [CD-ROM], Baan Business Innovation B.V., The Netherlands.

Best, D. P. (1996). The Fourth Resource – Information and Its Management, Aslib Gower, Aldershot, p 3.

Davenport, T. H. (1993). Process Innovation : Reengineering Work through Information Technology, Boston, Harvard Business School Press, ISBN 0-87584-366-2.

Doucek, P. (2005), "Information Management – Its Role in the Information Society", In: Sustainable Development Management. Bucharest : University POLITEHNICA of Bucharest, pp. 371-376. ISBN 973-748-022-8.

Earl, M. J. (1989). Management Strategies for Information Technology, Prentice Hall, University Press Cambridge, p. 24.

Galiers, R., Leidner, D. (2003): Strategic Information Management: Challenges and Strategies in Managing Information Systems. Butterworth-Heinemann; 3 edition, ISBN 0-7506-5619-0.

Hammer, M., Champy, J. (2001). Reengineering the corporation: A manifesto for business revolution, Harper Business – New York, ISBN 0-06-662112-7.

ISO/IEC 12207 Amd 1 Systems and Software Engineering - Software Life Cycle Processes Ammendment 1, International Organization for Standardization, Geneva, Switzerland, 2002.

ISO/IEC 20000 - Information technology – Service management – Part 1: Specification, International Organization for Standardization, Geneva, Switzerland, 2005.

IT Governance Institute: Cobit 4.0 (2006). Control Objectives, Management Guidelines Maturity Model, 2006, ISBN 1-933284-37-4.

IT Governance Institute: IT Governance Global Status Report (2006). pp. 32, ISBN 1-933284-32-3, [online], [cit. 2006-10-01], URL: <http://www.pwc.com/Extweb/pwcpublications.nsf/docid/D3E29 97D370F3C648025713300511A0>

Kern, T. (2001). Identification of the key business processes essential for successful reengineering of business systems in the process aspect. V: Jašková, Mária (editor). ECON '01 : [selected research papers], ([Sborník vědeckých prací Vysoké školy báňské v Ostravě. Řada ekonomická, Vol. 8, Year book of the Faculty of Economics, VŠB - Technical University Ostrava]). Ostrava: Technical University, Faculty of Economics, pp. 54-60.

Kern, T. (2005). Organizational structure without hierarchy in a dynamic global business environment. V: Lan, Yi-chen (ed.). Global information society: operating information systems in a dynamic global business environment. Hershey (PA): Idea Group, cop., pp. 27-41.

Kim, H., Fox, M. (2002). "Using Enterprise Reference Models for Automated ISO 9000 Compliance Evaluation," hicss, pp. 73, 35th Annual Hawaii International Conference on System Sciences (HICSS'02)-Volume 3, [online], [cit.2006-10-01],URL: <http://doi.ieeecomputersociety.org/10.1109/HICSS.2002.993991>

Kotelnikov, V. (2006).. Traditional Management Model, [online], [cit. 2006-10-01], URL: <http://www.1000ventures.com/business_guide/mgmt_traditiona l-model.html>.

Ladd, A., Curran, T., Keller, G. (1997). SAP R/3 Business Blueprint: Understanding the Business Process Reference Model, Prentice Hall, ISBN 0135211476.

Leibold, M., Gilbert, J. B., Gilbert, M. (2002). Strategic Management in the Knowledge Economy: New Approaches and Business Applications , Public Corporate Publishing & Wiley –VCH-VErlag GmbH & Co KGaA, , ISBN 3-89578-168-1.

Martin, W. J. (1995). The Global Information Society, Aslib Gower, Aldershot, p. 171.

Ministr, J., Fiala, J., Ráček, J. (2003). Efficiency Determination and Optimisation of Administrative Processes. Documentos de Trabajo. 1vyd. Cordóba, Španělsko : Universidad de Córdoba, pp. 2-6. ISBN 84-95723-11-5.

Novotný, O. (2005a). IS/ICT Management Reference Model. Portorož 16.03.2005 – 18.03.2005. In: Kaluža, J., Kljajčič, M., Leskovar, R., Rajkovič, V., Paape, B., Šikula, M. (eds.). Synergy of Methodologies. Maribor : University of Maribor, pp. 371–376, ISBN 961-232-175-2.

Novotný, O. (2005b). IS/ICT Management Reference Model – Open Issues. Bucharest 10.11.2005 – 11.11.2005. In: Sustainable Development Management. Bucharest : University POLITEHNICA of Bucharest, pp. 377–381. ISBN 973-748-022-8.

Oesterle, H., Brenner, W., Hilbers, K. (1993). Total Information Systems Management: A European Approach (John Wiley Series in Information Systems), John Wiley&sons, ISBN 0-471-93932-3.

Pink Elephant: PinkVerify™ Toolsets (2006). [online], [cit. 2006-10-01], 2006, URL: http://www.pinkelephant.com/en-US/PinkVerify/PinkVerifyToolset.htm.

Porat, M. (1978). Communication Policy in an Information Society. In: Robinson, G. O. (ed.), Communications for Tomorrow, pp. 3-60, New York: Praeger.

El Sawy, O. A. (2001). Redesigning Enterprise Processes for e-Business, McGraw-Hill, ISBN 0-07-057225-9.

Scott Morton, M., S. (1991): Organization of the 1990s – Information Technology and Organizational Trasformation, Oxford University Press, New York.

Taylor, R. S. (ed.) (1966). Information Management in Engineering Education. Bethlehem PA, Lehigh University Press.

Thomas, O., Scheer, A. W. (2006). "Tool Support for the Collaborative Design of Reference Models — A Business Engineering Perspective", hicss, Proceedings of the 39th Annual Hawaii International Conference on System Sciences (HICSS'06) Track 1, pp. 10a, [online], [cit. 2006-10-01], URL: <http://doi.ieeecomputersociety.org/10.1109/ HICSS.2006.489>.

The Stationery Office (2000). Service Support (It Infrastructure Library Series), ISBN 01-133-0015-8.

Van der Aalst, W. M. P., Dreiling, A., Gottschalk, F., Rosemann, M., Jansen-Vullers, M. H. (2006). Configurable Process Models as a Basis for Reference Modeling, In: Bussler, C. et al. (Eds.): BPM

2005 Workshops, LNCS 3812, Springer-Verlag, Berlin, Heidelberg, pp. 512–518, ISBN 3-540-32595-6.

Voříšek, J., Dunn, D. (2001). Management of Business Informatics – Opportunities, Threats, Solutions, Proceedings of "Systems Integration 2001" conference, VŠE, Praha, pp. 665–67, ISBN 80-245-0169-4.

Weber, K. C., Almeida, R. A. R., Scalet, D., Ortencio, V. V. (1999). "Software Standardization Process In Brazil," isess, pp. 9, Fourth IEEE International Symposium and Forum on Software Engineering Standards, [online], [cit. 2006-10-01], URL: <http://doi.ieeecomputersociety.org/10.1109/ SESS.1999.766573>.

About the Authors

Petr Doucek is professor at the Faculty of Informatics and Statistics, University of Economics, Prague. He is head of the Department of System Analysis. His research fields are: information management, project management, IS/ICT security and IS/ICT impacts on society.

Ota Novotny is assistant professor at the Faculty of Informatics and Statistics, University of Economics, Prague, Department of Information Technology. His research fields are: IS/ICT processes and services management, modelling, measurement and auditing.

Business Processes and Competence Profiles of Employees – A Joint Methodology

Tomaž Kern

tomaz.kern@fov.uni-mb.si

Matjaž Roblek

matjaz.roblek@fov.uni-mb.si

Janez Mayer

janez.mayer@fov.uni-mb.si

Benjamin Urh

benjamin.urh@fov.uni-mb.si

Abstract

This paper explores the methodology developed and verified in a number of research and development projects. The methodology makes it possible to increase the effectiveness of business processes and manage the competence profiles of the people participating in these processes.

The methodology is an efficient way of capturing process and employee data, and of entering these data into a unified business repository. The repository contains unified process models encompassing complex knowledge and skills pertaining to a particular process step and to the actual competences of the people working in the process. These entries serve as the basis for determining whether the knowledge and skills in particular process steps conform to needs, and for analysing the actual competences of employees performing particular organizational functions. The outcomes reveal a gap between the actual competences of the people participating in a particular process and the knowledge and skills needed for particular organizational functions resulting from that process.

It can be concluded that the use of a unified business repository not only makes it possible to capture and analyse data about the business system, but – more importantly – enables us to manage the system and its various aspects in a constantly changing environment.

Keywords: business processes, competence profiles, business repository, efficiency

1. Introduction

Characteristic of the companies of the so-called "Global Age" is the variety of production and the dynamics of change brought about by shifting business demands (Kern, 2003b, p. 97, Doucek, 2004, p. 67). This leads to turbulent business processes and constant changes. This is also the reason that continuous business processes become intermittent processes with fewer and fewer repetitions. Customers demand shorter delivery times and expect last-minute changes. At the same time, owners expect higher profits by reducing costs, simplification of work, and saving on equipment and stock. Such conflicting demands cause organizational difficulties, lessen efficiency and, consequently, the competitiveness of companies.

Managers try to achieve competitive advantages for companies by investing in equipment and technology. However, great changes, which are often radical, can frequently lessen or even nullify the effect of these efforts. There are many cases of longer production times (and greater costs), despite the automation of basic processes[1] after introducing expensive IT.

There are several reasons for the gap between total process time and the sum of the actual times involved in technical process activities. The main reason for this is that some activities do not add value to the business system (such as preparation, waiting, finishing work and transferring documentation and material among individuals). Plenty of time (and energy, resources and money) is spent on adaptation to and mastery of sequential or simultaneous activities. The analysis of the reasons for this situation shows that the majority of superfluous work is done due to the

---

1 Basic processes add value to the business system (production processes in factories, sale processes in shops, education processes in schools, etc.).

inadequate knowledge and skill (competences) of employees or the unsuitable organizational structure of the company.

This is often because many companies were formed under completely different circumstances. Employees' competences and organizational structure were aligned to meet the demands of a specific process, and there was thus no organizational gap when the process was set up. The dysfunction between required and actual competences, and the underlying organizational structures, appeared when these processes changed and people or structures did not manage to adapt to them.

Managers try to solve these organizational problems in two ways:

- The first solution is to reduce time and costs, and increase the quality of work through the formalization (detailed instructions) and improvement of business processes involving the adaptation of organizational structures, information support and job descriptions (Kern, 2003a, p. 101), (Urh, 2003, p. 456).
- The second way is to search for competent people who have adequate knowledge and skills, and who could be capable of designing and performing work independently. They also try to increase efficiency by developing adequate competences among employees (Mayer, 2004, p. 275).

According to these two possibilities, two approaches emerged. The first is the so-called "process approach" while the second is known as the "human resources approach". Both approaches are adequate. However, their weakness is that they are mutually exclusive. The reason for this is that the methods used in both approaches are divergent:

- The process approach is based on "hard methods" – data concerning time, frequency, probability, working hours, etc.
- The human resource approach is based especially on so-called "soft methods", which focus on people and their competences, their training and education.

The aim of the research was to find the common points of both methods and combine them into a new methodology.

2. Process Methodology (CPI, BPR, BPM)

Among the first to emphasize the importance of processes were Hammer and Champy, authors of the best-selling book *Re-Engineering the Corporation: A Manifesto for Business Revolution*, which caused a true revolution in the business world. Since the 1990s, many large business systems have tried to solve their problems through innovating their business processes (Davenport, 2000, p. 231). The most frequently used term in the literature is "Business Process Reengineering" – BPR, which requires radical business system changes in performing work and establishing processes. In addition to BPR, other approaches to business reorganization also gained ground, notably Continuous Process Improvement, Total Quality Management and others which are supported by particular methodologies.

A synthesis of different approaches to business process reorganization is contained in the guidelines related to BPM – Business Process Management (Scheer, 2000, p. 381, Holt, 2000, p. 103), which is the thematic follow-up to reengineering. Every business system needs to be organized in the form of processes. This involves development, design and establishment of the business, organization and information systems, i.e. business process management. It is a highly complex task involving many different aspects and – understandably – many different problems. Organizational, technical, economic, human resource, sociological and other intermingled and interrelated problems need to be solved. In time, the demands of the environment on the business system and the relationships within the system change, so the established situation constantly needs to be altered and supplemented. These changes could be called "organization and information reengineering of business systems from the process point of view".

It should be noted that business process or system reengineering projects differ from the majority of other projects. The main difference is that participants in the project are often part of the business system which is being reengineered. This means that those employed in the business system are actually changing the environment in which they work. During the preparation phase, consensus between key stakeholders needs to be reached regarding the problems involved in the business system reengineering project. Business system reengineering projects are related to three key interrelated areas:

- Organization
- IT
- Human resources

In accordance with the chosen methodology or approach, business process reengineering projects can be broken down into various phases, activities and tasks, depending on the approach selected (Valiris, Glykas, 2004, p. 446; Roblek, 2000, p. 66; Vakola, Rezgui, 2000, p. 241; Kern, 2006, p. 5).

2.1 Steps in the Representative Process Methodology

In the research, we applied the representative process methodology of business process reengineering, broken down into the steps shown in Figure 1.

Project preparation

- Definition of problems in the business system, proposals for alternative paths to solutions and identification of opportunities for project implementation
- Definition of the scope of changes and limitations that need to be taken into account in project implementation
- Definition of the "target goal"
- Structural definition of "objectives"
- Selection of internal and external stakeholders in the reengineering process and detailed planning of the project
- Organization of the reengineering project (project definition) and consensus regarding the system of communication during project implementation

Figure 1: Steps in the representative process methodology

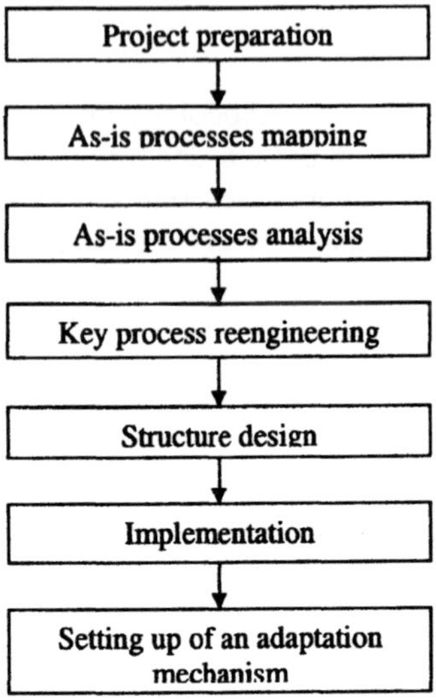

As-is processes mapping

- Mapping of the existing organizational structure
- Mapping of the existing information system
- Mapping of the existing human resources system
- Mapping of the existing processes, which is the most important activity in this step

As-is processes analysis

- Analysis of the data or attributes of the existing business system, results of the previous step – As-is processes mapping
- Benchmarking (e.g. comparison with the same business system in a different environment, business system analysis in past periods, etc.)

The analysis has to take into account the strategic guidelines of the business system adopted by the management of the system in which the business processes are undergoing reengineering. During the analysis, key factors in the environment that might have a major impact on the business system, without being significantly influenced by it, have to be identified.

Key process reengineering

- Selection and validation (on the part of the management – client) of key processes in the business system to be reengineered
- Definition of the level and degree of selected processes reengineering
- Preparation of alternative selected processes reengineering elaborated in cycles
- Development of reengineered key business processes models
- Variants of reengineered key business system processes selected and validated by the management – client

Structure design

- Setting up the appropriate organizational structure of the business system based on the proposed variants of the reengineered key processes
- Supporting key processes in the business system with an adequately structured information system
- Transition from the existing to the new human resources system, as the implementation of the reengineered business processes requires adequate human resources

Implementation

The key aspect of implementation is to make the proposed ideas "viable", which is the most time-consuming and difficult task in business process reengineering projects. This involves development of implementing project plans, which need to be validated by the business system management or the client, for the following:

- Implementing of the changed key processes
- Setting up organizational structures
- Building up information systems
- Implementing the competence-based human resource system.

Setting up an adaptation mechanism

In the recent period, business systems have often required implementation of a seventh step – namely setting up an adaptation mechanism in response to the increasingly dynamic environment in which modern business systems operate.

- Setting up a mechanism or a process that enables business systems to adapt to the changing demands of the environment

In the opinion of those working in the process, the major weakness of this method is that its primary goal is process efficiency, and it therefore proposes an "unnatural" set of activities to be performed in the framework of the proposed work function. The method does not take into account the limited capabilities of individuals; people are considered as "work tools" that can be "upgraded" to meet any level of complexity of the reengineered process.

3. HR Methodology (Competence Models)

The competence model was developed by D. McClelland (McClelland, 1973, p. 1ff), who published the well-known article entitled "Testing for Competence Rather Than for Intelligence". Application of competences in managerial practice was more widely accepted after the publication of the book *The Competent Manager* (Boyatzis, 1980, p. 76). By the end of the 1980s, the notion of competences was already well known (Svetlik, 2004, p. 21) and established in Western corporations.

Boyatzis defines a competence as an "underlying characteristic of an individual, which is causally related to effective or superior performance in a job, and competences can be: motives, traits, skills, aspects of one's self-image or social role, or a body of knowledge that one uses." However, for a more detailed scientific study of competences and their application in organizational practice, we need a more detailed definition. Boyatzis differentiates between:

- elements/tasks of a job that need to be competently performed – required competences; and
- features of an individual making this competency possible – actual competences.

On the basis of this differentiation, we can define a competence as the "sum of the behavioural patterns that an individual must command for efficient and effective performance" An individual competence is a written description of measurable work habits and personal skills used to achieve a work objective (Green, 1999, p. 5).

As we understand it, a competence is a behaviour enabling an individual to effectively perform a particular task. It is based on appropriate physical, social, psychological, personal and spiritual potential, interests, knowledge, skills, values and beliefs, and is above all reflected in the ability to fully exploit the internal and external resources available for attaining an objective.

Although particular competence components in an individual can be measured and evaluated directly (intelligence) or indirectly (personal features), we can never quite be sure how these will be manifested in a concrete (work) situation. A person can be very intelligent, but inefficient because he or she has no interest in the work being performed. A person can know a great deal, but be unable to put this knowledge into practice because he or she lacks the necessary implementation skills. The key question here is whether it is possible to clearly define the action taken by a person (competence) which is decisive for his or her efficiency in performing a particular process function (activity, task).

The level of a particular competence (efficiency) in a person can be inferred only from his or her concrete actions and results achieved. And the results can only be determined on the basis of criteria based on the complexity of the work. This means that – on the basis of the process analysis of all tasks (activities) making up an individual's organizational role – we need to clearly define the type and necessary level of all the competences required for the activities, and then determine whether the person concerned really possesses these competences and to what degree they are developed and demonstrated. However, it is also possible to proceed in reverse order. On the basis of the competences demonstrated by an individual, we can select an employee with the optimal scope of activities in the work process.

3.1 Steps in the Representative Competence Methodology

The representative competence methodology applied in the research involves the steps shown in Figure 2.

Figure 2: Steps in the representative competence methodology

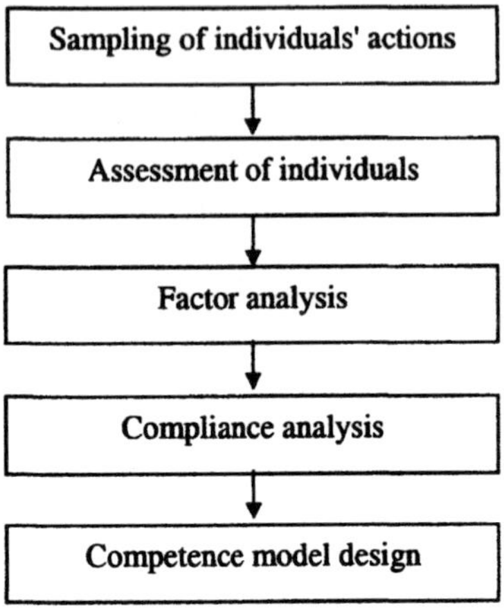

Sampling of individuals' actions

Classical methods of determining competences are based on interviews in which experts primarily aim to detect efficient and inefficient actions taken by individuals in concrete organizational roles. Data can be captured directly or with the help of a repertory competence list with preset descriptions. With either of the techniques, we can obtain descriptions of efficient and inefficient actions that are characteristic of the chosen organizational roles or wider work areas. In the classical method, questionnaires are prepared on the basis of the final set of competences. With the questionnaires, employees can evaluate the organizational behaviour of their supervisors, of colleagues at the same organizational level, their own organizational behaviour and that of their subordinates.

Assessment of individuals

Assessment provides a great deal of information, which in the classical method – for the sake of greater transparency – is usually reduced to key competences with the help of factor analysis. Furthermore, assessment provides an opportunity for weighing groups of competences and individual competences which correlate with the group. Factor analysis aims to simplify the complexity of relations between the multitude of variables under observation by revealing common dimensions or factors providing insight into basic competence structure.

Factor analysis
Factor analysis is an appropriate method of determining common key competences for a particular work area and for the entire organization. On the basis of the factor analysis results, we can design a competence model in which an organization defines the desired organizational behaviours to be demonstrated by employees in order to achieve efficient and effective performance.

Compliance analysis
The result of compliance analysis between actual and required competences shows harmony and discrepancy among the actual competences of the people participating in a particular process and the knowledge and skills needed for particular organizational functions resulting from that process. The degree of the match shows the likelihood of key tasks being performed efficiently, and the quality and universality of the employees' intellectual potential.

Competence model design
A competence model has many functions. It provides insight into the key competences demanded by the entire work process, and thus sets basic standards for personnel recruitment and deployment. However, the competence model serves its primary purpose only when the majority of key competences acquire high positive value, i.e. become active values in the organizational culture. The competence model should periodically be reassessed in order to remain topical and to reveal any gaps which might have occurred as the result of changes within and outside the organization.

The classical method (Spencer, Spencer, 2001, p. 91) has at least one important weakness and at least one important limitation. Its major weakness is that it neglects the process aspect of work, which is the only criterion measuring whether certain actions are relevant to above-average achievements in a particular activity, and that it reduces the number of competences, which – admittedly – facilitates analytic and diagnostic work but conceals less prominent competences, which are nevertheless important for the process. These two weaknesses can be eliminated in practice with the use of modern information tools. If we proceed only from effective and efficient behavioural patterns, we do not know exactly what work requirements and activities they are related to and thus can make only general assumptions about a person's (in)competence. In this manner, we can only determine general (un)suitability of an individual employee for a particular organizational role, but not for a particular task. If an employee does not meet the quality standards set for particular tasks, he or she need not be transferred to another position; we can only relieve him or her of those tasks that he or she is unable to perform to satisfaction, and add new tasks better suited to the employee's competences.

4. Combining Methodologies

In the past, there were no adequate methods, techniques and tools to enable the combination of both approaches in spite of the pressing need for such a methodology. In the projects on which the new methodology is based, we find out whether it is possible to gain information with a combination of process and human resource approaches with which to significantly increase the efficiency of companies in the future. A method based on the application of a business repository was thus developed (Kern, 2003b, p. 101; Roblek et al., 2005, p. 1039). The repository consists of the business premises, processes and structural models, at the same time containing data about the competences of people and competence profiles of their positions (Mayer et al., 2004 p. 6; Kern et al., 2006, p. 38). A unique business repository enables the analysis of a large quantity of data in real time. The method was tested in a real business environment.

4.1 The Common Point between the Two Methodologies

The steps in the two methodologies (Figures 1 and 2) reveal a common point which deserves further examination, namely the position or work role (Kern et al., 2005, p. 1203). Process methodology enables very precise definitions of activities which, if aggregated, constitute a detailed job description. On the basis of these activities, we can determine the complexity level of a position, but – unfortunately – the methodology does not allow us to measure the complexity of the activities themselves. On the other hand, we have the competence methodology, which is based on a detailed study of an individual's competences. If a certain set of competences is revealed as a trend in a certain set of individuals currently occupying the same position, the method assumes that this constitutes the complexity level of the position. However, it is not possible to determine whether the individuals under observation actually meet the complexity level requirements of the position. More simply:

- Process methodology determines the exact structure of a position's activities and then assumes that it is possible to find an employee with such "multitasking" abilities.
- Competence methodology determines the exact competence structure of individuals occupying particular positions, and then assumes that this constitutes the complexity level of the position. The new joint methodology eliminates this gap.

4.2. Steps in the Joint Methodology

In the joint methodology, the process and competence aspects of work are constantly interrelated. In the first step, we map the existing organizational roles from the point of view of organizational and human resource structure, the information and documentation systems and process aspects. Processes are mapped at a later stage of elaboration.

At the same time, we conduct detailed interviews with holders of the organizational roles under observation to determine those forms of organizational actions which lead to high performance effectiveness and efficiency. On this basis, we determine all the competences which the interviewees judge to be relevant for the process. All these competences are included in the repertory list. The final form of the repertory competence list is drawn up after the competences are tested for relevance (degree of importance, need, characteristics) to all key functions in the processes making up the organizational roles under observation. The testing is carried out by experts together with the employees who have the most detailed knowledge of these functions.

Thus we avoid the "halo effect", which is inherent in the classical method, because it neglects the exact analysis of the complexity of functions in the work process and relies on the general assumptions of those with a good knowledge of that process. Only through identifying a concrete process function (task) can we evaluate which competences are truly necessary for effective performance, and which are only seemingly important. A detailed study of particular functions in the work process is definitely a far more reliable criterion than general assumptions, as we can truly assess the suitability of employees for a particular organizational role only on the basis of a thorough, reliable and objective evaluation of competences. While the classical methodology is based only on the inner consistency of competences, our methodology is characterised by a consistent correlation between the objective work complexity and the subjective competences of those performing the work. The new, combined, methodology is an upgrade of process methodology and includes the steps in Figure 3.

Competence mapping in process activities

This involves identification of professional and leadership competences which an individual must possess to effectively perform an activity. As input, we use the content of the business repository (charts of business processes, organizational structure and hierarchy of activities in the business system under observation). In the initial phase, structures are designed on the basis of reengineered business processes; competence profiles of the employees are not yet taken into account – ("radical form of BPR").

Preparation of competence list (competence repertory)

The repertory list is the result of combined sets of competences identified for process activities (Mayer, 2003, p. 370). The repertory list combines competences into logical content clusters and is intended on the one hand, for determining the set of competences and their strengths for particular activities in an organizational role and, on the other hand, for assessing the personal competence profiles of individuals.

Figure 3: Business Processes and Competence Profiles of Employees – Joint Methodology[2]

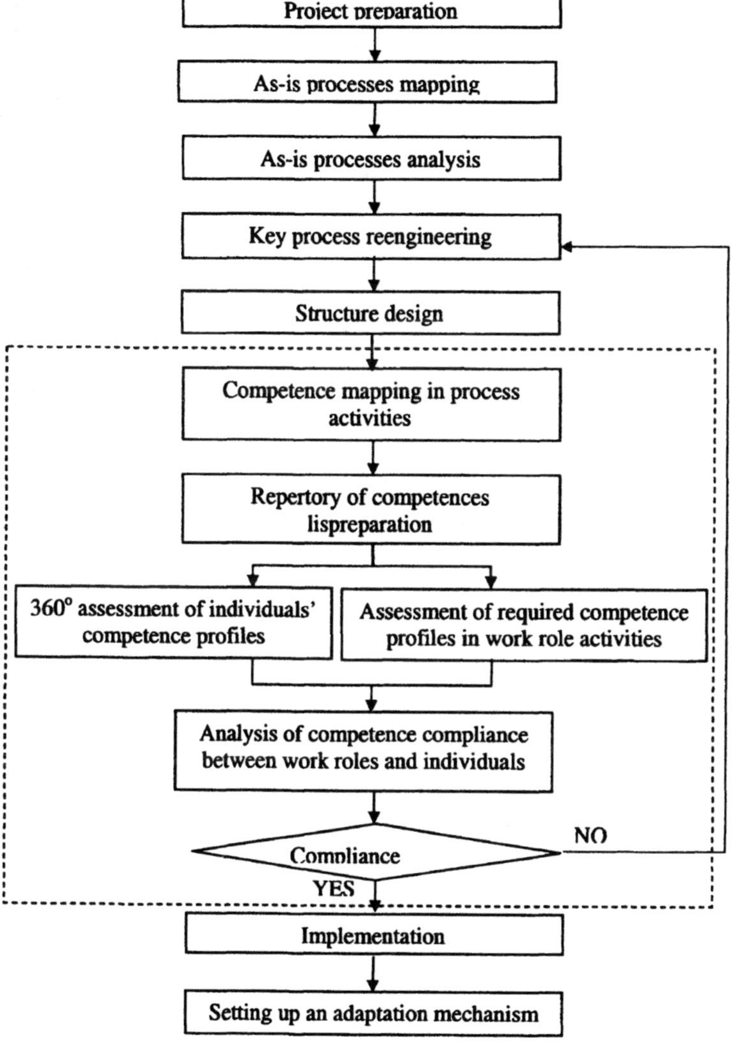

2 The methodology was developed and tested in targeted research projects (CRP) MORS No. M5-0048 and MORS No. M5-0171, and in the applicative project PROMETEJ, Iskratel.

360° assessment of individuals' competence profiles

This serves as the basis for compiling a complete competence profile of individuals under observation. The 360° Feedback Model is a process in which employees assess themselves on the basis of particular criteria, while at the same time – on the basis of the same criteria – they are assessed by their co-workers who know their efficiency (subordinate colleagues, supervisors and co-workers at the same organizational level). This feedback is intended to bring into an employee's awareness those behavioural patterns that he or she is not aware of but that are clearly visible to his or her co-workers. Through the 360° feedback analysis, employees learn how co-workers perceive their work, they identify their own weaknesses and then draw up a plan to increase their competence (Mayer et al., 2005, p. 20). The feedback obtained helps them to better manage their work and careers (Logar, 2004, p. 39). The data on actual competences is gathered and processed as follows:

- Descriptions of competences are turned into questions (grammatically speaking, the questions are in the 1st and 3rd person) for the 360° feedback method.
- In the first survey cycle, respondents answer the question "To what degree is my competence developed?" and assess their degree of development on a scale from 1 to 5.
- In the second survey cycle, respondents answer the question "To what degree is the competence developed in the person evaluated?" and assess it on a scale from 1 to 5. The questions are the same as in the first questionnaire.
- The answers are then processed into a verified competence profile of each individual participating in the selected process and holding a particular organizational function.
- The results serve as the basis for actual competence profiles of the employees.

These represent the available leadership and professional competences and their strength in the individuals under observation. They are intended for the analysis of competence compliance between organizational roles and individuals.

Assessment of required competence profiles in work role activities

This assessment follows the assessment of the competences (professional and leadership) needed for particular activities, which are aggregated in a work role with the help of the repository. The data on required competences are gathered and processed as follows:

- Selection of processes, partial processes and sets of functions within the processes.
- Determination of organizational roles within particular functions, and determination of the type of assignment.
- Determination of an individual's organizational role on the basis of the organizational and personnel structure map.
- The data about the relative importance of a particular competence is obtained through a survey based on the repertory list. For every observed function, the respondents assign the significance (importance, characteristics, strength) of every competence, usually on a 1–5 grading scale.
- The survey results are input into the repository.
- The model of the competences required by particular organizational roles is designed to be used in the analysis of competence compliance between organizational roles and individuals.

Analysis of competence compliance between organizational roles and individuals

The main purpose of the analysis is compliance between the actual competences of individuals and organizational roles in the business system under observation. The analysis involves a number of parameters but is nevertheless relatively simple, as it is carried out in the business repository. It analyses the following:

- Complexity of particular activities from the point of view of competences
- Complexity of the process from the point of view of competences
- Strength of particular competences in the process activities
- Significance of competences for the process
- Suitability of workers for assuming current work roles
- Actual competences of workers occupying positions with the competence profile of the position

4.3 Advantages of the Joint Methodology

Precise determination of the required competences makes it possible to determine and design the suitable (usually quite wide) complexity profile for an organizational role, which enables not only a comparison between the actual profiles, but also:

- a comparison between the competences of employees and the requirements of the entire process;
- suitability prioritization of employees for performing the entire process;
- determination of predominant competences in the work process;
- insight into the weaknesses in the actual competences in employees (for the entire process);
- comparison between the strength of the required competence and the lack of the actual competence;
- analysis of the complexity of organizational roles;
- prioritization of suitability of employees for assuming existing organizational roles;
- determination of key competences for particular organizational roles; and
- comparison between the actual competences of employees and the competences required by the organizational roles.

The result of the research and testing in a number of applied projects is a highly efficient HRM tool which can be used in the selection processes, career development, personnel mobility, work evaluation and formation of efficient work groups and organizational units. The databases thus obtained can be used for designing expert information tools to help HR experts and leaders in taking more reliable decisions regarding personnel issues.

In the selection process, with the knowledge of the entire work process and all actual competences, it is possible to select the most competent people for particular organizational roles or for positions which have not yet been adequately filled. It is also possible to create optimal (project) teams for particular tasks with the people available.

In the career development process, it is possible to tailor the tasks of individuals to the general profile of work area complexity. We can relieve individuals of the tasks for which they are not competent enough, and add those better suited with regard to their competences.

One of the challenges in organizations is the implementation of the personnel mobility process with people who work efficiently but have sunk into a routine and are consequently less creative. Insight into their (potential) competences and available opportunities might reveal possibilities for appropriate reassignments or shifts in organizational roles. It also makes it possible to identify "universal" people (generalists) capable of performing the majority of tasks in the process, who – when needed – can efficiently stand in for a number of co-workers.

5. CASE: Slovenian Military Administration – Selected Human Resources

In this case study, we mapped the business processes of the selected human resources. Altogether, 29 processes were mapped (m=29). The tool used in the mapping was ARIS. A multitude of processes were identified and activities mapped for each of them. Altogether, 166 different activities in the processes were mapped (n=166). Thus, a multitude of activities were obtained. An activity belonging to a process is expressed as the value of $b_{i,j}$:

$$b_{i,j} = \begin{cases} 1, a_i \in p_j;\ \textit{if activity } a_i \textit{ is in process } p_j \\ 0, a_i \notin p_j;\ \textit{if activity } a_i \textit{ is not in process } p_j \end{cases}$$

where $b_{i,j}$ = belonging of a_i to the process p_j
a_i = set of activities; i=1..n
p_j = set of processes; j=1..m

5.1 Example of Required Competence Analysis

The competences serving as the basis for the repertory list were mapped independently. Altogether, 133 competences were mapped (t=133). With the help of the repertory competence list, 33 work roles were analysed (s= 33), and the matching and strength of the competence for a particular activity within a work role were assessed ($c_{i,j}$):

for each w_k = role; k=1..s

$$c_{d,i} = \begin{cases} 1..5, o_d \in a_i;\ \textit{strength value from 1 to 5 if competency } o_d \textit{ is required by activity } a_i \\ 0, o_d \notin a_i;\ \textit{strength value 0 if competency } o_d \textit{ is not required by activity } a_i \end{cases}$$

where $c_{d,i}$ = matching of competence o_d over activity a_i; 0 (not required)..5 (highly required)
o_d = set of competences; d=1..t
a_i = set of activities; i=1..n

We defined a very simple criterion for identifying key competences (Ko) for particular work roles: key competences are the competences the maximal value of which over all activities exceeds the sum of average values and standard deviation values of all competences involved in a work task:

$$\underset{wk=1}{Ko} = \max_{d=1} c_{d,i} > \bar{x}\left(\max_{d=1..t} c_{d,i}\right) + \sigma\left(\max_{d=1..t} c_{d,i}\right)$$

Table 1: Example of key competences for a work role

Role: X for human resources		
Ref.No.	*Competence*	*Ko: max $c_{d,i}$ >4,00*
14.6	Professional independence	**5.00**
6.1	Good knowledge of MORS as a system	**4.67**
5.3	Knowledge of a wide range of regulations	**4.44**
2.4	Ability to derive essential information from the data	**4.33**
4.1	Freedom in professional decision-making	**4.33**
14.16	Knowledge of the Slovenian language	**4.33**
5.1	Simultaneous respect for a variety of legislative acts	**4.22**
1.2	Accuracy and consistency in performing tasks	**4.11**
2.1	Analytical thinking	**4.00**
4.2	Clear delineation of decision-making powers	**4.00**
7.18	Positive attitude when pressed for time	**4.00**
8.4	Mutual setting of priorities for task implementation	**4.00**
14.8	Knowledge of work organization	**4.00**
15.8	Time planning	**4.00**

5.2 Example of Actual Competence Analysis

The actual competence analysis was carried out with the 360° assessment and involved 44 candidates. The analysis involved an assessment of all 133 identified competences. The competence profiles of users (*Do*) were then input along with the competence requirements of the positions, and positive and negative deviations were determined:

for each w_k = role; k=1..s

$$e_{d,i} = \begin{cases} c_{d,i} \leq v_d;\ \textit{surplus of candidate competency } d \\ \qquad \textit{over the same competence of each role activity } i \\ c_{d,i} > v_d;\ \textit{shortage of candidate competency } d \\ \qquad \textit{over the same competence of each role activity } i \end{cases}$$

where $e_{d,i}$ = required value of competence $c_{d,i}$ matched with the actual value of candidate

$c_{d,i}$ = belonging and strength of competence o_d over activity a_i

v_d = strength of candidate's actual competences; d=1..t

Table 2: Example of a comparison between candidates' competences and competence requirements of work roles

Suitability of candidates for work roles: X for human resources					
Candidate	*P(MAX)*	*M(MAX)*	*P(POV)*	*M(POV)*	*RANG (M(MAX))*
7	150.555556	-8.11111	292.9583	0	1
12	100.666667	-15.2222	236.5361	-0.57778	2
15	141.222222	-15.2778	277.1917	-0.73333	3
3	83.8611111	-16.9167	217.8028	-0.34444	4
6	92.5555556	-19.1111	224.7306	-0.77222	5
10	**41.031746**	**-30.5873**	**160.9583**	**0**	**6**
33	97.4444444	-30.6667	221.2556	-3.96389	7
18	66.4722222	-30.8611	187.3111	-1.18611	8
23	40.4444444	-39	152.6167	-0.65833	9
4	49.9166667	-40.9722	159.8333	-0.375	10
16	36.6666667	-43.9722	143.6361	-0.42778	11
35	29.8888889	-47.1111	134.4611	-1.16944	12
28	37.05	-52.3556	135.7	-0.49167	13
21	27.7555556	-58.5111	121.775	-2.01667	14
1	25.5111111	-74.6667	105.8917	-4.53333	15
2	20.4055556	-78.3478	96.93	-4.35833	16
8	11.2222222	-92.4444	78.18889	-8.89722	17
9	13.5555556	-97.7778	72.39722	-6.10556	18
...	...	...	...	...	...
49	14.2222222	-106.028	71.98333	-13.275	20

In Table 2, Candidate "10", who currently occupies the work role, is marked in bold. Column P(MAX) shows the cumulative surplus of the candidate regarding all the competences required by the work role. Column P(MAX) shows the cumulative deficit of the candidate regarding all the competences required by the work role. Column P(POV) shows the cumulative surplus of the candidate, given the average values of particular competences for the work role, while column M(POV) shows the cumulative deficit of the candidate, given the average values of particular competences for the work role. These are cumulative values. However, it is possible to compare the complexity of the work role and abilities of the candidate down to the detailed level of a particular activity or a particular competence. Column RANG M(MAX) shows the ranking of candidates regarding the competence match, taking into account the cumulative deficit of competence values.

The results of the method were validated and confirmed by the candidates' supervisors as a supplement to the classic human resource deployment methods (in project CRP No.M5-0048 and in projects CRP No.M5-0048 and PROMETEJ).

6. Conclusions

According to certain advocates of competence models, their greatest value lies in a new logic which no longer builds the human resource systems around the positions and detailed descriptions of work operations, but on the basis of competences, demanding from employees a significantly higher level of independence, accountability, initiative and flexibility. What might possibly hinder the implementation of the competence model is excessive determination of positions with detailed descriptions of work operations, which supposedly requires the relatively stable business conditions that characterized business before the advent of globalization, while in turbulent environments we can rely only on competences – particularly key competences.

The results of research and applied projects show that competence models alone cannot replace the process aspects of an organization. However, we could also claim the opposite: process aspects alone cannot lead to radical improvements in performance. If we lose objectivity when evaluating the relationship between required and actual competences, we might end up looking for omnipotent or even "super" people, capable of finding an innovative solution to any problem and reaching an infallible decision at any given moment. In reality, original opportunities are identified through the synthesis of the exact process and subjective competence approaches supported by modern information tools. With their help, it is possible to quickly change process and competence profiles, and adapt them to newly emerging needs. In this way, we can constantly relieve individuals of old process functions and supplement them with new ones, or – in line with the development of his or her competences – combine certain functions and raise the level of their complexity according to new organizational roles.

The new methodology is particularly efficient, as it enables a comparison between the actual competence profiles of all employees working in an organizational unit and all the competences required by process functions, which enables perfect transparency of work process demands and available human resources.

Bibliography and References

Boyatzis, R. (1980): The Competent Manager, Wiley, New York.

Davenport, T. H., Beers, M. C. (2000): Process Think: Winning Perspectives for Business Change in the Information Age, Managing Information about Processes, pp. 228 - 249, Idea Group Publishing, London.

Doucek, P. (2204): IS/ICT Security Management in Information Society. ECON '04 (Selected Research papers), vol. 11, p. 67–74.

Green, P. C. (1999): Building Robust Competencies, Linking Human Resource Systems to Organizational Strategies, Jossey Bass, Inc. Publishers, San Francisco.

Hammer, M., Champy, J. (1993): Reengineering the Corporation: A Manifesto for Business Revolution. Harper Business. New York.

Holt, P. A.(2000): Business Process Management: Models, Techniques and Empirical Studies. Management Oriented Models of Business Processes. Springer-Verlag. Berlin. pp. 99–109.

Kern, T. (2003a): Organizational structure without hierarchy. *Strojarstvo*, vol. 45, no. 4/6, pp. 101–110.

Kern, T. (2003b): Business system repository as a universal business tool. V: Kaluža, Jindřich (ur.). 5th International Conference on

Strategic Management and its Support by Information Systems, Ostrava: Technical University of Ostrava, Faculty of Economics.

Kern, T., Roblek, M., Mayer, J., Urh B. (2005): Business processes and human resources competence profiles. In: Khosrowpour, M. (ed.). Information Resources Management Association, International Conference, San Diego, California, USA, May 15–18, 2005. Managing modern organizations with information technology. Hershey [etc.]: Idea Group, cop., pp. 1202–1204.

Kern, T., Mayer, J., Roblek, M., Urh, B., Logar, G. (2006): Projekt CRP MORS: elaborat projekta: verzija Z001. (Project CRP MORS: expert's detailed report of project: version Z001.). Kranj: Fakulteta za organizacijske vede.

Kern, T. (2006): Upravljanje procesov (metodološki del), (Business Prosess management (methodology)), Fakulteta za organizacijske vede, Kranj.

Logar, G. (2004): Uporaba procesnega pristopa pri oblikovanju kompetenčnega modela v podjetju (Modeling an organization competence model using the process approach), Univerza v Mariboru, Fakulteta za organizacijske vede, Bachelor thesis.

Mayer, J. (2003): Lastnosti uspešnih vodij (Characteristics of successful leaders). Organizacija, Kranj, year. 36, no. 6, pp. 368–375.

Mayer, J. (2004): Odkrivanje in kariera najobetavnejših ljudi v organizaciji. (The most promising people in an organization). In: Florjančič, J., Paape, B. (eds.). Personnel and Management: selected topics. Frankfurt am Main [etc.]: P. Lang.

Mayer, J., Kern, T., Roblek, M., Urh, B., Logar, G. (2004): Projekt PROMETEJ: elaborat projekta: verzija Z001. (Projekt PROMETEJ: expert's detailed report of project: version Z001) Kranj: Fakulteta za organizacijske vede.

Mayer, J., Roblek, M., Ban, J. (2005): Projekt KAIROS: elaborat projekta: verzija Z001. (Project KAIROS: expert's detailed report of project: version Z001) Kranj: Fakulteta za organizacijske vede.

McClelland, D. (1973): Testing for Competence rather than for Intelligence, American Psychologist, 28/1.

Roblek, M. (2000): Meta model preoblikovanja poslovnih procesov, Magistrska naloga (META model of BPR, Master thesis), Univerza v Mariboru, Fakulteta za organizacijske vede, Kranj.

Roblek, M., Kern, T., Urh, B. (2005): Business objects repository approach for managing changes in employee IT support. In: Khosrowpour, M. (ed.). Information Resources Management Association, International Conference, San Diego, California, USA, May 15–

18, 2005. Managing modern organizations with information technology. Hershey [etc.]: Idea Group, cop., pp. 1039–1041.

Scheer, A. W., Nuttgens, M. (2000): Business Process Management: Models, Techniques and Empirical Studies, ARIS Arhitecture and Reference Models for Business Process Management, pp. 376 – 390, Springer - Verlag, Berlin.

Spencer, L. M., Spencer, S. M. (2001): Competence at Work, John Wiley & Sons Inc.

Svetlik, I. (2004): Human resource management in the knowledge based organizations. In: Svetlik, I. Nadoh, J. (eds.). *Conference proceedings*. Ljubljana: Faculty of Social Sciences, pp. 21.

Urh, B. (2003): Business systems management with process performance management. In: Jašková, M. (ed.). ECON '03: [selected research papers], (Research works proceedings, Vol. 10, 2003, Economics set). Ostrava: Technical University of Ostrava, Faculty of Economics, pp. 455-466.

Vakola, M., Rezgui, Y. (2000): Critique of existing business process re-engineering methodologies: The development and implementation of a new methodology, Business Process Management Journal, Vol. 6 No. 3, pp. 238–250.

Valiris, G., Glykas, M. (2004).: Business analysis metrics for business process redesign, Business Process Management Journal, Vol. 10, Iss. 4, pp. 445 – 480, Bradford, 2004.

About the Authors

Tomaž Kern is an associate professor at the University of Maribor, Faculty of Organizational Sciences, and lectures on business processes and project management. He leads a team of experts. His bibliography includes over 200 scientific and technical papers and articles.

Matjaž Roblek holds a PhD in organizational sciences. He is a member of the Production Organization and Information Systems Laboratory at the Faculty of Organizational Sciences. He has participated in over 30 targeted research and applied projects.

Janez Mayer, PhD, assistant professor at the University of Maribor, Faculty of Organizational Sciences, is a doctor of psychology. He is the author of a special assessment procedure for measurements of intellectual potential of the most promising people in organizations.

Benjamin Urh holds an MSc in organizational sciences. He is a member of the Project and Process Management Laboratory at the Faculty of Organizational Sciences. He is author or co-author of over 20 scientific and technical articles, papers and other publications.

Unreliable Supplier Influence on Replenishment Process Optimization

Davorin Kofjač

davorin.kofjac@fov.uni-mb.si

Miroljub Kljajić

miroljub.kljajic@fov.uni-mb.si

Abstract

The modern business environment contains many factors that are more, or less reliable. One of them is an unreliable supplier in the supply chain. This paper introduces a system dynamics approach to the inventory control model for replenishment process optimization regarding inventory total cost. Also, two delivery algorithms are presented for supplier's delivery: a) orders are delivered in one batch and b) orders are delivered in several batches. The impact of unreliable delivery on a replenishment strategy and on inventory total costs is presented and discussed.

Keywords: inventory control, optimization, simulation, stochastic delivery, replenishment process.

1. Introduction

Inventory systems are often subject to randomly changing environmental conditions that may affect the demand for the product, the supply, and the cost structure. The environment represents various important factors such as the randomly changing economic conditions, market conditions that may affect the demand as well as the supply, and the cost parameters (Özekici and Parlar, 1999, p. 123ff). The contemporary business environment is dynamical and ever changing; therefore, it is hard to anticipate its behaviour. If, at a certain moment, a wrong decision is made, it can lead to long-term consequences for a company. To reduce the probability of making wrong decisions, simulation is often used to run several simulation scenarios. These are analyzed and assessed and the scenario closest to optimum is chosen on the basis of information currently available.

The source of uncertainty can be either the demand or the supply process. The demand and supply uncertainty can be divided into time and quantity deviations from the original plan. Time deviation occurs when customers place their orders earlier or later than expected. The quantity deviation occurs when order quantity is different from the one anticipated or delivered. Both deviations can also occur simultaneously. Because of the mentioned uncertainties, a new term must be introduced – "a warehouse", whose task is to compensate those variations (Minner, 2000, p. 2f). In other words – it should be a warehouse with an adaptive replenishment strategy, as deterministic approaches lead to problems in an uncertain environment (Reiner and Trcka, 2004, p. 218).

The warehouse, based on the material flow of supply, which is filling the warehouse, and of demand, which is emptying the warehouse, is affected by at least two unreliable factors. The supply can be unreliable because of an inability to deliver the required quantity, claims etc. (Zsidisin, 2003, p. 217f). In this paper, we will focus on the possibility that a supplier cannot deliver the ordered quantity in one batch; instead, it is delivered in several batches. The consequences are possible stock-outs and higher transportation costs if every batch must be paid for separately. We will also assume that there is only one supplier for each item, although many papers consider multiple suppliers (Kawtummachai and Van Hop, 2005, p. 231ff; Arda and Hennet, 2004; Choy et al., 2002, p. 213ff).

The demand uncertainty is dictated primarily by the stochastic behaviour of the modern business environment, where the demand can only be predicted in small time frames. The further we are away from the current moment, the harder it is to anticipate the demand. Unreliable demand negatively influences the replenishment process. If the demand is not known in advance and can only be predicted, it is a demanding task to make a right replenishment decision. So far, we have listed several factors that negatively influence the replenishment process. But also the warehouse capacity must not be neglected, and the fact that no stock-outs should occur.

To overcome uncertainty in the supply chain, one can use simulation to make a "what-if" analysis by running several simulation scenarios, thus anticipating possible future events. Computer-based simulation is seen as an integral business tool, giving flexibility and convenience to designing, planning and analyzing complex processes and/or systems. This is because computer-based modelling and simulation methods have the capability of representing the complex static structure as well as the dynamic behaviour of systems (Wang and Chatwin, 2004, p. 720ff; Kljajić et al., 2000, p.199ff; Dowlman et al., 2004, p. 40ff). Clearly, the imaginative and disciplined application of dynamic modelling and simulation provides a potentially useful mechanism through which managers can gain a comprehensive understanding of system behaviour, concentrating on core business processes such as order fulfilment, product development as well as customer acquisition, satisfaction, and retention (Fowler, 2003, p. 141).

This paper presents the simulation model used to solve replenishment strategy problems (when to place an order and how many products to order) in a medium-sized company in order to improve its replenishment processes. The main concern of the order manager is finding an ordering strategy that would produce minimal inventory costs without stock-outs. Barlas and Özevin (2004) have proved that people can be classified into different ordering behaviour patterns. The simulator's ability of visual presentation could prove to be one of its main advantages, as each subject is prone to a particular behaviour and the visualization of the process could facilitate learning new methodologies that the subject is not likely to try otherwise, thus making optimization of replenishment process faster and more efficient (Chwif and Barretto, 2003, p. 1994ff).

The paper is structured in the following way: Section 2 describes the problem in detail; in Section 3, the replenishment algorithm is described; in Section 4, simulation results are analyzed and discussed; Section 5 contains conclusions and suggestions for future research.

2. Inventory Control Problem Formulation

Items stored in a warehouse play an important role in the process of inventory optimization. They belong to different categories according to ABC and XYZ classifications. The ABC classification divides items into three categories according to their value, while the XYZ classification divides items into three categories according to the dynamics of their consumption (Silver et al., 1998, p. 32ff). The dynamics of item consumption and the item value must be considered to improve the inventory control processes. The consumption of items in category X is quite stable and can be well predicted, while the consumption of items belonging to category Z is not stable and cannot be predicted with any certainty. We believe there is a lack of optimization technology in use, and there are several possibilities for improving the inventory control processes. The warehouse staff solves these complex problems mostly by utilizing their experience.

2.1 Mathematical Formulation

As the production process and delivery are stochastic, future inventory dynamics cannot be determined with certainty and have to be anticipated "An anticipatory system is a system containing a predictive model of itself and/or of its environment, which allows it to change state at an instant in accord with the model's predictions pertaining to a latter instant." (Rosen, 1985, p. 339) In other words, anticipatory models will act according to the past states of the system and according to the desirable and possible future states as defined by function η:

$$x_{t+1} = \eta(x_1, x_2, ..., x_t, \hat{x}_s^t), \qquad (1)$$

where $\hat{x}_s^t$, $t+1 \leq s \leq t+k(t)$ is a prediction x_s done at time t, and $k(t)$ is the size of the forecasting interval at time t. If x is the inventory variable, then Eq. 1 is describing its past, present and future dynamics. Anticipation is done by running simulation scenarios, where replenishment algorithms predict future inventory dynamics based on production plans. Different algorithms yield different predictions and the algorithm with the best results (regarding Eq. 5) is used to change the state of a system, which will also affect its future states.

From the control aspect, the inventory optimization problem can be described with the following equation:

$$x(k+1) = x(k) + d(k) - p(k), k = 0,1,2,... \qquad (2)$$
$$x(0) = x_0$$

where $x(k)$ represents inventory level variable, $d(k)$ stochastic item delivery, $p(k)$ stochastic production process and x_0 the initial inventory level at $k = 0$. Production's demand is stochastic and discontinuous; its quantity keeps changing, and time varying gaps occur between two successive demands.

The delivery function *d(k)* is delayed for an average time of an order *o(k)* as defined by:

$$d(k) = o(k - \varphi(\tau_d)), \qquad (3)$$

where $\varphi(\tau_d)$ represents discrete uniform probability density function. When the assumption of deterministic demand is relaxed and demand is assumed to be stochastic, lead time becomes an important issue and its control leads to many benefits (Ben-Daya and Hariga, 2004, p. 76). In our case, time delays τ_d are stochastic for some items and tend to be very long (e.g. 2 to 3 months) thus representing a problem, because they are usually much longer than the time period in which the production plan can be predicted with a certainty. The items are delivered in several batches, but not more than three. The number of batches is defined by a uniform random generator in the range [1, 3]. The delivery time for each batch is calculated by the uniform random generator in the range [0, τ_d]. The batch sizes are defined by the exponential distribution.

To compensate for the stochastic delivery delay, the replenishment order policy *o(k)* has to be defined as:

$$o(k) = \gamma(x(k), d(k - \tau_d), p(k + \tau_p), x_{\min}), \qquad (4)$$

where τ_p represents a production plan horizon and x_{min} safety stock. It is necessary to find such *o(k)* to minimize the following cost function *c*:

$$c = \sum_{k=0}^{n} (c_c x(k) + c_p x(k) + c_t(w) d(k) + c_o o(k) + c_v d(k))$$
$$x_{\min} \le x(k) \le x_{\max}, \qquad (5)$$

where *c* represents the cost function consisting of: cost of capital c_c, cost of physical storage c_p, transport costs c_t, fixed ordering costs c_o, costs of taking over the products c_v, while *n* represents the number of simulation steps. The following restrictions have to be considered:

- maximum inventory level (x_{max}) for a specific item must not be exceeded,
- no stock-outs may occur (x_{min}).

The transportation cost is explicitly considered in the model as shown in Figure 1. Rather than assuming it to be a part of the fixed ordering cost or to be insignificant, we will take transport cost as a function of shipment lot size (Ertogral et al., 2007, p. 1597). In this case, transport cost c_t can be described by the following function:

$$c_t(w) = \begin{cases} 0, w = 0 \\ C_{t1}, w \in (0, W_1] \\ C_{t2}, w \in (W_1, W_2] \\ C_{tn}, w \in (W_{n-1}, W_n] \end{cases} \quad (6)$$
$$0 < C_{t1} < C_{t2} < \ldots < C_{tn}$$
$$0 < W_1 < W_2 < \ldots < W_n,$$

where C_{t1}, C_{t2}..., C_{tn} are transport cost constants, dependent on the transport weight w, and W_1, W_2, ..., W_n are weight constants.

Stock control problems, like the one previously described, are difficult to solve analytically. To improve the stock control process, an anticipatory simulation approach has been chosen, where the order manager's heuristics and computer replenishment algorithm were tested.

Figure1: Transport cost (c_t) as a function of the shipment size (w)

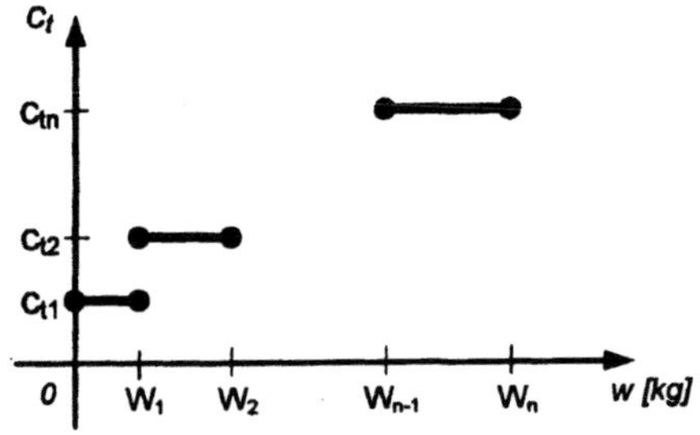

2.2 The Warehouse Model

Figure 2 represents the causal loop diagram (CLD) from which the influences of the elements can be observed. An arrow represents the direction of the influence, and the + or – sign its polarity. The + sign is used between two elements if the causal element has the same influence on the consequential element. The – sign is used if the causal element has an opposite influence on the consequential element.

There are two negative feedback loops in the causal loop diagram in Figure 2. The first interconnects *Stock, Ordering* and *Delivery* and it represents the fact that less is ordered if the stock level is high. The second interconnects *Delivery* and *Ordering* and represents the concept that less is ordered if more was ordered before. This loop considers orders which have not been delivered yet and will have an impact on the stock level later.

Figure 3 shows the warehouse simulation model built with Matlab (submodels are excluded). Matlab was chosen because it supports simulation with Simulink and offers a powerful computational engine, which provides a quick execution of the simulation runs.

Figure2: Causal loop diagram (CLD) of the inventory control model for replenishment policy optimization

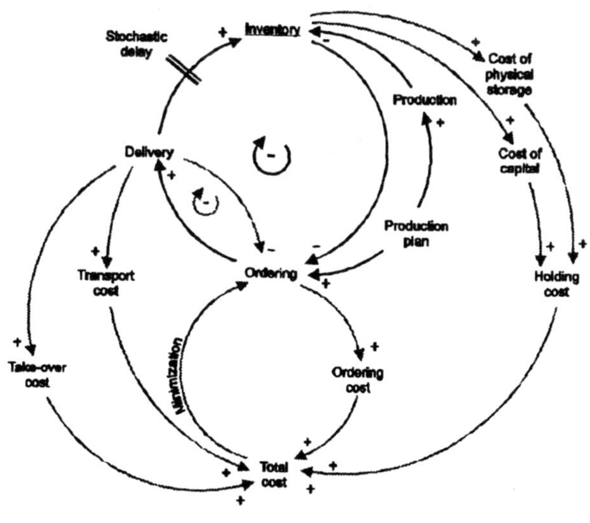

Figure3: Model of the warehouse with simulation based replenishment algorithms

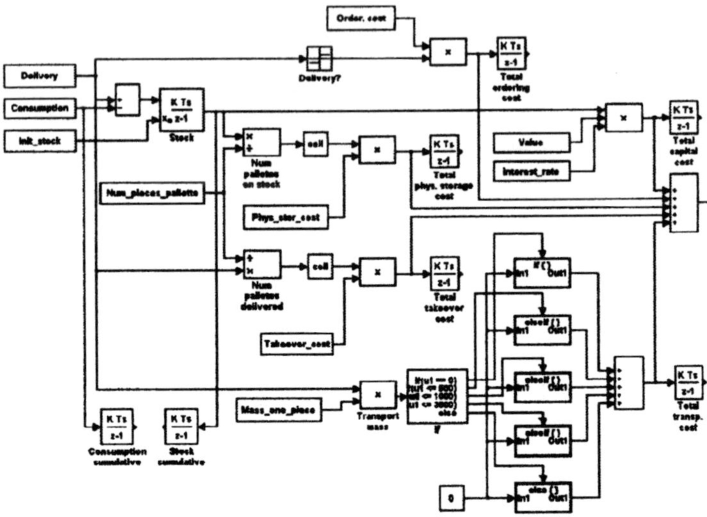

3. Replenishment Algorithm

Inventory management in a stochastic environment is usually based on simple control rules like reorder level policies of the (*s*, *nQ*) and (*s*, *S*)-type or like periodic order-up-to (*T*, *S*) policies. These basic policies are simple to apply in practice in order to control inventory and replenishment processes in an uncertain environment. They are also widely investigated in inventory theory, especially considering the performance of their specific structure and dealing with the problem of optimal determination of their parameters (De Kok and Inderfurth, 1997, p. 55).

Figure 4: Fixed review period algorithm as a function of inventory level and production plan

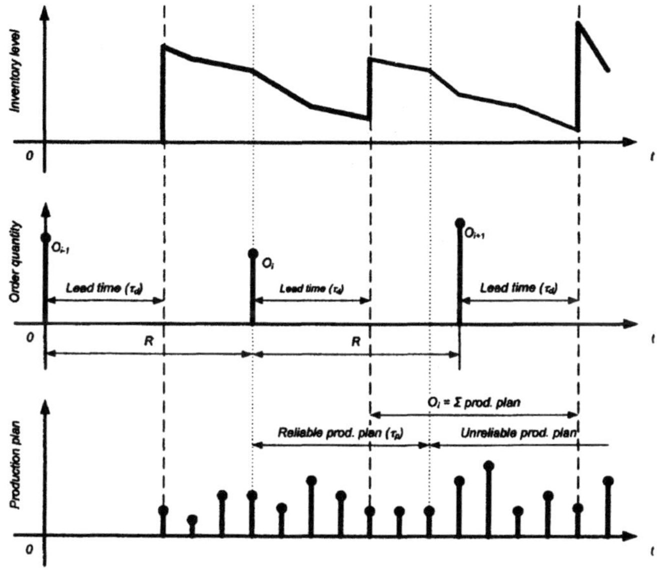

The Fixed review period algorithm (FRP) is similar to the *(R, S)* system (described in Silver et al., 1998, p. 239 ff.), where every *R* units of time, an order is made to adjust the inventory level to the order-up-to-level *S*. In contrast to the *(R, S)* system, *S* is not a fixed value in the FRP algorithm. The FRP is based on making a sum of demand for a specific item over a specific (fixed) period of time. The quantity of this sum is used in order quantity calculations together with past orders and stock-on-hand. This model is appropriate for products with large warehouse capacity and is presented in Figure 4.

Let us assume the specific period is fixed, e.g. five weeks, and it does not vary. This means that an order is placed every five weeks (*R* = *5*). If we assume the lead time is two weeks, and a production plan can be predicted with certainty for three weeks ($\tau_r = 3$), then we have a reliable prediction period of one week for the quantity to be ordered (*3* – *2* = *1*). For the rest of the review period (four weeks; *5* – *1* = *4*), the production plan is unreliable, and a production plan uncertainty factor must be considered.

Table 1 presents the numerical example of the FRP algorithm. The order quantity at Week 1 is the sum of the production plan from Weeks 3 to 7. The order quantity at Week 6 is the sum of the production plan from Weeks 8 to 12, and so on. The order quantity at Week 16 is symbolically represented with the letter *Q*, since the scope of the Table is not wide enough to make an exact sum. Stock on-hand and on-order stock are omitted from Table 1 in order to explain how the algorithm works, and are considered when running simulation scenarios.

Table 1: The numerical example of the FRP algorithm

Week	**1**	**2**	**3**	**4**	**5**	**6**	**7**	**8**	**9**
Production plan	10	6	11	0	0	3	5	0	7
Order quantity	19	0	0	0	0	33	0	0	0
Delivery	0	0	19	0	0	0	0	33	0

Week	**10**	**11**	**12**	**13**	**14**	**15**	**16**	**17**	**18**
Production plan	7	13	6	8	0	4	9	0	10
Order quantity	0	21	0	0	0	0	Q	0	0
Delivery	0	0	0	21	0	0	0	0	Q

4. Results

The experiment was performed with the historic data provided by the observed company. Four representative cases were examined in this study and their details are described in Table 2. Cases belong to different classes and inventory capacity is relevant only for Case 2. Case 2 is also the only item with variable lead-time.

The simulation of the actual warehouse process (RP – Real Process) was performed using real data of delivery, orders, and demand, while the simulation with inventory control algorithms (VP – Virtual Process) was performed using only real demand data; the ordering and delivery process in VP were controlled by inventory control algorithms.

Table 2: Details (class, capacity and lead-time) for cases examined in the study

Case	Class	Capacity (pieces)	Lead-time (weeks)
1	B-Y	irrelevant	6
2	B-X	1500	6-7
3	A-Z	irrelevant	6
4	B-Z	irrelevant	6

The RP simulation was run only once, whereas ten simulation runs were executed for every VP algorithm. Based on these simulation runs, average costs and average stock-outs were calculated. With several simulation runs and a calculation of average values, we have tried to minimize the influences of the random generator, which represent the stochastic environment. Out of all simulation runs, the maximum inventory level was considered as the capacity limit. For some cases, the capacity is not known and therefore the strategy with minimal highest stock level is favoured.

The simulation was run for a certain period in RP and VP, but also with subperiods of 24 weeks in the VP; depending on the algorithm, at each time-step (continuous review) or at each review period (periodic review) the simulation was run for 24 weeks, since this is the production plan prediction period, thus providing a replenishment schedule until the next review.

A Monte Carlo simulation was used for variation of production plan unreliability; the production plan variability was simulated by perturbations of its quantity every two weeks for ±5% by the uniform random generator. Variable lead times are simulated by an uniform random generator. If stock-outs occurred during the simulation, the missing quantity was transferred into the next period. The safety stock was also considered; it was equal to the average weekly demand.

Simulation results are shown in Table 3 and Table 4. Table 3 represents simulation results for delivery in one batch and Table 4 for delivery in several batches as described in Section 2.1. Results for stock-outs z, maximum inventory level S and total cost c are shown for each material. The best strategy for each item is indicated in bold and italics. At assessment of Case 2, one should pay attention to the inventory capacity of 1500 pieces, which must not be exceeded with maximum inventory level *S*.

Table 3: Simulation results for delivery in one batch

Case	**Variable**	**VP**						
		2	**3**	**4**	**5**	**6**	**7**	**8**
1	z	0.00	0.00	0.00	0.00	***0.00***	0.30	0.60
	$S*10^3$	1.16	1.16	1.39	1.39	***1.79***	1.62	2.15
	$c*10^6$	1.31	1.18	1.08	1.00	***0.96***	0.99	1.00
2	z	4.50	2.46	***1.58***	1.72	1.12	1.24	1.14
	$S*10^3$	1.09	1.16	***1.24***	1.55	1.56	1.64	2.05
	$c*10^6$	1.44	1.38	***1.31***	1.28	1.21	1.18	1.17
3	z	0.00	0.00	***0.00***	0.16	0.40	0.62	0.56
	$S*10^4$	0.37	0.47	***0.40***	0.51	0.56	0.61	0.75
	$c*10^6$	1.45	1.47	***1.45***	1.50	1.58	1.56	1.58
4	z	0.00	0.00	0.00	0.00	***0.00***	0.28	0.10
	$S*10^3$	1.54	1.54	1.95	1.95	***1.54***	2.05	2.74
	$c*10^5$	3.65	3.21	3.12	3.07	***2.88***	3.33	3.25

Case	**Variable**	**VP**					**RP**
		9	**10**	**11**	**12**	**13**	
1	z	0.72	0.80	1.48	1.74	1.70	0.00
	$S*10^3$	1.72	1.89	1.89	2.57	2.69	4.95
	$c*10^6$	1.02	0.98	1.00	1.00	1.08	5.15
2	z	0.38	0.96	0.54	0.36	0.04	0.00
	$S*10^3$	2.19	2.26	2.59	2.54	2.64	1.26
	$c*10^6$	1.16	1.14	1.15	1.17	1.17	1.95
3	z	1.02	0.96	1.52	1.30	1.72	0.00
	$S*10^4$	0.71	0.88	1.14	1.15	1.04	0.64
	$c*10^6$	1.77	1.80	1.89	1.94	2.30	3.26
4	z	0.20	0.14	0.34	0.56	0.54	0.00
	$S*10^3$	2.35	1.97	2.74	3.05	3.06	1.21
	$c*10^5$	3.28	3.23	3.00	3.39	3.49	3.23

Table 4: Simulation results for delivery in several batches

Case	Variable	VP						
		2	**3**	**4**	**5**	**6**	**7**	**8**
1	z	0.00	0.00	0.00	0.00	***0.00***	0.12	0.26
	$S*10^3$	1.69	1.74	2.07	1.99	***2.03***	2.33	2.34
	$c*10^6$	1.71	1.61	1.45	1.34	***1.32***	1.32	1.28
2	z	2.60	***1.58***	0.90	0.76	0.74	0.96	0.74
	$S*10^3$	1.23	***1.38***	1.57	1.62	1.63	1.60	1.92
	$c*10^6$	2.10	***1.99***	1.87	1.75	1.66	1.61	1.56
3	z	0.00	0.00	***0.00***	0.02	0.14	0.38	0.28
	$S*10^4$	0.63	0.81	***0.70***	0.79	1.04	0.94	0.83
	$c*10^6$	1.94	1.96	***1.92***	1.97	2.05	2.00	2.03
4	z	0.00	0.00	0.00	0.00	***0.00***	0.16	0.08
	$S*10^3$	1.94	2.61	2.61	2.00	***2.65***	2.72	2.97
	$c*10^5$	4,77	4,39	4,09	4,15	***3,90***	4,28	4,14

Case	Variable	VP					RP
		9	**10**	**11**	**12**	**13**	
1	z	0.46	0.30	0.96	0.72	1.26	0.00
	$S*10^3$	2.46	2.42	2.46	2.73	2.69	4.95
	$c*10^6$	1.30	1.23	1.23	1.23	1.29	5.15
2	z	0.24	0.74	0.34	0.36	0.08	0.00
	$S*10^3$	2.38	2.46	2.47	2.36	2.50	1.26
	$c*10^6$	1.50	1.42	1.39	1.39	1.34	1.95
3	z	0.60	0.64	0.66	0.80	0.94	0.00
	$S*10^4$	1.18	1.08	1.24	1.20	1.36	0.64
	$c*10^6$	2.20	2.23	2.32	2.33	2.68	3.26
4	z	0.26	0.08	0.30	0.30	0.34	0.00
	$S*10^3$	3.02	2.79	3.17	3.26	4.61	1.21
	$c*10^5$	4,02	3,95	3,73	4,12	4,23	3,23

Simulation results indicate significant total cost reductions regarding RP for all cases at delivery in one batch (Case 1 - 81%, Case 2 - 33%, Case 3 - 55%, Case 4 - 11%). At delivery in several batches, total cost reduction was achieved for Case 1 and Case 3 (74%, 41%), while total cost increased for Case 2 and Case 4 (1.7%, 20%) due to the higher transport cost, since every delivery is paid separately. Such significant cost savings indicate a big possibility for replenishment process optimization, even though, in reality, this would mean savings of only a few percent.

We should point out that every VP simulation strategy produced stock-outs for Case 2; this is probably due to the variable lead time, which is an additional uncertainty factor, together with delivery in several batches. Also, every VP simulation strategy produced higher total cost regarding RP for Case 4 at delivery in several batches; one can presume that the current order manager's replenishment strategy is better than the ones proposed by the optimization algorithm.

For illustration of simulation results in Table 3 and Table 4, we will focus only on Case 1, the results of which are graphically presented in Figure 5 and Figure 6.

Figure 5 represents simulation results for delivery in one batch and Figure 6 for delivery in several batches. Stock-outs did not occur at ordering at every two, three, four, five and six weeks for delivery in one batch. The best simulation strategy is ordering at every six weeks. The total cost was reduced by 81%; it was reduced drastically due to the very high initial inventory level for the RP, as opposed to the near-optimal inventory level of the VP as shown in Figure 7. For delivery in several batches, stock-outs did not occur at ordering at every two, three, four, five and six weeks. The best simulation strategy is ordering at every six weeks, where the total cost was reduced by 74%. Such a drastic total cost reduction is again due to the fact mentioned before.

Figure 5: Simulation results for delivery in one batch for Case 1

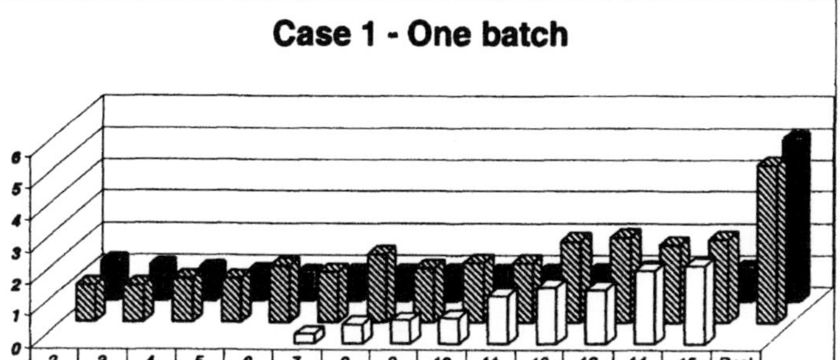

	2	3	4	5	6	7	8	9	10	11	12	13	14	15	Real
z						0,3	0,6	0,72	0,8	1,48	1,74	1,7	2,28	2,44	
S * 1.000	1,159	1,159	1,388	1,388	1,788	1,616	2,154	1,72	1,888	1,888	2,572	2,69	2,45	2,631	4,946
c * 1.000.000	1,308	1,176	1,079	1,001	0,961	0,986	0,995	1,016	0,98	0,995	1,003	1,079	1,114	1,104	5,152

Strategies

Figure 6: Simulation results for delivery in several batches for Case 1

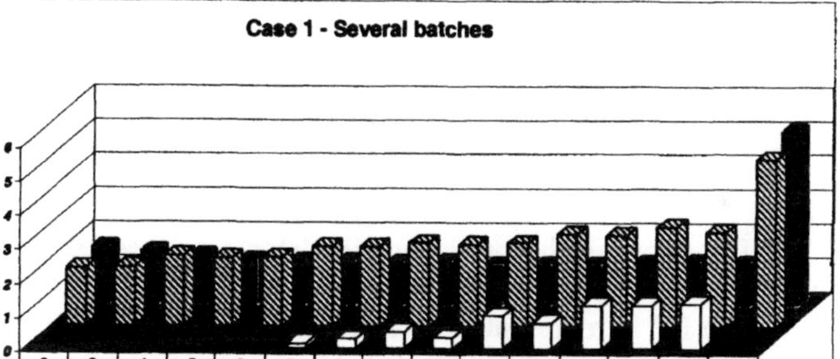

	2	3	4	5	6	7	8	9	10	11	12	13	14	15	Real
z						0,12	0,26	0,46	0,3	0,96	0,72	1,26	1,26	1,32	
S * 1.000	1,689	1,735	2,065	1,992	2,028	2,334	2,337	2,462	2,416	2,462	2,731	2,69	2,939	2,779	4,946
c * 1.000.000	1,7062	1,6063	1,4487	1,3439	1,3169	1,3192	1,2786	1,3018	1,2306	1,2313	1,2278	1,2851	1,3162	1,3005	5,1518

Strategies

Figure 7: Comparison of stock-on-hand, supply and demand dynamics for the RP and the VP for Case 1

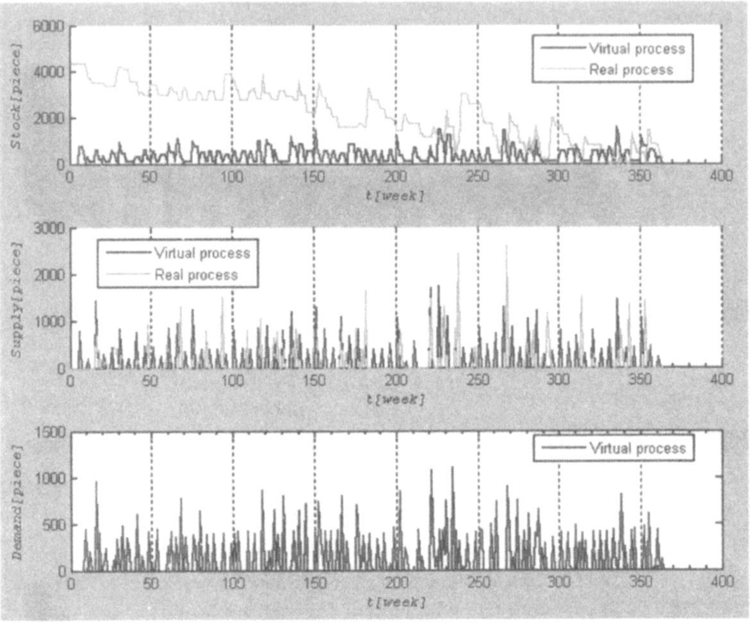

The benefits of using the presented simulator are presented in Figure 7, which can be used to indicate similarities or differences between the RP and VP. The RP is represented by a brighter line and the VP by a darker one. The first graph presents stock level dynamics, the second delivery dynamics and the third the consumption dynamics throughout simulation time. The supply dynamics graph indicates some similarities in the ordering strategy – some peaks (representing order quantity) are very similar but with some time delay. The simulator also allows us to compare two methodologies used in the ordering process: heuristics of the warehouse operator and algorithm based on simulation. In this figure one can observe, from the inventory level dynamics, the order manager's "learning by experience". Namely, starting from a high inventory level, the order manager's replenishment strategy slowly improves over time, approaching the strategy obtained by simulation. From the obtained results we can deduce about the usefulness of the simulation method for the order manager's training on the new replenishment strategy.

5. Conclusion

This paper has researched inventory optimization by using an FRP replenishment algorithm. The SD approach was used in the modelling and validation of the inventory control model. The simulation model was built using Matlab – Simulink. The observed company's representative cases were analyzed and the simulation results show potential, since a cost reduction of a few percentage points is usually considered a success. Nevertheless, the simulation model still needs to be validated meticulously, although the logical validation has already been accepted by the research team.

The delivery in several batches did not affect replenishment intervals except in Case 2, where the replenishment interval changed from four to three weeks. The reason is the inventory capacity; it was not exceeded at replenishment at three weeks, but instead at four weeks, while delivering in several batches. The replenishment interval remained the same for the rest of the components. As expected, the deliveries in several batches produced a higher total cost and, thus, lower cost reduction, or even a cost increase in some cases. Transport cost represents a high percentage among all cost categories and therefore influences the total cost the most. Therefore, it is critical to find a replenishment policy that minimizes the transport cost in our cases.

The advantage of optimization with the presented method is in its speed, with which we have achieved the results. The solution is available almost instantly and stressing this is very important, as staff is usually under severe pressure and inclined to make more mistakes in their decision-making process. The consequence of using methods described in this paper is the near-optimal item quantity in inventory, which assures undisturbed production and minimal inventory control costs.

Management today is faced with more decision factors than they feel they can cope with. Managers face great uncertainty about the operating environment and what could happen as a consequence of various decisions. The simulator presented in this paper can simulate various scenarios, undertake "what-if" analyses and help to determine potential outcomes and strategies, so as to reveal the truly best options.

Acknowledgements

This research was supported by the Ministry of Higher Education, Science and Technology of the Republic of Slovenia (Program No. UNI-MB-0586-P5-0018).

Bibliography and References

Arda, Y., Hennet, J. C. (2004). Optimizing the ordering policy in a supply chain. *11th IFAC Symposium on Information Control Problem in Manufacturing* (INCOM'2004), Salvador da Bahia (Brésil), 5-7 April 2004.

Barlas Y., Özevin, M. G. (2004). Analysis of stock management gaming experiments and alternative ordering formulations. *Proceedings of the 22nd International Conference of the System Dynamics Society*, Oxford, England, UK, July 25-29. Retrieved December 14, 2007 from
http://www.systemdynamics.org/conferences/2004/SDS_2004/PAPERS/286BARLA.pdf

Ben-Daya, M., Hariga, M. (2004). Integrated single vendor single buyer model with stochastic demand and variable lead time. *International Journal of Production Economics*, 92(1): 75-80.

Choy, K.L., Lee, W. B., Lo, V. (2002). An intelligent supplier management tool for benchmarking suppliers in outsource manufacturing. *Expert Systems with Applications*, 22: 213–224.

Chwif, L., Barretto, M. R. P. (2003). Simulation models as an aid for the teaching and learning process in operations management. *Proceedings of the 2003 Winter Simulation Conference*, New Jersey, USA, December 7-10: 1994-2000.

De Kok, T. & Inderfurth, K. (1997). Nervousness in inventory management: Comparison of basic control rules. *European Journal of Operational Research*, 103(1): 55-82.

Dowlman, N., Lang, M., McEntegart, D., Nicholis, G., Bacon, S., Star, J. & Byrom, B. (2004). Optimizing the supply chain through trial simulation. *Applied Clinical Trials*, 13(7): 40-47.

Ertogral, K., Darwish, M. & Ben-Daya, M. (2007). Production and shipment lot sizing in a vendor–buyer supply chain with transportation cost. *European Journal of Operational Research*, 176(3): 1592-1606.

Fowler, A. (2003). Systems modelling, simulation, and the dynamics of strategy. *Journal of Business Research*, 56(2): 135-144.

Kawtummachai, R., Van Hop, N. (2005). Order allocation in a multiple-supplier environment. *International Journal of Production Economics*, 93-94: 231-238

Kljajić, M., Bernik, I., Škraba, A. (2000). Simulation approach to decision assessment in enterprises. *Simulation*, 74(4): 199-210.

Minner, S. (2000). *Strategic safety stocks in supply chains*. Springer Verlag.

Özekici, S., Parlar, M. (1999). Inventory models with unreliable suppliers in random environment. *Annals of Operations Research*, 91: 123-136.

Reiner, G., Trcka, M. (2004). Customized supply chain design: Problems and alternatives for a production company in the food industry. A simulation based analysis. *International Journal of Production Economics*, 89(2): 217-229.

Rosen, R. (1985). *Anticipatory systems*. Pergamon Press, New York.

Silver, E. A, Pyke, D. F., Peterson, R. (1998). *Inventory management and production planning and scheduling*. John Wiley & Sons.

Wang, Q., Chatwin, C. R. (2004). Key issues and developments in modelling and simulation-based methodologies for manufacturing systems analysis, design and performance evaluation. *The International Journal of Advanced Manufacturing Technology*, 22(8): 720-729.

Zsidisin, G. A. (2003). A grounded definition of supply risk. *Journal of Purchasing & Supply Management*, 9: 217-224.

About the Authors

Davorin Kofjač gained his Ph.D. from the Faculty of Organizational Sciences in Kranj. Currently, he is working as a researcher at the Faculty of Organizational Sciences in Kranj. His research interests include modelling and simulation, artificial intelligence and operational research.

Miroljub Kljajić gained his Ph.D. from the Faculty of Electronics in Ljubljana in 1974. He is a professor at the Faculty of Organizational Sciences in Kranj in the area of systems theory, cybernetics and computer simulation. He has been the principal investigator in many national and international modelling and simulation projects. As author and co-author he has published more than 20 scientific articles recognized by the scientific community.

Documentation Management in Health Care: A Synthesized Approach in Nursing

Uroš Rajkovič

uros.rajkovic@fov.uni-mb.si

Olga Šušteršič

olga.sustersic@vsz.uni-lj.si

Jože Zupančič

joze.zupancic@fov.uni-mb.si

Abstract

Documentation can be viewed as an information model for organizing and managing processes. This chapter presents a synthesized system approach used in the development of electronic documentation in the health care environment, based on the example of nursing. A nurse plans the nursing process after gathering and evaluating information regarding the patient's health status. Documentation is thus considered to be a basis for the successful work of the health team and a way of ensuring quality. A prototype software model for e-documentation in community nursing will be described.

Keywords: document management, health care, nursing, community healthcare, software solution

1. Introduction

A system approach in an organizational and informational context brings specific challenges in terms of the complete management of complex systems (Kaplan, 1997, p. 4 f; Bengtsson et al., 2007, p. 37 ff). Systems in healthcare, of which nursing is a part, similarly belong within this framework (van Bemmel and Musen, 1997, p. 159; McEwen and Wills,

2007, p. 465). Along with the system approach, it makes sense to use the potentials of contemporary information and communications technology (ICT) and to study the possibility of adding value in managing complex systems, especially in terms of the effective use of resources and quality assurance.

The e-documentation of any process is an information model, which uses ICT for organizing and managing the process according to established goals. Nursing documentation consists of patient and family data. Nurses use these data to plan the nursing process, which in short covers assessing patients' nursing problems, making nursing diagnoses, implementing nursing interventions and evaluating the work (Gordon, 1994; McEwen and Wills, 2007, p. 481). The documentation of the nursing process is the basis for the successful work of a nurse, and also represents an element of quality assurance in nursing (Ball et al., 2000, p. 139 ff; Rajkovič et al., 2000, p. 529 ff; Saba and McCormick, 2000, p. 233 ff; Potter and Griffin Perry, 2003, p. 97 ff; Müller-Staub et al., 2007, p. 76 ff).

Existing nursing documentation mainly consists of words, and only rarely includes graphs and images. It provides a dataset that serves as a base for a software solution (Šušteršič et al., 2002, p. 184 ff; Klein, 2003, p. 1 f). As long as such documentation is kept manually, ICT possibilities are not exploited. It makes sense to use the object-oriented approach to the reengineering of the documentation into electronic form (McFadden and Hoffer, 1994, p. 167 ff; Barry, 1996, p. 29 ff; Kroell and Birthe Garde, 2005, p. 139 ff), which enables more suitable structuring and processing of data. It is thus a matter of structuring the documentation in terms of an object orientation, whereby classical data are combined with models and procedures for their implementation, e.g., graphic presentation of numerical data (Kaplan, 1997, p. 11 ff). At the same time, when reengineering the documentation, possibilities and needs appear for the reengineering of basic processes (Jacobson et al., 1994; Ferioli and Migliarese, 1997, p. 150 ff; Chang, 1999; Meystel and Albus, 2002, p. 16 ff) in the organizational sense, in this case, in the field of nursing.

We wish to propose a model that will serve for the reengineering of classical documentation into e-documentation. With a suitable object-oriented organization and use of contemporary ICT it is thereby possible to achieve a higher level of quality especially with regard to the integral treatment of a patient (Eldh et al., 2007, p. 114 ff). The active computer model itself supports the work of the nurse and, at the same time, reduces the possibility of mistakes at work (Kurihara et al., 2007, p. 360 ff).

This chapter is based on findings and models developed within the framework of a ***Project for preparation of a model tool for establishing quality with the aid of documentation in nursing*** at the Ministry of Health of the Republic of Slovenia. Below, the elaboration and implementation of the proposed model, as well as testing of the prototype software for community nursing are presented.

2. Analysis of Existing Documentation in Nursing

Using the survey research, we first analyzed the current state of documentation in nursing in selected primary, secondary and tertiary health organizations in Slovenia. The sample included three residential homes for elderly people, the Ljubljana Health Centre with five units and the University Clinical Centres in Ljubljana and Maribor. We distributed 386 questionnaires, of which 286 (response rate of 74.1%) were returned.

From the results of the survey on the use and suitability of nursing documentation we can conclude both the actual state of the documentation itself and the process of documenting, and also the perception (opinions, considerations) of existing problems and possible solutions on the part of those surveyed.

The majority of documents (86%) are prescribed on the level of the institution. The only exceptions are community nursing and residential homes for elderly people. Documentation for community nursing is prescribed and unified throughout the country, while residential homes for elderly people have a uniform computer-supported information system. Rather less than 13% of documents are computer supported. Among different types of documents, the following were most frequently listed: nursing care plan, referral/discharge document, continuation notes and variance report, admission document and report on an undesired event.

It can be concluded that these five most frequently used documents should be unified first, taking into account the specificities of individual services, given that, with contemporary ICT, we can generally provide effective support to documentation and increase the use of computers in health care.

From the perspective of content, a process method of work is only used in 32% of nursing documentation. Over 52% use only a fragmented process approach. It appears that existing documentation is, to a large extent, at fault here, since the majority use only those elements that the documentation enables. It is therefore sensible to reengineer the documentation in a way that will enable documenting of all phases of the nursing process.

Minimal datasets on patients are recorded by three quarters of the survey participants. One of the reasons that the percentage is not higher is the unsuitability of the existing documentation.

Discussions with a patient, observation of a patient and measurements are used as a source of data for completing documentation in more than half of the cases. Slightly less than half have also stated nursing documentation as a regularly used source of data. It is sensible, then, to consider links between other health documentations and nursing documentation.

In the opinion of the surveyed nurses, they see the purpose of documentation or documenting mainly in the continuity of nursing, security for members of the nursing team and patients and an account of the work of individual members of the nursing team. The content thus supports the work, with emphasis on the legal security of members of the nursing team, and the patient.

Among reasons for the non-use of nursing documentation, according to a quarter of nurses, are understaffing and insufficient knowledge of the nursing process, and among unspecified reasons in the questionnaire, the fact that existing documentation is unsuitable was most often noted.

In terms of the influence of nursing documentation, the following are highlighted: the quality of nursing, standardization of work and reducing the possibilities of mistakes. With improved documentation, we expect most changes in the quality of collaboration inside the health team and in the distribution of work and responsibilities among nurses and other health team members.

The results have shown that reengineering of documentation using ICT can and should positively influence the quality of nursing care. Because of unified documentation in the community nursing, we have decided to begin the reengineering of documentation in this area.

3. Process Method of Work in Nursing

The basis for developing e-documentation is the nursing process. Figure 1 shows a schematic presentation of the process method of work in the IDEF1 standard. The division in the figure differs from the literature (McEwan and Wills, 2007, p. 162 ff), and Table 1 shows the link between the two models. A major difference is in the stage of evaluation due to standardization restriction. The IDEF1 standard does not allow any process to appear in the scheme more than once. There is also a difference due to the cybernetic feedback loops, which are of crucial importance from a systemic point of view for system management, in this case, nursing.

The user interface of the prototype supports this process method in the nurse's job sequence. Only a few elements must be added, which are specific to community nursing (Rajkovič and Šušteršič, 2000). These are elements such as entering referrals for community care visits to patients or families and for planning dates of home visits. Home visits can only be planned on the basis of referrals received from a general practitioner or on the basis of instructions for implementing community nursing. Later on, the same steps apply for each home visit as in the already mentioned process scheme.

Figure 1: Schematic presentation of the process method of work in nursing according to the IDEF1 standard

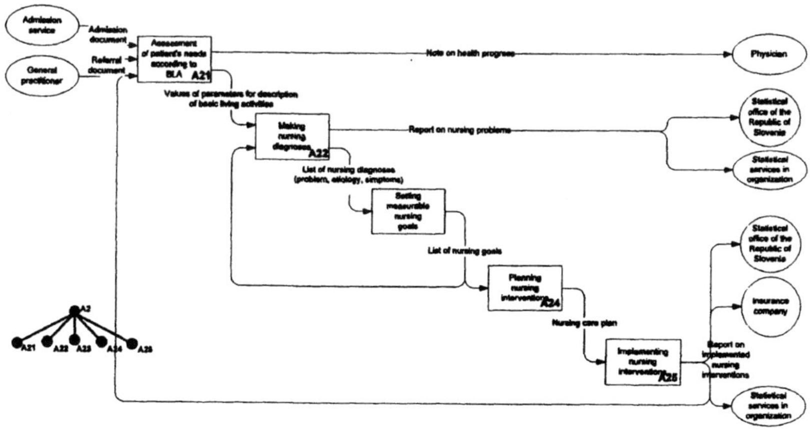

Table 1: Comparison of phases of the nursing process and the schematic presentation in Figure 1

Stages of nursing process	Sub-processes of the process method of work in Figure 1	
1. Assessment	A21	Assessment of patient's needs according to basic living activities
2. Diagnosis	A22	Making nursing diagnoses
3. Planning	A23	Setting measurable nursing goals
	A24	Planning nursing interventions
4. Implementing	A25	Implementing nursing interventions
5. Evaluation	A21	Assessment of patient's needs according to basic living activities
	A22	Final evaluation; making changes in the list of nursing diagnoses

4. Model of Database

The base for a software solution is a database that enables data archiving and the accessing of data. A critical analysis of nursing documentation was a starting point in the database design process (Handler and Hieb, 2003, p. 1 ff).

In paper form, the documentation is often mainly unstructured. Thus, words in sentences can be entered. A problem occurs when seeking data in a longer text. The legibility of the writing often presents an additional difficulty. Similarly, the statistical processing of such data for research, education and other purposes can become unreasonably difficult (ICN, 1999, p. ii).

The higher level of data structuring in an electronic form enables a higher usability of the acquired data. The nurse is reminded, with the entry fields, of all data that are desired in the documentation. The nurse is also forced to gather and record important data in the compulsory fields. This results in an electronic form of data that enables electronic processing.

Additional fields for entering comments and data, which were not envisaged in the original structure, are also important. These fields serve in the prototype solution also as information for further development – which data must be additionally structured for electronic processing.

For ease of overview, we have grouped similar data according to their semantic relations. Tree-structured data for describing a patient and his or her family are shown in Tables 2 and 3.

A relational database suitable for storing data in electronic form was developed. It enables a simple entry of data, reduces duplication of data and provides fast extraction (Madsen, 2005, p. 139 ff; Klein et al., 2007, p. 478 ff). The entity-relationship diagram of the proposed database is shown in Figure 2.

It is worth highlighting some particularities in the database diagram. The nursing diagnosis is directly bound to the subject of nursing. In the nursing diagnosis we record to which basic living activity it is bound and we are aware that after the evaluation of the nursing care plan, it may remain in the care plan throughout one or more of the following visits.

The subject of nursing can be a patient or a family. In the case of a visit to a family or a visit to a patient living with other family members, we also see a list of all family members who live together. From this list, we can access data on an individual member or on the whole family.

We see elements of the diagnostic therapeutic program as a list of previously determined nursing interventions, which must be carried out independently in relation to the established nursing problems, nursing diagnoses or nursing goals.

In electronic documentation, a user uses a password-protected login. While it was necessary to sign some of the documents in paper form, in the electronic version, data on the user are automatically recorded. For example, when the user records that an individual nursing intervention has been carried out, it is automatically recorded who entered the data for the individual activity, and when.

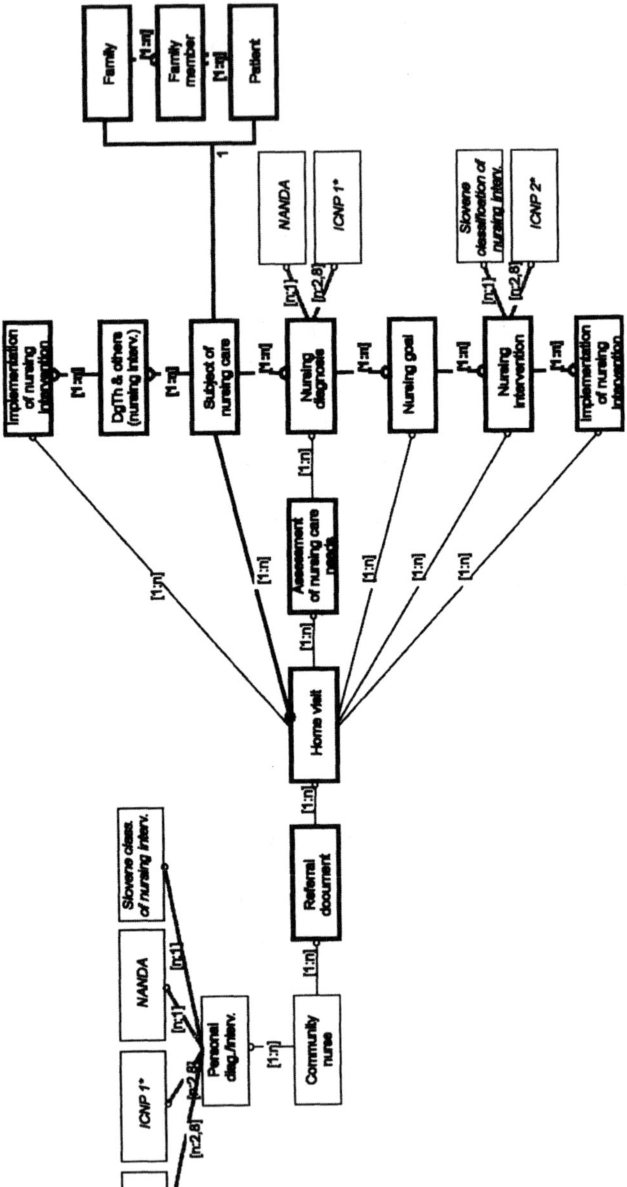

Figure 2: Entity-relationship diagram of the proposed database

Table 2: Tree structure of data groups on a patient

Patient
- Basic data
  - Basic data (name, surname, sex etc.)
  - Addresses
  - Admission data
  - Selected physicians
  - Education and employment
  - Health insurance
  - Nursing attributes
    - Chronic non-contagious diseases
    - Genetic diseases
    - Disability
    - Other
  - Notes
- Other data
- Family
  - Patient's data in regard to the family
  - Family data
    - List of family members
- Visits
  - Home visits;
    possible viewing of data from an individual visit
- Childbirth and development
  - Newborn infant
    - Data on birth
    - Measurements at time of birth
    - Data at time of discharge from hospital
    - Other data
  - Infant and pre-school child
  - School pupil and teenage years
  - Age independent child's data
- Pregnancy/postnatal
  - List of pregnancies
  - Data on selected pregnancy
  - Data on selected delivery
    - List of born children
- Document of nursing care

Table 3: Tree structure of data groups on a family

```
Family
├─General data
│  ├─Demographic data
│  └─List of family members
├─Home visits
└─Document of nursing care
```

5. Software Solution

The steps that comprise the desired course of work of the community nurse (CN) required for each home visit are in accordance with the process method of work in nursing. When the CN selects a patient or a family and one of the planned home visits, a screen image is shown for the individual home visit. In the upper part, data on the selected patient or family are shown, and below, the individual steps of the nursing process supported through four tabs: nursing anamnesis, assessment of patient's/family's need, planning and implementation. We will describe later how the evaluation phase is supported.

We have grouped criteria for an overall assessment of a patient's needs in a tree structure based on the fourteen basic living activities (Henderson, 1997, p. 623 ff; Bohanec et al., 2000, p. 191 ff; Šušteršič et al., 2003, p. 212 ff). It is a professionally accepted and well-known division as it has been confirmed in our survey. A list of parameters opens for each basic living activity of which we wish to remind the CN for gathering relevant data. These parameters are taken from the profession, and in nomenclature, we followed the Slovene translation of the International Classification of Nursing Practice (Cibic et al., 2000).

With each parameter, there is a field with free text for the entry of values, e.g., with the parameter of excessive body weight, we can insert the body mass index. In addition, with each parameter, we can also determine the degree of a problem according to a five-point scale (no problem, minor problem, medium problem, major problem, very severe problem).

The CN chooses the values in relation to the assessed state with individual nursing subjects. From the values describing degrees of problems for parameters under the same basic living activity, the degree of a problem for that individual basic living activity is calculated. These calculated values are then shown in the phase of planning. We will later show how we have used these grades in supporting the evaluation phase.

Thus, for example, the value of the parameter "appetite" has an impact on "diet", this impacts the basic living activity "diet and drinking", which affects the "physical basic living activities" and, consequently, the "overall assessment" of a patient. Values of the higher-level parameters in the tree structure of parameters are calculated. The CN records values only for final parameters in the tree structure, that is, parameters on the tree leaves. After a simple calculation, we then obtain the grade of a nursing problem for an individual basic living activity, or a total overall assessment.

Under the tab planning, we compose a nursing care plan in a tree structure. At the first level, we see a list of basic living activities and with each of them we see a calculated degree of a problem. On the second level, we can add to each basic living activity an arbitrary number of nursing diagnoses. To each nursing diagnosis we must further add at least one nursing goal, and to each nursing goal at least one nursing intervention (Figure 3).

Figure 3: Schematic presentation of a nursing care plan in a tree structure with explanation of individual levels

Degree of a problem, basic living activity
Nursing diagnosis
Nursing goal; with timeframe
Nursing intervention ... frequency

The nursing diagnosis is made according to the PES system (Problem, Etiology, Symptoms). In denoting a problem, the nurse can get help from the International Classification of Nursing Practice (ICNP beta 2) or the classification of the North American Nursing Diagnosis Association (NANDA) (Gordon, 1994; ICN, 1999, p. iii ff; Šušteršič et al., 1999, p. 243 ff; Rajkovič et al., 2003, p. 166 ff).

Nursing interventions are described by name and the frequency of performing them. Nurses denote interventions with the aid of the Slovene classification of nursing interventions and the ICNP beta 2.

The nurse can store the most often used nursing diagnoses and interventions in her/his personal directory. In the prototype, this is a planned solution, which can be simply supplemented with the catalogues that the International Council of Nurses propagates as lists of the most often used nursing diagnoses and interventions for an individual field of nursing.

Under the implementation tab we see all planned nursing interventions, those carried out need only to be marked.

For the needs of evaluation, we can record comments on individual nursing interventions, e.g., ongoing evaluation or values of measurements, materials and time used.

After carrying out nursing interventions, it is necessary to reassess the condition at the end of the visits. Assessments of the condition between two visits can also be compared. The evaluation phase is supported with the following visualization elements: a comparison of overall assessments that shows progress for every parameter, and a progress graph for a selected parameter throughout all previous visits. CN uses these measurements of changes in patient's needs to evaluate nursing goals and other elements of the nursing care plan.

When comparing assessments, we can compare the grade of nursing problem for the recorded and calculated criteria for two entries of overall assessments. We can thus compare two home visits, analyze the condition in the time between visits, or compare the overall assessment before and after visits are made, and analyze the impact of the interventions carried out on the change of condition.

Where we have a number of assessments, it is also possible to show a time series of levels of a nursing problem for an individual parameter – what sort of level of nursing problem was shown through all assessments of the condition, e.g., "appetite".

With these elements, we wish to support the evaluation phase. The result of the evaluation phase is reflected in the changed nursing care plan. This means in practice to seek inappropriate elements in the nursing care plan, supplement them, exchange or remove them, and plan a new part of the nursing care plan for the new focus of problems.

The tabs are similar for home visits to the family, differing only in the parameters by which we describe the overall assessment. Instead of basic living activities, we divided the parameters of families into the following groups: socio-economic state, health anamnesis, relations within the family and with the wider environment and functions of the family.

Computer support is provided by a completed prototype software solution. The solution used is a type of client-server and enables the use of laptop computers, which the CN can use directly in the field.

The software is accompanied by a user's manual. It contains instructions for installing the program and organizational and informational instructions for the direct use of the prototype software. It is basically intended as an aid to the work of the CN in using the software.

6. Testing the Model in Practice

We wanted to check the following categories in testing the proposed solutions:

- Success in implementing the nursing process in accordance with individual phases,
- Strengths and weaknesses of the use of hierarchical models of basic living activities in the process,
- Suitability of the structure of data in nursing documents with an emphasis on the nursing care plan,
- Accordance of the data model and links among data with the current method of work or existing documentation,
- Interface with other processes.

In the alpha phase of testing, after completing the writing of the manual, we checked the operation of the program in compliance with the manual, using simulation of real data. This was first carried out by the programmer and then by two working groups.

Beta testing of the software took place in the community nursing units of the Ajdovscina Health Centre and the Ljubljana-Bezigrad Health Centre. At both locations, we placed software of a client-server type. Each participant in the testing, a CN, thus had available her/his own computer supported worksite. Data inserted at locations were gathered on the server.

We began with an introductory seminar at each location, which covered:

- Presentation of the program in accordance with the process method of work,
- Presentation of the manual and annex and
- Test entry of data.

The CNs then had a month to become familiar with the program and to try some test entries. During this time, we solved some open questions in relation to terminology, the new model and the software solution.

In order for the CN to become accustomed to work with the program, during the month they entered test data daily (1 or 2 entries daily). This was the introductory period, which was intended to make a significant contribution to CNs being subsequently able to carry out the extensive plan of testing.

As a last step, we presented a detailed plan of testing. More than 80 entries in the period of one month provide the framework for testing various subjects with various needs and difficulty of work.

At a new meeting, we then discussed possible difficulties and proposals of improvements and examined the entered records.

A SWOT analysis was carried out, which we performed with the help of the participants of testing at a final meeting.

Advantages:

- Providing users with integral nursing of high quality;
- Timely recognition of some dangers that threaten the patient;
- Systemically arranged data of a relatively large quantity, which provides an easily viewed information picture;
- Encouragement for the CNs' own professional development.

Weaknesses:

- Insufficient ICT equipment;
- In dealing with patients with existing solutions, we do not cover some administrative needs (e.g. reading health insurance cards);
- Too many patients per day prevent concurrent insertion of data into the computer (work norms are frequently exceeded);
- Lack of professional knowledge;

- The question is raised as to whether we know and can suitably use the available data.

Opportunities:
- To be more attuned to the user by means of the available data and be able to offer a higher quality of nursing;
- Users can be better informed and educated;
- Timely recognition of conditions;
- Production of guidelines for professional treatment and higher quality services for users;
- Including family and others in the nursing process;
- Motivation of staff.

Dangers:
- Insufficient ICT equipment of community nursing services could hold back the use of the system;
- Lack of permanent professional training and willingness of nurses to change could negatively affect the use of such a system;
- Changes in existing methods of work often trigger resistance in staff;
- Commitment to the computer rather than to the patient.

Although the model and its prototype are already suitable for use in practice, we will continue to take certain comments into account and make the necessary changes. Extended testing will follow, which means monitoring use of the model in practice in a larger number of community nursing institutions throughout a longer period of time.

7. Conclusion

The presented model of e-documentation covers the treatment of patients and families both from the aspects of processes and data. On this basis, a prototype organizational and informational solution of nursing documentation for the community-nursing segment has been developed, tested in practice, and critically evaluated.

The added value that contemporary ICT can contribute to nursing has been presented, deriving primarily from a structured information picture, which monitors the patient and the nurse in the nursing process (Hammond and Cimino, 2006, p. 269 ff; Abdelhak et al., 2007, p. 44 ff). It is worth highlighting in particular the use of hierarchical models in the treatment of basic living activities. The model of calculating the grade of a nursing problem, which the computer carries out concurrently in relation to the condition of the patient, thus enables an integral overview of the patient, and systemically links apparently separate problems. It is thus a direct contribution to reducing the possibility of overlooking something important. E-documentation relies on the nursing record of the patient as a part of the overall health record of the patient (Hammer et al., 2003, p. 212 ff; Leskovar et al., 2003, p. 259 ff). This way, we avoid duplication of data and the associated excessive work and obtain an overall information picture, which significantly contributes to a greater security for the patient and members of the nursing team.

We will continue the work not merely by extending testing and analysis of this model, but also by developing a similar model for documenting nursing in hospitals and dispensaries.

Acknowledgements

The authors thank the Ministry of Health of the Republic of Slovenia for financing the research work. We are also sincerely grateful to all institutions and individuals who took part in the project.

Bibliography and References

Abdelhak, M., Grostick, S., Hanken, M. A., Jacobs, E. (2007). Health Information: Management of a Strategic Resource, Third Edition, Saunders Elsevier, Philadelphia.

Ball, M. J., Hannah, K. J., Newbold, S. K., Douglas, J. V. (eds.) (2000). Nursing Informatics. Where Caring and Technology Meet. 3rd ed., Springer, Berlin.

Barry, D. K. (1996). The Object Database Handbook, John Wiley & Sons, Inc., New York.

Bengtsson, M., Müllern, T., Söderholm, A., Wåhlin, N. (2007). A Grammar of Organizing, Edward Elgar, Cheltenham.

Bohanec, M., Zupan, B., Rajkovič, V. (2000). Applications of Qualitative Multi-Attribute Decision Models in Health Care, Int J Med Inf, (58-59): 191-205.

Chang, R. Y. (1999). Process Reengineering in Action: A Practical Guide to Achieving Breakthrough Results, Jossey-Bass/Pfeiffer, San Francisco.

Cibic, D., Dogša, I., Filej, B., Šlajmer-Japelj, M., Šušteršič, O. (2000). International Classification of Nursing Practice (in Slovene language: Mednarodna klasifikacija prakse zdravstvene nege), Kolaborativni center SZO za primarno zdravstveno nego, Maribor.

Eldh, A. C., Ekman, I. and Ehnfors, M. (2007). Communication Errors as Definitions of Patient Participation Lacks Patient's Point of View. ACENDIO 2007, 6th European Conference of Acendio, Nursing Communication in Multidisciplinary Practice. Eds.: Oud, N., Sheerin, F., Ehnfors, M. and Sermeus, W., Amsterdam: Oud Consultancy; pp. 114-117.

Ferioli, C., Migliarese, P. (1997). The Organizational Relational Model: Proposal and Result. Decision Support in Organizational Transformation. Eds.: Humphreys, P., Ayestaran, S., McCosh, A. and Mayon-White, B., London: Chapman & Hill.

Gordon, M. (1994). Nursing Diagnosis. Process and Aplication. 3rd ed., Mosby, St Louis.

Hammer, S. V., Moen, A., Børmark, S. R. and Husby, E. H. (2003). A Hospital Wide Approach to Integration of Nursing Documentation in the Electronic Patient Record. Proceedings of the 8th International Congress in Nursing Informatics. Eds.: de Fatima Marin, H.M., Marques, E.P., Hovenga, E. and Goossen, W., Rio de Janeiro: International Council of Nurses; pp. 212-216.

Hammond, W.E., Cimino, J. J. (2006). Standards in Biomedical Informatics. Biomedical Informatics, Computer Applications in Health Care and Biomedicine, Third Edition. Eds.: Shortliffe, E.H. and Cimino, J.J., New York: Springer; pp. 265-311.

Handler, T.J. and Hieb, B.R. (2003). The Gartner 2004 Criteria for the Enterprise Computer Based Patient Record, Gartner Group. http://www4.gartner.com/resource/118300/118364/118364.pdf

Henderson, V. (1997). Basic Principles of Nursing Care, International Council of Nurses, Geneve.

ICN - International Council of Nurses. (1999). International Classification of Nursing Practice, Beta, International Council of Nurses, Geneve.

Jacobson, I., Ericson, M., Jacobson, A. (1994). The Object Advantage : Business Process Reengineering with Object Technology, Addison-Wesley Pub. Co., Reading.

Kaplan, R.M. (1997). Intelligent Multimedia Systems, John Wiley & Sons, Inc., New York.

Klein, G. O., Sottile, P. A., Endsleff, F. (2007). Another HISA – The New Standard: Health Informatics – Service Architecture. MEDINFO 2007, Proceedings of the 12th World Congress on Health (Medical) Informatics, held in Brisbane, Australia. Eds.: Kuhn, K. A., Warren, J. R., Leong, T. Y., Amsterdam: IOS Press; pp. 478-482.

Klein, J. (2003). Predictions for 2004 in Healthcare and Life Sciences, Gartner Group. http://www4.gartner.com/resources/119000/119010/119010.pdf

Kroell, V., Birthe Garde, A. (2005). Strategy for Documentation in Nursing at a National and at a Local Level in Denmark. ACENDIO 2005: Documenting Nursing Care. Eds.: Oud, N., Sermeus, W., Ehnfors, M., Bern: Verlag Hans Huber; pp. 139-142.

Kurihara, Y., Asai, N., Ishimoto, E., Kawamata, S., Nakamura, S. (2007). A Survey of the Effects of the full Computerized Nursing Records System on Sharing Nursing Records Among Health Professionals. MEDINFO 2007, Proceedings of the 12th World Congress on Health (Medical) Informatics, held in Brisbane, Australia. Eds.: Kuhn, K. A., Warren, J. R., Leong, T. Y., Amsterdam: IOS Press; pp. 360-363.

Leskovar, R., Baggia, A. and Vukovič, G. (2003). Building and Scheduling Teams in Hospitals. ECON '03, Research works proceedings, Vol. 10. Ed.: Jaškova, M., Ostrava: Technical University of Ostrava, Faculty of Economics; pp. 259-269.

Madsen, I. (2005). How to Avoid Redundant Data in an Interdisciplinary Electronic Patient Record. ACENDIO 2005: Documenting Nursing Care. Eds.: Oud, N., Sermeus, W., Ehnfors, M., Bern: Verlag Hans Huber; pp. 139-142.

McEwen, M., Wills, E.M. (2007). Theoretical Basis for Nursing, 2nd ed., Lippincott, Philadelphia.

McFadden, F.R., Hoffer, J.A. (1994). Modern Database Management., 4th ed., The Benjamin/Cummings Pub. Co., Inc., Redwood City.

Meystel, A.M., Albus, J.S. (2002). Intelligent Systems: Architecture, Design and Control, John Wiley & Sons, Inc., New York

Müller-Staub, M., Lavrin, M.A., Needham, I., Odenbreit, M., van Achterberg, T. (2007). Improved Quality of Nursing Documentation: Results of a Nursing Diagnoses, Interventions and Outcomes Implementation Study. ACENDIO 2007, 6th European Conference of Acendio, Nursing Communication in

Multidisciplinary Practice. Eds.: Oud, N., Sheerin, F., Ehnfors, M., Sermeus, W., Amsterdam: Oud Consultancy; pp. 76-80.

Potter, P.A., Griffin Perry, A. (2003). Basic Nursing., 5th ed., Mosby, Inc., St Louis.

Rajkovič, V., Šušteršič, O. (eds.) (2000). Information System for Community Nursing (in Slovene language: Informacijski sistem patronažne zdravstvene nege), Založba Moderna organizacija, Kranj.

Rajkovič, V., Šušteršič, O., Leskovar, R., Bitenc, I., Zelič, I. (2000). Increasing Quality of Nurses' Work by an Information System: Community System Case. Nursing Informatics 2000. Eds.: Saba, V., Carr, R., Sermeus, W., Rocha, P., Auckland: Adis International Ltd; pp. 529-536.

Rajkovič, V., Šušteršič, O., Rajkovič, U., Porenta, A., Zupančič, M.J. (2003). How E-Representation brings International Classification of Nursing Practice Closer to User. ACENDIO 2003. 4th European Conference of ACENDIO. Making nursing visible. Ed.: Oud, N., Bern: Verlag Hans Huber; pp. 166-170.

Saba, V. K., McCormick, K. A. (2000). Essentials of Computers for Nurses: Informatics for the New Millennium, McGraw-Hill, New York.

Šušteršič, O., Rajkovič, V. and Kljajić, M. (1999). An Evaluation of Community Nursing Process in the Frame of the International Classification for Nursing Practice. ICNP and Telematic Applications for Nurses in Europe, The Telenurse Experience. Ed.: Mortensen, R.A., Amsterdam: IOS Press Ohmska; pp. 243-249.

Šušteršič, O., Rajkovič, V., Leskovar, R., Bitenc, I., Bernik, M., Rajkovič, U. (2002). An Information system for Community Nursing, Public Health Nurs, (19): 184-90.

Šušteršič, O., Rajkovič, V., Kljajić, M., Rajkovič, U. (2003). Improving Nursing Care Documentation by Computerised Hierarchical Structures. Proceedings of the 8th International Congress in Nursing Informatics. Eds.: de Fatima Marin, H.M., Marques, E.P., Hovenga, E. and Goossen, W., Rio de Janeiro: International Council of Nurses; pp. 212-216.

Van Bemmel, J.H., Musen, M.A. (eds.) (1997). Handbook of Medical Informatics, Springer-Verlag, Berlin.

About the Authors

Uroš Rajkovič has a BSc degree in information systems management from the University of Maribor, Faculty of Organizational Sciences, where he is employed as a teaching assistant. His main research field is information systems in nursing care.

Olga Šušteršič has a PhD degree in information systems management from the University of Maribor, Faculty of Organizational Sciences. She is an associate professor of nursing care, community and dispensary nursing care and computer science in nursing at the University of Ljubljana, College of Health Studies. She is participating in numerous national and international research projects regarding nursing care.

Jože Zupančič has a PhD from the University of Ljubljana, Faculty of Electrical and Electronic Engineering. He is a professor of information systems at the University of Maribor, Faculty of Organizational Sciences. His primary research interests are information systems development methods and tools, information systems management, and user acceptance of information systems.

Production Processes, Atmospheric Pollution and the Greenhouse Effect

Marjan Senegačnik

marjan.senegacnik@fov.uni-mb.si

Drago Vuk

drago.vuk@fov.uni-mb.si

Dušan Mežnar

dusan.meznar@tvm.si

Abstract

The present article is concerned with some aspects of the relationship between production and ecology. The classical economic view on environmental protection was unfavorable, but such a manner of thinking has fortunately disappeared in the main and the ecological component nowadays is an important constituent of production processes. Among environmental problems, particular attention in this paper is devoted to atmospheric pollution. A brief historical review of emission control development tries to demonstrate that, when adequate measures are taken, an important improvement can be reached. This is shown by using the example of automotive emissions, where progress in emission control devices has enabled a substantial reduction of the emissions of carbon monoxide, nitrogen oxides and hydrocarbons. The problem of the greenhouse effect currently presents probably the most serious environmental threat. The reduction of greenhouse gas emissions will be a very difficult task. However, many successful examples of the lowering of classical pollutant emissions prove that possibilities to master the problem of the greenhouse effect do, in fact, exist.

Keywords: environmental protection, production processes, environmental legislation, atmospheric pollution, emissions, greenhouse effect

1. Introduction

The ecological dimension nowadays is an important component of production processes. Nearly all human activities result in some kind of pollution. Activities of gaining material goods and energy as well as their consumption cause interruptions to natural flows, and distortions in the natural equilibria. In earlier historical periods and in the lower stages of production development, these influences were localized and did not present a general problem. Important negative changes appeared with the industrial revolution era. The consumption of fossil fuels has led to increasing atmospheric pollution. Substantially enhanced production capacities have had on the one hand positive consequences in a considerably higher standard of living and economic prosperity, but, on the other hand have resulted in the accumulation of more and more waste. In addition, the building up of infrastructures and other objects presents an important environmental burdening. The results cannot only be seen in the natural environment which, in certain locations has been practically destroyed, but also some consequences have spread over very large areas, or even globally. Such examples are ozone holes and the greenhouse effect (Vuk, 1999, p. 261ff).

When the first environmental problems appeared and their sources were identified, some measures were taken. However, for a very long time, it remained characteristic that environmental care for production companies only meant an undesired obligation or even nuisance, which, wherever possible, was avoided. From the view point of the classical economy, this seemed logical, as environmental expenses (e.g., the construction of a purifying plant) incur only costs which do not result in higher prices for products and, thus, mean only a financial loss. The role of legislators (authorities, but also the role of civil society should not be forgotten) was crucial, as increasingly restrictive legal demands contributed essentially to the reduction of pollution. Production companies were forced to fulfil legal requirements. One possibility to avoid environmental expenses (costs of adequate solid waste management, water treatment plants and appropriate cleaning of gaseous emissions etc.) was so-called ecological dumping - the moving of production units to undeveloped countries where environmental legislation was much more lax. Fortunately, nowadays, this is generally no longer practised by the developed markets (Vuk, 1998, p. 113ff).

The awareness of environmental threatening is increasing, and it is evident that the relationship between human beings and the environment must be changed. This has also influenced producers' manner of thinking, and activities connected with environmental care no longer present only some kind of unavoidable burden and unnecessary costs. On the contrary, environmental care has become one of the essential components of production processes and can even be put into force as a competitive advantage. Environmental demands do mean certain limitations in processes, but they can also be considered as a challenge for development.

2. Environmental Aspects of Production

The influence of the manufacturing processes on the environment can be divided into three phases:

- Manufacturing process
- Use of the product and
- End-of-life product (waste)

Customers as product users, irrespective of their ecological awareness, are interested in buying products which, during the second and third phase, produce minimal pollution. Considering the products which use energy for their functioning (electrical devices, cars etc.), it is self-evident that users, for economic reasons, would prefer articles whose energy consumption is as low as possible. The lower energy consumption is wholesome for the environment, too. Considering the end-of-life products, it is also less complicated and cheaper for users when the product is designed in such a way that, after becoming waste, its degree of pollution is minimal. Therefore, pure economic reasons can often motivate consumers to choose products which are friendlier to the environment; nevertheless, the purchase price of these articles may be slightly higher. Furthermore, the number of customers with a higher degree of environmental awareness is continually increasing. Therefore, environmental care is becoming a more and more significant component of production processes. Not only is the quality of a product important but also its environmental friendliness. It can also be said that these two aspects are mutually interweaving and supplementing. This can be illustrated by the increasing number of organizations which, after the acquirement of a quality standard (ISO 9000 series), endeavour to fulfill also the requirements of environmental standards (ISO 14000 series) (Vuk, 2000, p. 145ff).

Nowadays, it is not only important that products and services are producing a low degree of pollution but also that a company or a trade mark is recognized as friendly to the environment. For an illustration of this, some examples can be taken from the automotive industry. An automobile is a typical example of a product which is environmentally problematic during its life time as well as after becoming waste. Legislation related to the noxious impacts of cars on the environment is becoming more and more restrictive. Manufacturers are obligated to respect the legislative demands; otherwise they would no longer be able to sell their products on a particular market. However, the fulfilling of legislative demands relating to pollution entails great effort and costs, which should be invested in development. Therefore, it is logical that manufacturers will try, to a certain degree, to resist this pressure. On the other hand, development of more environmentally friendly technologies and products can help a company to gain an important competitive advantage. Those manufacturers who are capable at an early stage of fulfilling the more restrictive emission limits can profit from this. The situation is also similar in other industrial branches and fields and even in non-profit organizations. However, some differences exist: environmental aspects are in some fields more and in other fields less expressed, but, nowadays, important everywhere.

During the preparation of environmental regulations and standards, the relationship between legislators (authorities) and production companies is, on the one hand a battle but, on the other hand also a cooperation. Anyhow, it presents the moving force of the development of cleaner, less polluting products. Figure 1 tries to show this relation.

Figure 1: Symbolic representation of the relationship between legislators (authorities, but also other factors such as civil society should be considered) and manufacturers (automotive and accompanying industries) in the process of the preparation of automotive emission regulations.

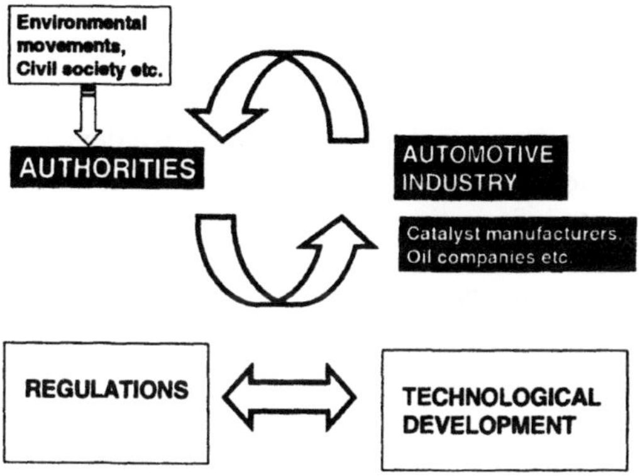

Environmental legislation and regulations present the basis or a necessary condition. Every production company which is not able to fulfil these legal requirements is practically out of the running. As environmental legislative demands are becoming more and more severe, it is anything but easy to satisfy them. Nevertheless, it is still possible to make some additional contribution to the benefit of the environment, which is not explicitly required by legislation. This contributes to the integral image of a company as an ecologically conscious organization and this aspect is becoming more and more important. Therefore, nowadays, organizations are spending much effort and financial means on environmental activities, although they are not obligated to do so. The International Environmental Standards (ISO 14000) and the European Union's Eco-Management and Audit Scheme (EMAS) can be classified among such activities. This is a way of helping an organization to build up a reputation and gain credibility with customers, suppliers, partners etc.

One of the main principles of modern waste philosophy could be expressed by the following statement: »The best waste is waste which has not been generated at all«. This concept should be followed during the projection of processes. Environmental aspects must be respected as one of the essential factors. For every particular phase of a process, its environmental influence should be estimated. Information on the following aspects is necessary:

- Quantities of waste produced (solid waste, waste water and gaseous emissions)
- Hazardous potential of waste
- Eventual other negative influences on the environment (radiation, noise, vibrations)
- Efficiency of process
- Consumption of energy etc.

Ecological bookkeeping, which is also a legislative demand, is very useful in achieving a systematic survey of the environmental aspects of a process. Only with adequate information is it possible to manage processes from an environmental point of view and to search for possibilities to minimize the degree of pollution (Vuk, 2000, p. 137ff).

Large-scale enterprises usually have at their disposal special professionals or departments responsible for environmental policy. Besides this, it is important that particularly top managers are aware of environmental problems and possess adequate knowledge to make the relevant decisions. Nevertheless, also employees in lower, less responsible positions must be acquainted with the environmental aspects of their role in the working process. Only in this way can they make an efficient contribution to reducing pollution and securing a better relationship between the environment and the entire company. This means that they not only obey regulations and prescriptions, but should always perform their work in such a manner that negative impacts on the environment are minimized.

As an example in the following chapter, a brief historical review of automotive emissions and their contribution to the atmospheric pollution is given. It can be seen from this review that the identification of a problem, the accepting of adequate measures and their consistent implementation can lead to the desired goal – a considerable lowering of noxious emissions and a certain amelioration of the environment.

3. Brief Historic Review of Emission Control

Atmospheric pollution increased parallel with the technological development of society. The discovery of new material and energetic resources and their exploitation was, on the one hand, the mobile force of technological development and enabled a higher standard of living, but on the other hand, also resulted in increased pollution. Serious changes in the environment and disturbances in natural circles and equilibria were observed as a consequence of the use of fossil fuels. As early as in the 13th century, there was a report of poor air quality in London because of coal burning. The use of coal was actually forbidden by a particular law which proved to be completely inefficient. In the 17th century in London and the environment, a series of damage to plants was observed, which was recognized as a consequence of the increased consumption of coal. The situation was aggravated further after the beginning of the development of the chemical industry. Besides pollution caused by coal burning, other noxious emissions appeared, particularly emissions of hydrogen chloride. Owing to serious vegetation lesions in northern England in 1863, the first office for atmospheric pollution inspection was founded. This was an important milestone in the history of environmental protection (Treshow and Bell, 2002, p. 5f).

In the second half of the 19th century, the beginning of forest decay was observed in the vicinity of smelting works in Central Europe and in Great Britain. Sulphur dioxide, generated from the Sulphur contained in ores, was identified as the main perpetrator of the damage (Treshow and Bell, 2002, p. 6).

During the 20th century, because of an enormous development of industry and energetics, the degree of pollution increased continuously. Owing to the massive use of motor vehicles, the contribution of traffic to the entire pollution process was becoming more and more important.

The consequences of heavy emissions, particularly those deriving from road traffic, first broke out in the Los Angeles basin in California in the form of very aggravated air quality with particularly smog problems. This was the result of very dense traffic and, on account of the specific local topographic and climatic conditions, the situation got even worse. Wind from the ocean coast on the one side and a mountain barrier on the other side create conditions which, particularly in the case of hot, sunny weather, enable smog formation – the so called Los Angeles type of smog (Botkin and Keller, 2003, p. 505f). The main smog precursors are nitrogen oxides (NO_x) and hydrocarbons (C_nH_m), both constituents of automotive exhaust. Under the influence of sunshine, smog is formed - a brownish fog which considerably limits visibility. The role of ozone in this process is also important.

Road traffic was identified as the main cause of the smog problem. The first measures to reduce automotive emissions were performed during the 1950s in California. The search for solutions was becoming more and more systematic. It was characteristic that certain measures were first accepted in California but these were then very soon followed by similar regulations on the US federal level. Emission regulations became more and more exacting. They were developed through cooperation, agreements and sometimes even battles between legislators (authorities) and manufacturers (automotive industry and accompanying industry: oil companies, catalyst suppliers etc.).

The progress in emission control devices can be illustrated by the comparisons of pollutant quantities, emitted from a typical vehicle from the particular period. Emissions from a typical US car before the introduction of any measures were: 8.1 grams of hydrocarbons per kilometer, 0.45 grams of nitrogen oxides per kilometer and 54 grams of carbon monoxide per kilometer (U.S. Environmental Protection Agency: 1994). In California in 1964, certain emission regulations were established to come into force for all new cars for the model year 1966. Similar regulations were then accepted on the US federal level in 1966 for the model year 1968. During the 1960s, manufacturers were able to satisfy emission standards through particular variations in engine functioning (carburettor air preheating, recirculation of exhaust gases, spark timing etc.).

In 1970, in the USA, the Environmental Protection Agency (EPA) was founded and the Clean Air Act Amendment was accepted. This was probably one of the most important milestones in the history of the automotive pollution reduction. Thus, for the model year 1975, emission boundary levels were lowered considerably: 0.93 grams hydrocarbons per kilometer and 9.3 grams of carbon monoxide per kilometer. (Mondt, 2000, p. 81). It was not possible to satisfy these legislative demands without the introduction of catalytic converters in the automotive exhaust system. At first, oxidizing catalytic converters were used, which efficiently reduced emission of carbon monoxide and hydrocarbons but did not have any effect on the emissions of nitrogen oxides. For the model year 1981, new limits came into force: 0.25 grams of hydrocarbons per kilometer, 2.11 grams of carbon monoxide per kilometer and 0.62 grams of nitrogen oxides per kilometer. Simultaneous decomposition of hydrocarbons and carbon monoxide (oxidation) and nitrogen oxides (reduction) was only attainable with the introduction of modern, three-way catalytic converters. These need for their operation an oxygen sensor (a lambda sonda) and electronic regulation of the engine.

Figure 2: Comparisons of EURO 1 standard (1993) and EURO 4 standard (2005) boundary values for emissions of carbon monoxide (a), hydrocarbons and nitrogen oxides (b) and particulate matter (c) (DieselNet 1, 2006; Senegačnik et al., 2003, p. 201).

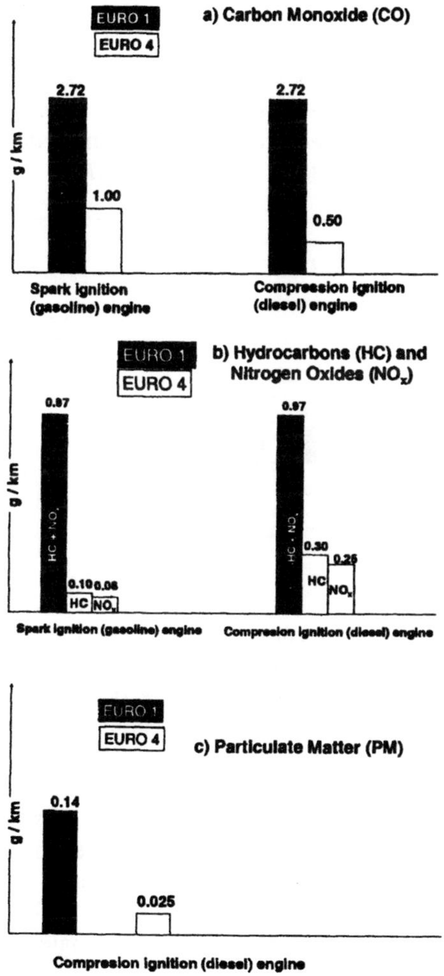

The introduction of catalytic converters required the use of unleaded gasoline, as continence of lead in fuel destroys the converter because of lead adsorption on the catalyst surface.

All these limitations of emissions described here are related to personal cars, the majority of which, in the US (at least until recently), were equipped with a spark ignition (gasoline) engine. However, parallel to this, an important development of catalytic converters for compression ignition (diesel) engines was made, too.

Figure 3: Annual emissions of lead into atmosphere in millions of tons in USA in the period 1970-1995. Total emissions and emissions from road traffic are shown (estimated according to literature data) (Botkin and Keller, 2003, p. 499; EPA, 2000).

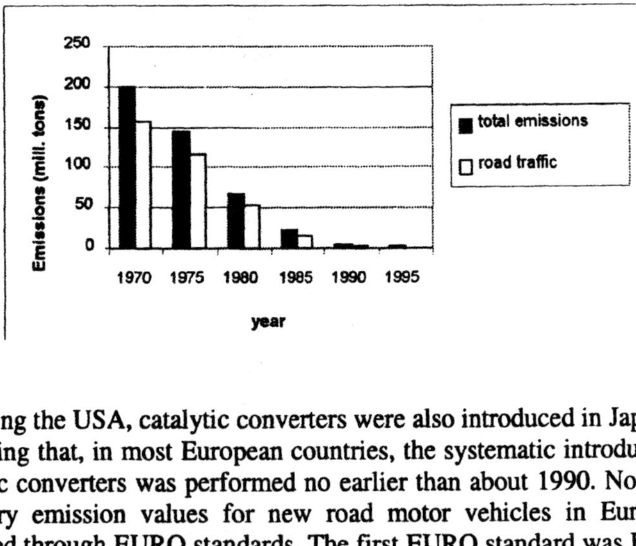

Following the USA, catalytic converters were also introduced in Japan. It is interesting that, in most European countries, the systematic introduction of catalytic converters was performed no earlier than about 1990. Nowadays, boundary emission values for new road motor vehicles in Europe are regulated through EURO standards. The first EURO standard was EURO 1 from 1993. Emission standards permit lower and lower emission boundary values, as can be seen from Figure 2. This is feasible because of an impressive technological progress of the emission control devices, which is the result of an enormous effort invested in research and development. It can be stated that more than 20 cars produced in 2006 emit the same quantity of pollutants into the atmosphere as a single car from the 1970s did (ACEA, 2006).

A review of particular pollutants emission data for the USA concerning the period of the last few decades, based on the literature data, shows that emissions are stabilizing or even dropping. However, this does not mean that the problem of these pollutants has finally been solved, but this fact can prove that, when adequate measures are enforced, progress is achieved. This is very evident considering emissions of lead. After the introduction of catalytic converters in 1975, which require the use of unleaded gasoline, emissions have decreased rapidly, as can be seen from Figure 3.

When considering the emissions of carbon monoxide, the reduction was not as striking as in the case of lead. Nevertheless, after 1970, when emissions had reached the maximum (total of about 120 million tons) until 1998 they dropped to about 80 millions tons. This was undoubtedly the effect of the introduction of catalytic converters and their further improvement (Botkin and Keller, 2003, p. 494). It should be taken into consideration that the number of vehicles and entire distances driven all this time were increasing and yet emissions, in spite of this fact, decreased. Figure 4 shows the total emissions of carbon monoxide in the USA and those deriving from traffic for the period 1970- 1998) (Botkin and Keller, 2003, p. 494; EPA, 2000).

Figure 4: Annual emissions of carbon monoxide (CO) into the atmosphere (in millions of tons) in the USA for the period 1970-1998. Both total emissions and the contribution of road traffic are shown (estimated according to literature data) (Botkin and Keller, 2003, p. 494, EPA, 2000).

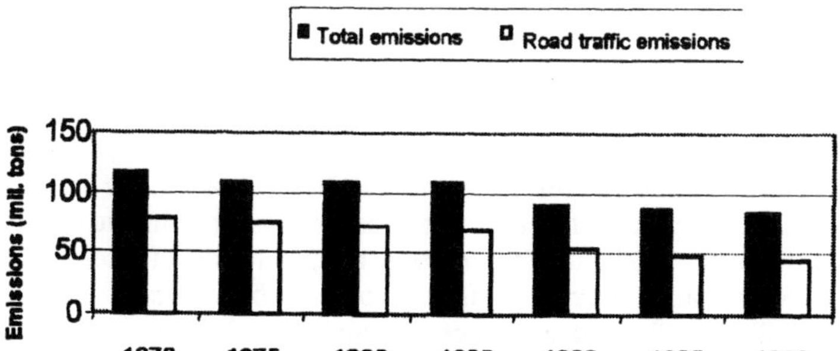

As mentioned above, the problem of substances harmful to the human health has by no means been solved ultimately. According to an OECD study, in Europe, between 2 to 6 per cent of all cases of death and disease can be linked with known impacts of pollution, and there are probably some other noxious effects which have not yet been recognized (European Commission, 2006, p. 11). Nevertheless, the discussed example of automotive pollution control shows that important changes can be achieved in the case of a systematic approach.

4. Emissions of Carbon Dioxide and the Greenhouse Effect

In the previous chapter, it was shown that, by introducing adequate measures, it is possible to lower emissions efficiently. This was quite successfully done in the case of the so-called classical pollutants. Here, it should be mentioned that classical pollutants are designated substances which are poisonous or in some other way noxious to human health or to the environment. Such compounds are carbon monoxide, nitrogen oxides, hydrocarbons, sulphur dioxide etc. However, more dramatic is the situation related to the greenhouse gas emissions. This is undoubtedly one of the most pressing environmental problems and many people who are not particularly interested in ecological issues are concerned about the greenhouse effect and global warming. Contrary to the emissions of classical pollutants (sulphur dioxide, carbon monoxide, nitrogen oxides, hydrocarbons, soot) the problem remained unobserved for a very long time. The consequences are now very evident, but various judgments exist among scientists. However, the opinion that it is not possible to avoid global warming and climatic changes connected with it, is prevailing. It is only a question of how radical these changes will be. Climatologists, on the basis of average temperatures from the past few decades and by using simulation models, predict different scenarios for the next climatic changes. All these forecasts agree that the earth's temperature will rise, but the expected temperature increase differs considerably. Which of these scenarios will actually happen depends mainly on the future degree of pollution (Kajfež-Bogataj, 2006, p. 54ff; Mitchel, 2003, p. 217ff). Therefore, it is urgent that efficient measures be implemented to minimize the impact of the greenhouse effect (Perčič, 2001, p. 14f).

The greenhouse effect is, to a certain extent, spontaneously present on the earth. However, human activities – particularly various emissions into the atmosphere – provoked the hypertrophy of this effect, which then itself provoked many noxious consequences. This is the so-called anthropogenic (human made) greenhouse effect. Table 1 shows the contribution of emissions of various gases to the anthropogenic greenhouse effect.

Table 1: Contribution of emissions of various gases to the anthropogenic greenhouse effect (Botkin and Keller, 2003, p. 467).

Gas	Contribution (per cent)
Chlorofluorocarbons (CFC)	15-25
Methane (CH_4)	12-20
Ozone (O_3) (tropospheric)	8
Dinitrogen oxide (N_2O)	6
Carbon dioxide (CO_2)	50-60

As can be clearly seen from Table 1, carbon dioxide emissions contribute to more than one half of the anthropogenic greenhouse effect. Carbon dioxide is the final product of consumption of every carbon containing fuel. Unlike classical pollutants (carbon monoxide, hydrocarbons, nitrogen oxides), carbon dioxide emissions cannot be lowered by any filter, cleaning device or catalytic converter. The only way to reduce them is lower fuel consumption or the use of alternative fuels. Carbon dioxide is not directly noxious to human health. Therefore, carbon dioxide was not considered as a pollutant from the classical view point and its emissions were not treated as problematic at all. However, enormous quantities of carbon dioxide are produced every day all over the world by the use of fossil fuels. Intensive cutting of trees, particularly in tropical regions, presents an additional contribution to the net emissions, due to a deficit in photosynthesis. These factors have provoked serious disturbances in natural circles. The result is an increase of carbon dioxide concentration in the atmosphere, which causes global warming and climatic changes. The increasing frequency of storms causing great damage is believed to be first of all a consequence of anthropogenic greenhouse gas emissions. It is urgent that adequate measures are taken to keep the changes at least within certain limits, even if they cannot be avoided.

Alternative fuels seem to be a very promising solution for the future, for example fuel cells or internal combustion engines using hydrogen, and are therefore the subject of intensive investigations. However, for the near future, widespread use of such energy sources seems quite unrealistic. It is clear that effective changes must be done now and may by no means be postponed. Some kinds of alternative energy sources can be used nowadays without requiring greater technical or infrastructural changes, for example, biological fuels (biodiesel etc.). For this purpose, EU state members are also obligated to attain a certain share of biological fuel in their entire consumption. For countries like Slovenia, it will not be easy to assure the necessary quantities of biological fuels (Knez et al., 2004). Nevertheless, most important is the rationalization of the use of energy. This is connected with various changes in different fields, such as industry, energetics, traffic, waste treatment etc.

Figure 5: Contributions of various sectors to total greenhouse gas emissions in Slovenia in 2004: 1 – energetics, 2 – traffic, 3 – use of fuel in industry and construction, 4 – use of fuels in households and commercial sector, 5 – industrial processes, 6 – agriculture, 7 – waste, 8 – other (Mekinda Majaron, 2006).

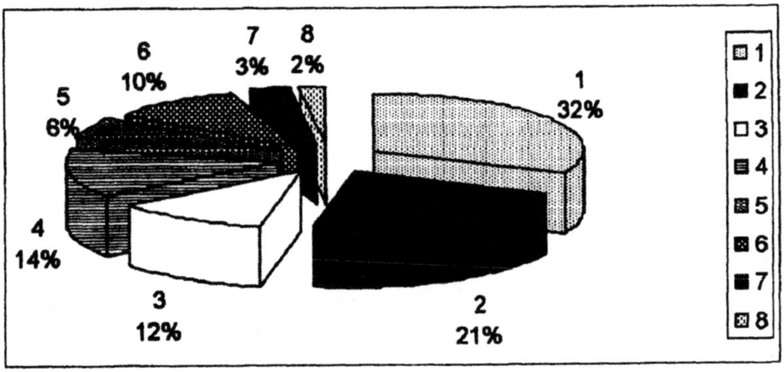

Slovenia is one of those states which are subscribers to the Kyoto Protocol and have certain difficulties to fulfil its requirements. Figure 5 shows the contribution of various sectors to the total greenhouse gas emissions in Slovenia. The emissions deriving from traffic are particularly alarming. The contribution of traffic is lower than the contribution of energetics, but the tendencies are less favorable.

5. Perspectives and Conclusions

It seems more and more certain that, to some extent, global heating and climatic changes are unavoidable. So, in the future, many measures should be performed to accommodate this situation; and another group of activities is necessary to minimize these climatic changes. Elevated temperatures will cause an alteration of precipitations regime and thus influence soil humidity. Agriculture is, then one of those fields which will be particularly affected by these changes and certain modification will be indispensable. However, as mentioned above, the extent of climatic changes will depend on the intensity of the greenhouse gases emissions. Therefore, it is urgent to implement effective measures which will help to keep all these changes in sufferable limits. It has been estimated that costs of these meteorological alterations will be enormous and the economy will also be hurt considerably. Thus, also for economic reasons, it is important to reduce greenhouse gases emissions as efficiently as possible. This will result in a lower degree of climatic changes, and so less accommodation activities will be necessary, as Figure 6 tries to show schematically. This means that also the expenses incurred by these processes will be lower.

The Kyoto Protocol can be regarded as the core of a systematic battle against greenhouse pollution. However, the problem is that some big countries which contribute on a large scale to the total greenhouse gas emissions do not participate in the Kyoto Protocol. Besides this, some states which have joined the Protocol have not succeeded in reducing emissions to the expected extent.

Figure 6: a) The result of greenhouse gas emissions is shown in climatic changes which require numerous accommodations particularly in fields such as agriculture. This is connected with enormous costs. b) Efficient measures in lowering greenhouse gas emissions will help to reduce climatic changes and less accommodation will be necessary.

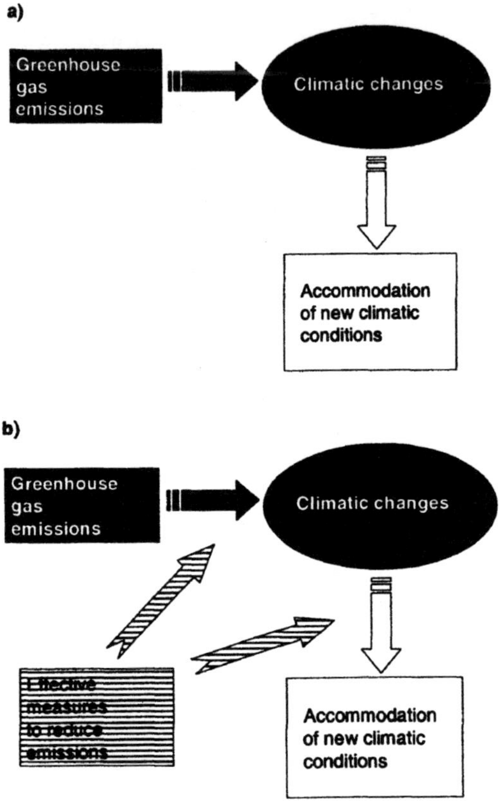

Among the countries which have difficulties to fulfil the obligations under the Kyoto Protocol is also Slovenia, as was discussed above. The contribution of a particular small country cannot essentially contribute to the solution of the problem. In the case of classical pollutants, an individual country can, with the efficient implementation of emission control, improve local air quality to a great extent. Contrary to this, the greenhouse effect is a global phenomenon. However, in spite of this, it is important that every state invests the maximal effort to reduce greenhouse gas emissions. This includes various activities: the preparation and realization of appropriate legislation and taxing policy as well as informing and education. As can be seen from Figure 5, the contribution of the households to the total anthropogenic emissions of greenhouse gases in Slovenia is about 15 per cent and, the situation in Europe as a whole is similar (Environment for Europeans, 2006, p. 3f). Furthermore, when considering emissions deriving from traffic, the greater part of them are linked to individual cars. Therefore, every person as an individual should be aware that he or she can actively contribute to reducing greenhouse gas emissions, and that this is not only the task of the authorities.

The historical review of the battle against classical pollutants is encouraging, and proves that essential improvements can be attained when systematic measures are taken, and a similar course must be followed in the case of greenhouse gases, too.

Bibliography and References

ACEA, (2006): Improving Air Quality – a Key Interest, European Automobile Manufacturers Association (ACEA): http://www.acea.be/euro_standards .

Botkin, B. B., Keller, E.A. (2003): Environmental Science: Earth as a living planet, John Wiley & Sons Inc.

DieselNet 1 (2006): Emission Standards – European Union: Cars and Light Trucks: www.dieselnet.com/standards/eu/ld.html .

Environment for Europeans (2006): Europe warms to Commission climate change campaign, Environment for Europeans – Magazine of the Directorate-General for the Environment, September 2006, pp. 3-4.

European Commission (2006): Healthy people in a healthy environment – Environmental impacts on health: better understanding for better protection, Office for Official Publications of European Communities, Luxembourg.

Kajfež – Bogataj, L. (2006): Glede spreminjanja podnebja Slovenija ni izjema (Changes of climate: Slovenia is not exception – published in Slovene), Proteus, 69, pp. 54-61.

Knez, Ž., Habulin, M., Primožič, M., Stanjkovič, D. (2004): Poročilo o opravljenem delu na industrijskem projektu Biodizel (Report of research work on industrial project Biodiesel – in Slovene),

University of Maribor, Faculty for Chemistry and Chemical Technology.
Mekinda Majaron, T. (2006): Kazalci okolja v Sloveniji, Izpusti toplogrednih plinov, Agencija za okolje Republike Slovenije (ARSO) (Indicators of environment in Slovenia, Greenhouse gases emissions, Agency of Environment of the Republic of Slovenia):http://eionet-si.arso.gov.si/kazalci/index_html .
Mitchell, T. D. (2003): Pattern scaling: An examination of the accuracy of the technique for describing future climates, Climatic Change, 60, pp. 217-242.
Mondt, J. R. (2000): Cleaner cars: the history and technology of emission control since the 1960s, Society of Automotive Engineers, Inc.
Perčič, T. (2001): Pred vrati apokalipse ali o možnostih klimatskega prestrukturiranja (At the door of apocalypse or about possibilities of climatic rearrangement – in Slovene), Dialog, Vol. 37 (No. 9-10), pp. 14-26.
Senegačnik, M., Vuk, M., Ogris, O. (2003): EURO 1-5 Standards and their Role in Automotive Emissions. In: Kaluža, J. (ed): Strategic Management and its Support by Information Systems, Proceedings of the 5th International Conference, 3.-5. September 2003, Horni Bečva, Czech Republic.
Treshow, M., Bell, J. N. B. (2002); Historical perspectives, In: Bell, J. N. B., Treshow, M. (eds.): Air pollution and plant life, John Wiley & Sons, Ltd. (pp. 5-22).
Vuk, D. (1998): Management, Vol.3 (No.2), pp. 113-119.
Vuk, D. (1999): Sodobna produkcija in okolje (Modern production and environment – published in Slovene), Založba Moderna organizacija, Kranj.
Vuk, D. (2000): Uvod v ekološki management (Introduction to ecological management – published in Slovene), Založba Moderna organizacija, Kranj.

About the Authors

Marjan Senegačnik is an assistant at the University of Maribor, Faculty of Organizational Sciences. His research field is technological systems with fundamentals of ecology.

Drago Vuk is a professor at the University of Maribor, Faculty of Organizational Sciences. His main research field is environmental aspects of production processes. He is the author of a number of scientific papers which have 12 citations in the journals indexed by the SCI and SSCI bases.

Dušan Mežnar obtained his PhD degree from the University of Maribor. He has held managerial positions in many important Slovenian companies such as Lesna Slovenj Gradec, Metal Ravne and Paloma Sladki vrh. He is now general manager of Tovarna vozil Maribor, Viator & Vektor Group. The main topics of his research work are the influence of globalization on the development of Slovenian companies, crisis management and integral processes.

Enterprise Resource Planning Systems and E-Commerce Knowledge Acquiring in the Procurement and Selling Processes

Mateja Podlogar

mateja.podlogar@fov.uni-mb.si

Abstract

The chapter consists of the following students' educational themes that address the procurement-selling process: new business models, business processes reengineering, information technology with emphasis on Enterprise Resource Planning systems (ERP systems) and e-commerce. Firstly we address the issue, that these days, we cannot educate our students without directly involving them in practical work in enterprises. For this reason, ERP systems and e-commerce teaching is based on a prototype developing method, and its contribution to acquiring knowledge, which is needed to transform traditional processes into electronic ones, is presented. These prototype solutions are not the product of some imaginary business but they present real life examples of business and are strongly connected to practice. ERP systems and e-commerce knowledge acquiring is executed over different courses, which gradually drive students to achieve the following aim: students of informatics need to have, besides informatics knowledge, also a knowledge of business processes and new business models, which is necessary for the totally different business enterprise of today.

Keywords: Enterprise Resource Planning systems, teaching, e-commerce, business process, procurement, selling, reengineering, new business model, student, practice.

1. Introduction

Enterprise Resource Planning systems (ERP systems) and e-commerce is nowadays of strategic importance to an enterprise's competitive position in the new information economy. Examples of major e-business process categories include procurement, selling and production management, in addition to internal communication and support services (Mesenbourg, 2002).

ERP systems and e-commerce are significantly changing the ways in which businesses operate. When introducing ERP systems and e-commerce to business processes, it is important to pay attention to the reengineering of those processes which are the basis of deriving greater benefit from e-commerce, such as cost and time reduction, process simplification and error reduction whilst executing business quality improvements. Today, a great number of enterprises are aware of how e-commerce solutions, which are based on ERP systems, can lead to integration along the entire supply chain. E-procurement and e-selling promise a great opportunity for closer relationships between buyers and suppliers (Podlogar, 2007 p. 42ff) and enable business processes to take directions between buyers and suppliers (Esichaikul & Chavananon, 2001, p. 261). Because of the strategic importance of the procurement and selling processes, we have chosen these two for our ERP systems and e-commerce teaching.

Many enterprises' business processes with their suppliers and buyers are organized in numerous arrangements. First, these processes have to be reengineered, uniformed and incorporated into collaborative processes, which will then enable successful e-commerce processes and, in turn, give access to all data at the time when all business partners will need them. Collaboration is improved, especially by e-commerce and process reengineering, in addition to reviewing an enterprise's internal processes, including process review of activities outside its borders, with all supply chain business partners. It is important to have, on the one side, buyers who are able to create orders on-line and, on the other side, suppliers who are able to deliver goods in time in cooperation with logistics partners who are able to deliver ordered goods on time to the right place (Lesničar, 2002, p. 9ff; Poirer & Bauer, 2001, p. 88ff).

For successful e-business processes, it is also important to choose an information technology that would offer effective support to enhancing business processes. Growing technology opportunities (Web-enabled ERP systems, tracking technology such as RFID and others), with an emphasis on technology, and process complexity and compatibility, are the most important issues in organizing effective and efficient e-business processes. Enterprises that are healthier in the sense of information technology also have better organized e-business processes (Podlogar, 2007 p. 42ff; Podlogar & Pucihar, 2004 p. 279ff). By using reliable, open and Web-based information technology, which supports business processes and also enables enterprises to be flexible, we can optimize the entire supply chain and achieve successful e-commerce implementation right through it.

Unlike in the past, enterprises nowadays are not willing to wait the typical one to three years' time needed for the implementation of new information technology. To meet rapidly changing business needs, enterprises have to find ways to implement most or parts of ERP systems and e-commerce solutions in a matter of months, not years. We must find ways to integrate academia and industry into teaching IS (Lytras and Carroll, 2007, p. 11). The aim of this chapter is to present the possibility of a faster knowledge sharing between a student and an enterprise. We assume that the faster knowledge sharing cannot be done without directly involving the student in practical work in an enterprise. For this reason, teaching is based on a prototype developing method. Also its contribution to acquiring knowledge, which is needed to transform traditional processes into electronic ones, is presented.

We need to emphasize that these prototype solutions are not the product of an imaginary business but they present real life examples of business and are strongly connected to practice. ERP systems and e-commerce knowledge acquiring is executed over different courses, which gradually drive students to achieve the following aim: students of informatics need to have, besides informatics knowledge, also a knowledge of business processes and new business models, which is necessary for the totally different business enterprise of today.

2. Fundamentals of E-Procurement, E-Selling and E-Business Process Integration

Both the e-procurement and the e-selling process are closed loop processes, where buyers and suppliers exchange information regarding product and service offering, and negotiate and carry out business transactions (Podlogar, 2007, p. 42ff; Dai & Kauffman, 2001, p. 5ff; Gebauer & Segev, 2001, p. 4ff; Shaw *et al.*, 2000, 397ff).

Many advantages and opportunities can arise from the field of e-procurement and e-selling. Enterprises must take very careful steps to prepare business processes for the successful implementation of e-commerce. By gaining an understanding of the most important e-commerce factors, such as time and cost, process reengineering, process simplifying, and the volume of e-transactions, enterprises have to organize themselves in a way that ensures success. With the change-over from the classical business model to the electronic one, the processes have also changed. These changes together with e-commerce success factors in mind are most important for the successful operation of e-commerce (Podlogar, 2007, p. 42ff; Podlogar, 2006, p. 180ff). Enterprises are being forced to redesign their traditional processes of sales, procurement, service, and marketing by trying to redefine the buyer/supplier relationship within a comprehensive, integrated buyer/supplier relationship management process (Norris *et al.*, 2000, p. 35f).

All the above facts and the perception of the new information technology opportunities are very important for an enterprise to achieve e-business process integration. In mind of these information technology opportunities, we would like to stress information technology such as ERP systems, and if possible, Web-based.

In the literature, we can find a lot of ERP system definitions. The ERP system definition presented by Wallace & Kremzar (2001, p. 4f), is the most accurate and also broad enough to be used in the frame of business process integration:
An enterprise-wide set of management tools that balances demand and supply,

- containing the ability to link buyers and suppliers into a complete supply chain,
- employing proven business processes for decision-making, and
- providing high degrees of cross-functional integration among sales, marketing, manufacturing, operations, logistics, purchasing, finance, new product development, and human resources, thereby
- enabling people to run their business with a high level of buyer service and productivity, and simultaneously lower costs and inventories; and providing the foundation for effective e-commerce.

The following are some descriptions of ERP systems (Wallace & Kremzar, 2001, p. 4f), which are not definitions, but certainly good examples to emphasize the importance of ERP, especially in the procurement and selling fields:

- ERP is an enterprise increasing its sales by 20 percent in the face of an overall industry decline. Discussing how this happened, the vice president of sales explained: "We're capturing lots of business from our competitors. We can out-deliver them. Thanks to [ERP], we can now ship quicker than our competition, and we ship on time."
- ERP is a Fortune 50 corporation achieving enormous cost savings and acquiring a significant competitive advantage. The vice president of logistics stated: "ERP has provided the key to becoming a truly global enterprise. Decisions can be made with accurate data and with a process that connects demand and supply across borders and oceans. This change is worth billions to us in sales worldwide."
- ERP is a purchasing department generating enormous cost reductions while at the same time increasing its ability to truly partner with its suppliers. The director of purchasing claimed: "For the first time ever, we have a good handle on our future requirements for components raw and materials. When our buyers demand changes, we ---ourselves and our suppliers--- can manage changes to our schedules on a very coordinated and controlled basis. I don't see how any enterprise can do effective supply chain management without ERP."

If we want to implement e-commerce successfully, an ERP of one enterprise has to be connected with the ERP of other business partners through the whole supply chain. In the future, it is clear that enterprises will work together in extended value chains. Successful enterprises will be part of a networked team of business partners dedicated to delivering buyer value.

In the following, ERP systems and e-commerce knowledge acquiring in the procurement and selling processes is presented, based on three alternative models for achieving extended enterprise as described by Norris *et al.* (2000, p. 35ff):

- A model in which parties connect with each other through third party aggregators of buyers and/or sellers-who create and manage marketplaces (Figure 2).
- A model in which each enterprise's e-sell channel connects directly to the e-buy channel of the next enterprise upstream in the production process (Figure 3). Industry standards (XML, HTML ...) are important here, especially in heavily regulated industries.

- A model in which each enterprise's ERP system connects directly to the ERP systems of suppliers and buyers (Figure 4). Because this is an Internet-based model with open standards, an enterprise could connect through Web-based technology with each supplier and each buyer.

3. ERP Systems and an E-Commerce Teaching in the Procurement and Selling Processes

Because of ERP systems and e-commerce complexity, knowledge transmission as a part of an educational process is a critical activity. The knowledge transfer has to be done firstly in the field of process reengineering as a basis for e-commerce, and a field that enterprises are faced with all the time. Secondly, it has to be done in the field of ERP and e-commerce systems adoption. Students will only understand ERP and e-commerce systems operating if they have knowledge of both fields.

We assume that, if we provide the proper literature for ERP systems and e-commerce knowledge acquiring in the procurement and selling processes to the students, it is not enough. We need to assure practical experience which is based on real-life problems at the enterprise. We are talking about the Living Lab concept (Figure 1). The Living Lab concept originated from the high tech industry and has been adopted as a research instrument to construct the research setting in a qualitative research environment (Boutellier *et al.* 2007, p. 10). It allows the researcher to position him or herself in the research environment and to take various viewpoints such that of an enterprise, a governmental institution, a technology provider or an individual participant in the research field (Bjørn-Andersen *et al.*, 2007; Frößler *et al.*, 2007, p. 8f) In this concept we have three key actors: laboratories, business and students, who are linked together with the same purpose, which is exploring, researching, prototyping and testing. The problem that they are dealing with is answering the following questions: What do the users want? and How can it be achieved?. With this concept, a strong connection between practice, research and education can be established. The next wave which can be observed is global knowledge exchange from a regional point of view. Here, the Living Lab open innovation community launched by the European Union has to be mentioned. This is an open forum for the development of Living Lab services around Europe (http://www.cdt.ltu.se/~zcorelabs).

Figure 1: The Living Lab concept

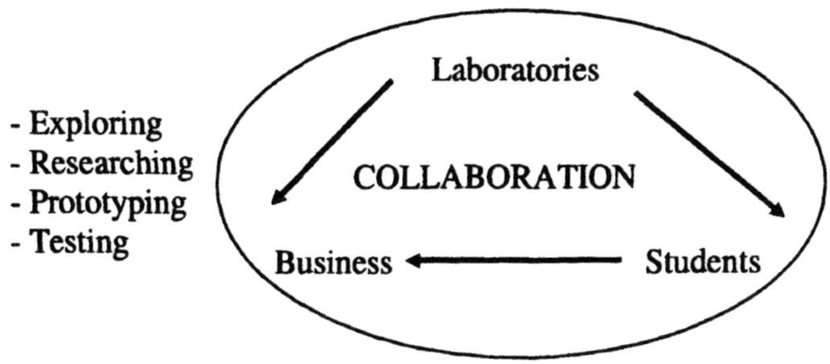

In this view of the Living Lab concept and three different models for achieving an extended enterprise, the following ERP systems and e-commerce teaching cases from the Faculty of Organizational Sciences, University of Maribor, are presented.

In our faculty, we transfer knowledge of ERP systems and e-commerce in the following subjects: information systems, organizational process design, e-commerce and information system projects. We are trying to strongly connect all our teaching in these courses to the real-life problems inside and between more enterprises. Also teaching is implemented by use of different ERP systems for hands-on experience and through students' prototype development projects for application in interested enterprises. Here, we need to stress that our students have the chance to experiment with the world-reknown ERP systems such as SAP ERP, Oracle EBS, MS Dynamics Navision, and others. They can also use other new information technology such is RFID technology for their experimenting on e-commerce field. At the end of the seminar, students present their results achieved by prototype developing to subscribers at these enterprises. This concept of ERP systems and e-commerce knowledge acquiring in the procurement and selling processes is shown in Figure 2. As we have already mentioned, the problems are oriented to procurement and selling processes. Why we choose these two processes, was explained in section 2.

Figure 2: Concept of ERP systems and e-commerce knowledge acquiring in the procurement and selling processes

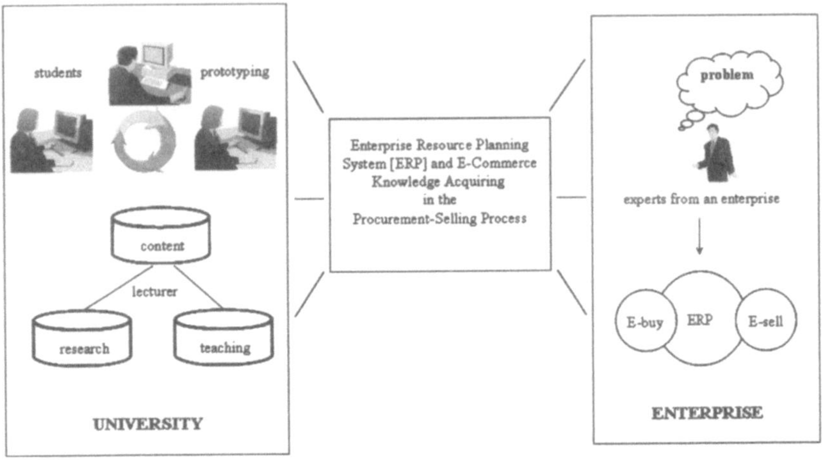

Based on the real-life problem in procurement or selling process, students try to find suggestions/solutions for, how to successfully implement ERP systems and e-commerce within a practical environment. They elaborate different prototypes as a result of the seminar. Parallel with work at the enterprise and prototype developing, students also have lectures, where they gain theoretical knowledge for an IS development methods, IS elements and the use of information technology for better organizational effectiveness.

In the following, firstly an ERP teaching case based on the processes inside an enterprise is described. Then two models for achieving an extended enterprise, which are explained at the end of section 2, are presented.

3.1 An ERP Systems Teaching Case Based on the Processes Inside an Enterprise

In this first case, students make their prototypes inside one enterprise (Podlogar & Basl, 2006, p. 186f). The problem is chosen from the procurement or selling process. Both scenarios in this teaching case consist of different steps. Students go through them and gain practical experience with ERP systems usage, based on two prepared cases. In this case, SAP ERP and MS Dynamics Navision are ERP systems that are offered to students. In Figures 3 and 4, both scenarios and their main steps are demonstrated.

Figure 3: Procurement process scenario

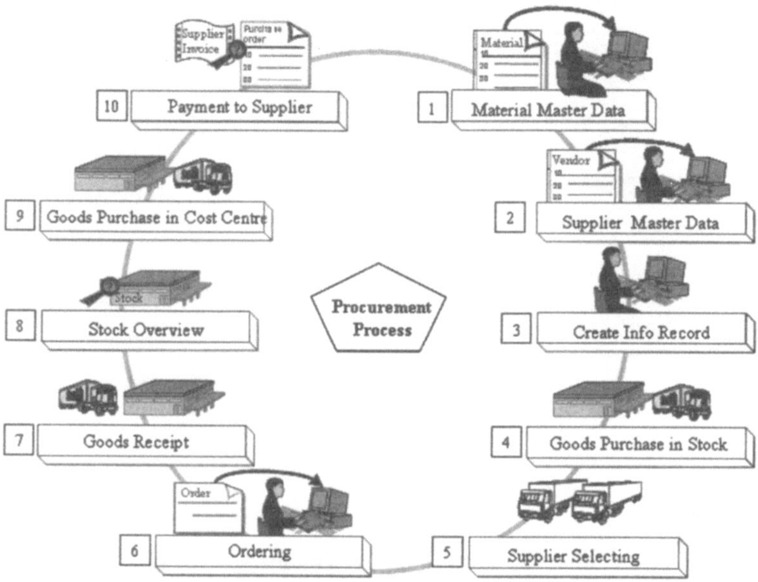

Figure 4: Selling process scenario

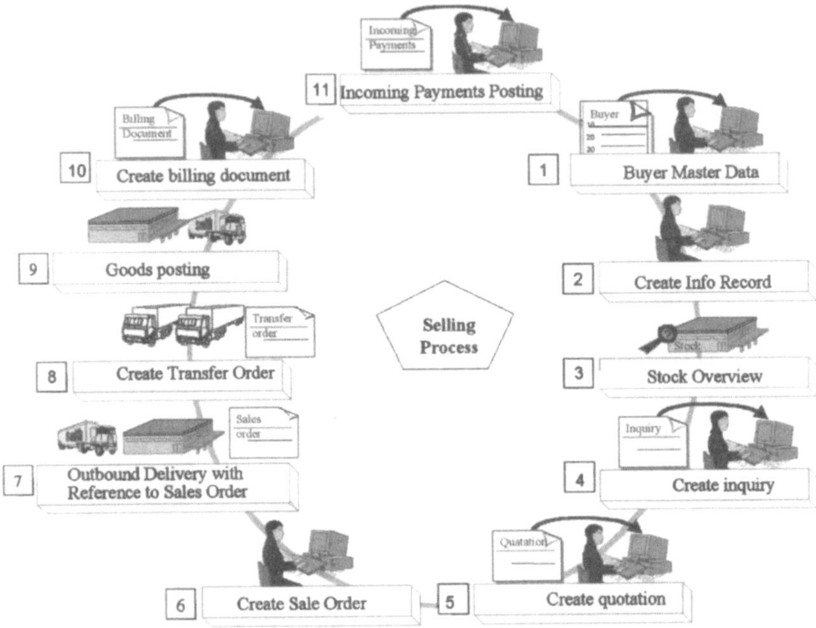

Both above cases give students a basic knowledge of how they can implement a selected process/problem from the business environment, in an ERP system such as SAP ERP or MS Dynamics Navision.

3.2 An ERP Systems and E-Commerce Teaching Case for Extended Value Chain, Where Buy-Side Front End Connects to Sell-Side Front End

This teaching case is based on a model in which each enterprise's e-sell channel connects directly to the e-buy channel of the next enterprise upstream in the production process. The prototype was done by student Valjavec in the frame of his diploma work (Valjavec *et al.*, 2003, p. 69ff). Important in this case is that student used two different ERPs: MS Dynamics Navision and SAP ERP and achieved e-commerce integration between them (Figure 5). From this case, students gain more than just ERP systems knowledge acquiring, they also gain a lot of XML and HTML knowledge that is necessary for different ERP systems integration and for achieving e-commerce between two or more business partners.

The following is a short description of two different ERP systems' integration (Podlogar & Basl, 2006, p. 188). One enterprise represents the buyer's perspective and used SAP ERP for internal business. The other enterprise represents the supplier's perspective and used MS Dynamics Navision for internal business. E-transactions between businesses require the sender and receiver to understand the message in the same way. An XML-based procurement/selling documents in one enterprise must be acceptable for another enterprise. As we already mentioned, the greatest problem is that the enterprises use different ERPs, which cannot communicate with each other unless some kind of connection is established. In the prototype, buyer and supplier exchanged a purchase order, purchase invoice, purchase receipt, sales order, sales invoice and shipment notification in electronic form. The interaction between the two different ERP systems was established by using a BizTalk Server, which enables e-procurement/e-selling document exchange based on XML format, which is understandable to different ERP systems.

Figure 5: Two different ERP systems' integration: MS Dynamics Navision and SAP ERP.

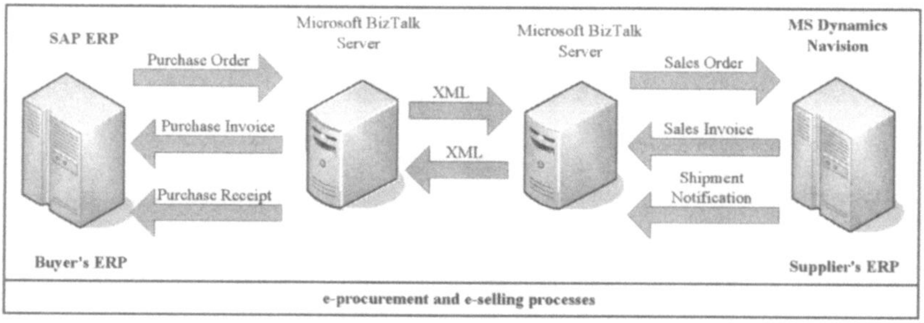

3.3 An ERP Systems and E-Commerce Teaching Case for the Extended Value Chain, Where Parties Connect with Each Other through Third Party-Aggregators of Buyers and/or Sellers Who Create and Manage Marketplaces

In this teaching case, students are using e-commerce technology (in our case, Oracle EBS) for the extended value chain, where parties connect with each other through third party-aggregators of buyers and/or sellers who create and manage marketplaces. Students develop a prototype e-solution in order to demonstrate a trading process on an e-marketplace for the selected enterprises. As with all our teaching cases explained in this section, this case is also used to develop a realistic scenario. Figure 6 (Gričar *et al.*, 2005, p. 105f) presents an example of one such scenario designed and performed with an e-marketplace. In this trading scenario, a supplier creates the catalogue where buyers search for products and services. A buyer creates a buyer's auction where selected suppliers are invited to participate. Invited suppliers acknowledge auction participation. After the auction is opened, suppliers place bids. When the auction is closed, the buyer awards the supplier that placed the winning bid. This is followed by the buyer's order creation and closed with the supplier's order confirmation.

Figure 6: Teaching case for the extended value chain, where parties connect with each other through third party-aggregators in the e-marketplace

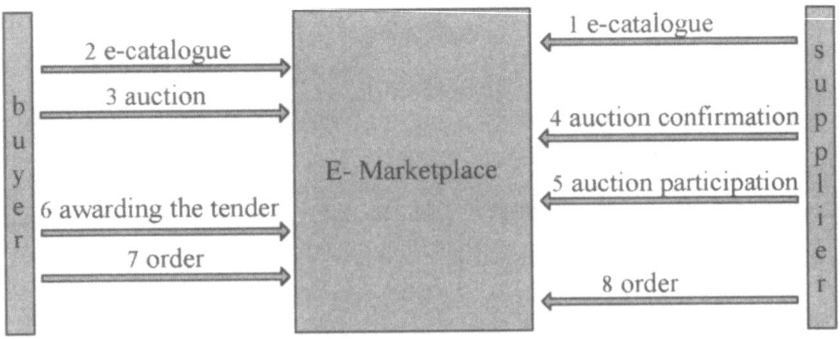

Besides all the above cases in the ERP systems and e-commerce field, we are also trying to implement other information technologies such as RFID

(Radiofrequency Identification) for ensuring traceability through the supply chain. Based on a cooperation between the Slovene enterprise (Oria Computers) and our e-Procurement laboratory, e-Center, Faculty of Organizational Sciences, University of Maribor, in September 2005, we jointly announced an "e- Living Lab Supply Chain RFID" initiative (http://www.elivinglab.org/RFID/). At the end of the last year we went one step further and, together with the Identification and Electronic Data Exchange Institute - GS1 and University of Ljubljana, Faculty of Electrical Engineering, Laboratory for Telecommunications, RFID Group, launched the initiative for "Establishment of RFID/EPC Center"(www.rfid-epc-center.si). We believe that this is the beginning of establishing a really strong connection between usage, research and developing in the field of e-supply chain.

4. Conclusions

In this article, we have demonstrated how ERP systems' and e-commerce knowledge acquiring in the procurement and selling processes need to be done with the strong cooperation between universities (lecturers, students, laboratories) and business. Exploring, researching, prototyping and testing can be done effectively and in the shortest time (this is a necessity with enterprises) as is possible only in this kind of environment. Prototype solutions including all new information technology opportunities and based on business process reengineering from the realistic business problem starting point is the proper method to achieve this knowledge acquiring. The presented ERP systems' and e-commerce knowledge acquiring in the procurement and selling processes is applicable to different types of business processes such as planning, manufacturing, order fulfilment or service and support.

We have described how, by incorporating ERP into higher education, students can identify better with the real world, because they transfer learned concepts and principles from the classroom into real-life business practice and complexity. Only if universities are aware of the many challenges and undertake a thoughtful and directed approach to ERP dissemination within their schools can the benefits begin to accrue.

Also, the Living Lab concept, where collaboration between researchers, developers and users is based on three levels: communications, coordination and cooperation, is explained. This concept leads to both sides (enterprises and students) gaining the proper knowledge for achieving effective and efficient supply chain integration as follows:

- faster order processing;
- reduced inventory;
- improved cash flow,
- reduced steps order handling;
- improved communication;
- enhanced coordination;
- fewer stock shortages; and
- faster processing.

At the end, we would like to stress that the synergy effect produced by efficient integration and usage of both an enterprise's experiences and students' knowledge, including new information technology opportunities such as the Internet, the Web, a host of enabling technologies and ERP systems, is no longer only a competitive advantage. For most of the enterprises and universities, it is already a condition they have to assure in order to be able to compete in the new information economy.

Bibliography and References

Bjørn-Andersen, N., Flügge, B., Ipenburg, F. v., Klein, S., Tan, Y.-H. (2007). ICT Challenges in Cross-Border Trade: The ITAIDE Perspective. *Paper presented at the European Conference on Information Systems (ECIS 2007)*, St. Gallen. [Accesssed 6 May 2007]. Available from World Wide Web: < http://www.ecis2007.ch/panel_ict_challenges.php>.

Boutellier, R., Flügge, B., Raus, M. (2007). Challenges of Global Trade and the transfer to enabled Business models in the Swiss Socks Market, *Proceedings of 20th Bled eConference eMergence:Merging and Emerging Technologies, Processes, and Institutions*, Bled, Slovenia, Markus, L. *et al*, Editors, Moderna organizacija, Kranj, June 4 - 6.

Dai, Q., Kauffman, R. J. (2001). Business models for internet-based e-procurement systems and B2B electronic markets: an exploratory assessment, *Proceedings of Thirty-Fourth Annual Hawai'i International Conference on Systems Sciences* (HICSS-34), Maui, HI, 1 – 10, January 3 – 6.

Esichaikul, V., Chavananon, S. (2001). Electronic Commerce and Electronic Business Implementation Success Factors, *Proceedings of 14th Bled Electronic Commerce Conference, e-Everything: e-Commerce, e-Government, e-Household, e-Democracy,* Bled, Slovenia, O'Keefe, B. *et al*, Editors, Moderna organizacija, Kranj, 259 – 275, June 26 - 26.

Frößler, F., Rukanova, B., Higgins, A., Klein, S., Tan, J. H. (2007). Inter-Organisational Network Formation and Sense-Making: Initiation and Management of Public-Private Collaboration, *Proceedings of 20th Bled eConference, eMergence: Merging and Emerging Technologies, Processes, and Institutions,* Bled, Slovenia, Markus, M.L. *et al*, Editors, Moderna organizacija, Kranj, 1 – 18, June 3 - 6.

Gebauer, J., Segev, A. (2001). Changing shapes of supply chains – how the internet could lead to a more integrated procurement function, Fisher Center Working Paper 01-WP-1041, Submitted to *Revue Internationale de l'Achat.* [Accesssed 6 May 2007]. Available from World Wide Web: http://citm.haas.berkeley.edu/publications/papers/wp-1041.pdf: 1 – 17.

Gričar, J., Pucihar, A., Lenart, G. (2005). Active Learning Model for Teaching B2B E-Marketplaces, *Journal of Information Systems Education,* **16**(1): 103 - 108.

Lesničar, T. (2002). e-Commerce influence on supply chains, *Master thesis,* University of Ljubljana, Faculty of Economics, Ljubljana.

Lytras, D. M., Carroll, J. M. (2007), Editorial. International Journal Teaching and Case Studies, **1**(1/2): 10-14.

Mesenbourg, T. L. (2002). *Measuring electronic business,* February. [Accesssed 17 November 2006]. Available from World Wide Web: <http://www.census.gov>.

Norris, G., Hurley, J. R., Hartley, K. M., Dunleavy, J. R., Balls, J. D. (2000). *E-Business and ERP, Transforming the Enterprise,* John Wiley & Sons, Inc., Canada.

Poirier, C. C., Bauer, M. J. (2001). *e-Supply chain: using the internet to revolutionize your business,* Berrett-Koehler Publishers, Inc., San Francisco.

Podlogar, M. (2007). E-procurement success factors : challenges and opportunities for a small developing country, *E-procurement in emerging economies : theory and cases.* Hershey [etc.]: Idea Group, Pani, A.K. & Agrahari, A.: 42-75.

Podlogar, M. (2006). Simplifying the procurement process by using e-commerce. *International journal of internet and enterprise management,* **4**(2): 180-198.

Podlogar, M., Basl., J. (2006). SAP ERP case study at the University of Maribor, Slovenia and at the University of Economics, Prague, Czech Republic, *Journal of Management, Informatics and Human Resources,* **39**(3): 184-191.

Podlogar, M., Pucihar, A. (2004). Electronic commerce in the procurement process: experiences and the frequency of use. Informatics and management: selected topics, Frankfurt am Main [etc.]: P.Lang: 279-295.

Shaw, M., Blanning, R., Strader, T., Whinston, A. (2000). *Handbook on electronic commerce,* Springer-Verlag Berlin, Germany.

Valjavec, A., Podlogar, M., Bogataj, K. (2003). Connecting two different ERP systems: Microsoft Business Solutions-Navision and SAP. *Proceedings of 16th Bled eCommerce Conference, eTransformation,* Bled, Slovenia, Wigand, R.T. *et al.*, Editors, Moderna organizacija, Kranj, 69 – 72, June 9 - 11.

Wallace, T. F., Kremzar, M. H. (2001). *ERP: Making It Happen. The Implementer's Guide to Success with Enterprise Resource Planning,* John Wiley & Sons, Inc., Canada.

Other Internet sources:

http://www.elivinglab.org/Objectives.htm
http://www.cdt.ltu.se/~zcorelabs
http://www.Aladin.units.it
http://www.elivinglab.org/RFID/

About the Author

Mateja Podlogar is an assistant professor at the University of Maribor, Faculty of Organizational Sciences. Her research fields are e-commerce in supply chains, ERP systems, RFID systems, e-business models, business process reengineering and information systems auditing.

Incorporation of a Human Resource Strategy into the Business Strategy

Vesna Novak

vesna.novak@fov.uni-mb.si

Abstract

Strategy is the basic framework within which an organization is able to preserve its continuity, while gaining competitive advantage by conscious adaptation to the change in the environment. This article emphasizes that effectiveness of strategic management greatly depends on the extent to which the development and implementation of a company's strategy include the human resource function. Therefore, it is vital to provide constant co-operation of the managers at all levels to ensure congruity among general management, line management and human resource management. This makes all those involved reconcile their decisions, plan their activities and the allocation of resources, and participate in the implementation and evaluation of all human resource-related activities, which in turn contributes to an increase or maintenance of the company's strategic advantage.

Keywords: human resource strategy, business strategy, human resources, management

1. Introduction

A company's life cycle includes a number of interacting factors that impact its development. They uncover and dissect the secrets of progress, while shedding light on the reasons for regression. The fact that the present is chaotic and unpredictable requires that managers adapt to this, forming an active standpoint and viewing the chaos as a source of potential success. What is needed is by no means merely adapting to the demands of the global market but rather introducing a coherent system of change into a company's business practices. It is therefore vital that a human resource strategy is actively linked to a business strategy as its equally important complement.

Hellriegel et al. (2001, p. 369) believe that different human resource activities help organizations achieve their strategic goals, thus having an impact on a company's profitability, and the lives of its employees and the wider social community. As human resources are the ones that implement the business strategy, many authors (Lipičnik, 2002, p.445; Porter, 1997, p. 48ff; Baron and Kreps, 1999, p. 1ff) believe that it is precisely they that represent a company's competitive advantage.

Without knowing the state of affairs and staff projection in an organization, and on the workforce market, it may happen that the planned business strategy cannot be carried out due to lack of appropriate experts or an appropriate workforce. Moreover, without being well acquainted with strategic orientation (and cooperation in the process of setting it), it may happen that activities and processes employed by a human resource department do not support company business operations. It may be said (Heneman III and Judge, 2006, p. 32) that a human resource strategy is both an outgrowth of, and a contribution to, a company's business strategy. Therefore, it is necessary to examine the compatibility of human resource strategy with business strategy. Human resource strategy should be translated into a concrete medium-term plan and made efficient through solid annual planning of human resources and the activities which are to be performed in human resource management and the entire organization regarding its employees (Novak and Florjančič, 2005, p. 64).

The human resource function began to rise in significance only after 1980, when numerous authors (Schuler and Huber, 1993, p. 10; Noe et al., 1994, p. 49; Sadler, 1995, p. 113; Schmitt and Chan, 1999, p. 231; DeNisi and Griffin, 2005, p. 72) recognized the need to form a comprehensive human resource strategy, which is to be harmonized with the business strategy. Thus, the influence of human resource experts has been changing, and they are beginning to take on an important role in the formation and implementation of the business strategy (Guest and Peccei, 1994, p. 219ff), acting as important advisers to the top managers (Baron and Kreps, 1999, p. 512).

In Slovenia too, new circumstances demand transformation of the role played by the human resource function, which should support the process of developing a business strategy. It ought to become an internal consultant in the company, a support to its general management in strategy formation, and an aid to its line managers, who take responsibility and decision-making into their own hands. Therefore, all activities of the human resource department should be focused on increasing the company's competitive ability, which means that human resource directors must cease to behave protectively or defensively in relation to general management. They should no longer be merely persons who have to do with people, but businesspersons; no longer merely those in charge of a particular function, but partners in a team of managers.

2. Company Strategy

Numerous definitions of strategy can be found in the relevant literature, e.g.:

- Broadly speaking, strategy is the definition of an organization's basic strategic aims and objectives and the directions of action, as well as deployment of the resources needed to achieve these goals; in narrower terms, it is the decision-making rules used in choosing among the combinations available to the management (Pučko, 2002, p. 284).
- Strategy is any business orientation promising realization of the planned goals if pursued (Možina, 2002, p. 14).
- Strategy is the definition of the main action programmes that a company would use to accomplish its long-term goals in line with its mission (Stoner, 1978, p. 100).
- Strategy is the pattern of decisions taken by a company. Thus strategy originally referred to the skills and the decision-making process of the general (executive) (Wensley, 2001, p.161).

Trying to define a uniform view of strategy, we may sum up that strategy is the basic framework within which an organization is able to preserve its continuity, while gaining competitive advantage by conscious adaptation to change in the environment.

Strategies relate to different levels of management, thus falling into (Hellriegel et al., 2001, p.200):

- corporate or general strategy,
- business strategy, and
- functional strategy.

Corporate strategy pertains to the whole organization and is the strategy of its highest level. It determines a company's basic orientation and the industry or markets in which it would compete (Wheelen and Hunger, 1995, p. 150). Corporate or general strategy is determined by top management (Kreitner, 2007, p. 201), on the basis of a company's concept of strategic development, its vision and doctrine. Business strategy pertains to an organization's business units (e.g. branch divisions). The core of a business strategy is the definition of how such a unit would create competitive advantage. What managers at this level have to achieve is to align the business strategies with corporate strategy. Functional strategy facilitates realization of the corporate and business strategies in a particular functional area (human resources, production, innovation, finances, etc.). Being in a sense strategies of the lowest level of management, functional strategies are often called operational strategies. Among them, the human resource strategy is the most important one (DeNisi and Griffin, 2005, p. 54), as it is closely connected with all other functional strategies as well as the business and corporate strategies, allowing all other strategies in an organization to be carried out. Therefore, it must become an integral part of the business strategy or be closely connected with it.

Heneman III and Judge (2006, p. 19) mention the mutual connectedness of the business and the human resource strategy. They are formed interactively: the business strategy by taking into account the human resource capacities and capabilities, and the human resource strategy by containing elements that support the implementation of business strategy. According to various authors (DeNisi and Griffin, 2005, p. 48; Noe et al., 1994, p. 48), the first step in strategy formation is a SWOT (strengths, weaknesses, opportunities and threats) analysis. Thus, for each strategy, managers must analyse its advantages and disadvantages, determine its risks and potentials, and finally assess whether it fits into the context of their company's needs and capabilities. The strategy of human resources must also be regarded, as this alone enables assessment of how efficiently a selected corporate strategy would be implemented.

3. Human Resource Strategy

A strategy of human resources defines a set of human resource related activities that would support delivery of an organization's strategies and thus achievement of its business goals. It is a set of key decisions on how human resources in an organization would be handled (Heneman III and Judge, 2006, p. 19). Therefore, human resource managers must understand their organization's business operations, and know the ways in which human resource activities would help the company achieve its business goals (DeNisi and Griffin, 2005, p.32).

To form a successful human resource strategy, it is necessary to define the mission and purpose of human resource management, to analyse the internal and the external environment, to analyse and assess the existing strategies, and to define the company's capabilities and capacities. Both the strategic goals and the indicators with which to monitor their realization must be defined.

Today's organizations are continually being faced with unpredictable situations. For a greater effectiveness, it is vital to provide a well-trained, highly motivated and creative workforce capable of adapting to such change. The human resource function has therefore increasingly been viewed as part of strategic planning (Schmitt and Chan, 1999, p. 231; Beardwell and Holden, 1997, p. 24), and a concern of all executives (Florjančič et al., 2004, p. 62). This view is shared by Baron and Kreps (1999, p. 512), who believe that all general managers, and especially top managers, need to be "human resource literate."

Considering the fact that the strategic importance of the human resource function only began to be recognized after 1980 (DeNisi and Griffin, 2005, p. 32), an international study in the human resource management field made in 2001 is interesting. Comparison among certain European states indicates that Slovenia (the study included 205 Slovenian organizations with over 200 employees each) ranked almost equal with those countries with a rather strong tendency towards strategic planning. According to the results, Sweden was the country with the highest percentage of organizations having formed an – either written or unwritten – human resource strategy (74.4% and 14.8% respectively), while Germany had the lowest such percentage (26.7% and 36.7% respectively). 10.8% of Swedish organizations had no strategy, while in Germany this percentage amounted to 36.6% (Svetlik, 2002, p. 385). In Slovenia, 53.8% of the organizations held a written strategy, 32.5% an unwritten one, and 13.7% none. The results are presented in Chart 1.

Chart 1: International comparison of written and unwritten human resource strategies

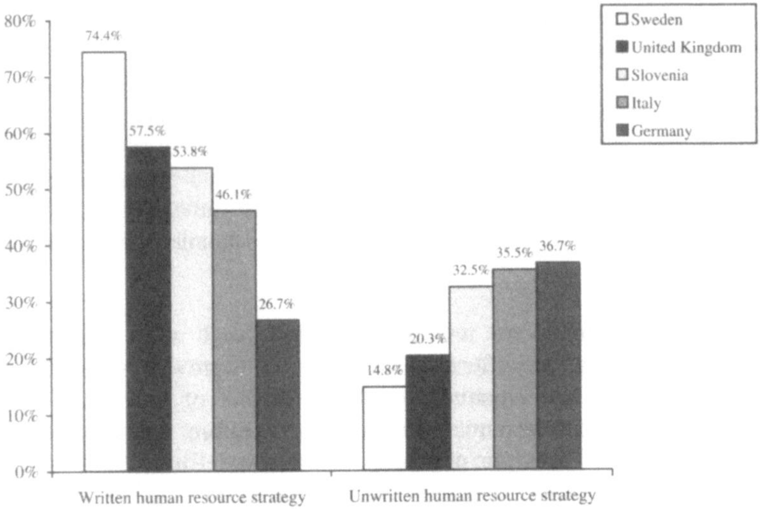

Comparison between Slovenia, the European Union, and the transitional countries (see Table 1) shows that, as for human resource strategy existence, Slovenian organizations are even ahead of the European Union, and far ahead of the organizations in transitional countries.

Table 1: Comparison of human resource strategy existence between Slovenia, the EU, and the transitional countries (Svetlik, 2002, p. 385)

		SLOVENIA	EU	TRANSITIONAL COUNTRIES
HUMAN RESOURCE STRATEGY	written	53.8%	50.5%	35.8%
	unwritten	32.5%	28.2%	34.4%

Existence of a mutual impact between a company's overall and human resource strategies is a highly important fact that top managers must not ignore. The policies and practices of a company's human resource management must be linked with its overall strategy, as today competitive advantage can only be gained by constant innovation and improvement in line with the strategic orientation (Porter, 1997, p. 54).

If the managers disregard this, the employees might be incapable of pursuing a given strategy. Therefore, human resource managers must also understand their company's business operation. This is reflected in one of the roles played by the human resource manager in the achievement of the company's business goals and, thus, business success. What is meant is Ulrich's role of the human resource manager as a "strategic partner" (Ulrich, 1997, p. 24f). In this role, the human resource manager must ensure that the business strategy and the human resource strategy are harmonised. A key role in this is played by employee empowerment, which should be directly linked to the strategic goals, the working process, and individuals' own competency and responsibility.

4. The Study

4.1 Intent and Implementation of the Study

Our intent in conducting the study was to examine the advantages and disadvantages of human resource strategy development practices in Slovenian companies, to determine the link of the human resource strategy to the business strategy, and to propose ways of improving the current state.

The technique used in establishing the current state in Slovenian companies was the questionnaire. The basic sample consisted of large companies according to one criterion (over 250 employees). Large companies were chosen based on the argument that they have a greater impact on the Slovenian economy than do smaller ones, which makes them more relevant for the study of economic policies and measures. As we wished to question enough managers to be able to make relevant conclusions, the sample included 300 companies, chosen randomly by the Slovenian Chamber of Commerce and Industry. The managers were questioned in June 2003. The questions were of the closed type with answers to be selected from a list, which yielded pre-categorised and measurable data that could be technically processed. The data from the returned questionnaires (46%) were entered into a database and prepared for further statistical processing.

4.2 Study Results

Written or unwritten human resource strategy

Work within particular sectors is usually organized on the basis of the adopted goals, by way of anticipating the tasks necessary for their realization. It would be sensible to form the goals of a human resource department within a human resource strategy. We therefore wished to find out how many of the questioned Slovenian companies held a written human resource strategy.

The study showed that 62.6% of the companies had such a strategy in written form: 56.5% as part of their business strategy and 6.1% as an independent document. 26% of the managers replied that their company did have a human resource strategy but an unwritten one, which means that the strategy is not formal and it is not known how it relates to the human resource activities. 11.5% of the companies had not worked out a strategy at all. The results are presented in Chart 2.

Chart 2: Answers to the question: "Does your company have a written human resource strategy?"

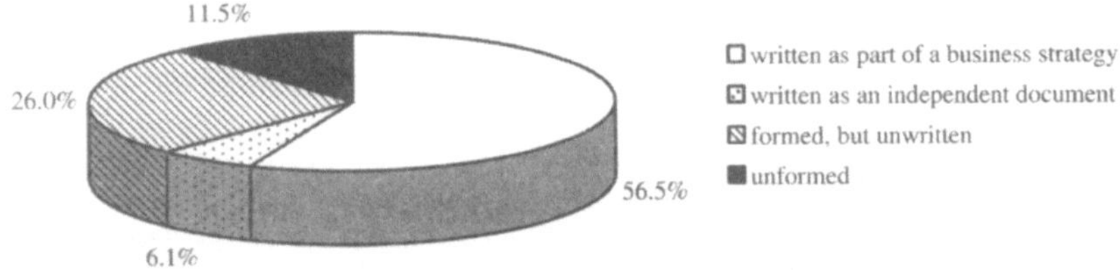

A more detailed analysis showed that human resource strategy (non)formation in Slovenian companies depended on the human resource director's level and field of education. Such a strategy remained unformed by no less than 40% of the directors with a secondary education, by 32% of those with a 2-year higher education, by 18.7% of those with a 3-year higher education, and by only 2.5% of those with a bachelor's degree, while a human resource strategy had been both formed and written down by all the directors with a postgraduate degree (see Table 2). The results permit conclusion that a more extensive knowledge makes managers realize that formation of a human resource strategy is vital for a sound functioning of a human resource department.

Table 2: Impact of the human resource director's level of education on the formation of a human resource strategy

	Human resource strategy written as part of a business strategy	Human resource strategy written as an independent document	Unwritten human resource strategy	No human resource strategy
Secondary education	20%	20%	20%	40%
2-year higher education	16%	-	52%	32%
3-year higher education	62.5%	6.3%	12.5%	18.7%
Bachelor's degree	67.5%	7.5%	22.5%	2.5 %
Postgraduate degree	100%	-	-	-

Differences in strategy formation also depend on whether the studies completed by the human resource director are directly related to human resource management, indirectly related to it or not related to it at all,* as shown in Table 3.

* Today's requirements for human resource directors include completion of studies within which specialization in human resource management is possible. In Slovenia, these primarily include work organization, sociology and psychology. The studies completed by human resource directors thus fall into three categories: those directly related to human resource management (work organization, sociology, psychology), those indirectly related to it (law, economy, administration and social work), and unrelated ones (other courses of study). According to our study, 42.6% of the human resource directors in Slovenian

Table 3: Impact of the human resource director's field of study on the formation of a human resource strategy

	Human resource strategy written as part of a business strategy	Human resource strategy written as an independent document	Unwritten human resource strategy	No human resource strategy
Field of study directly related to human resources	64.8%	7.4%	24.1%	3.7%
Field of study indirectly related to human resources	51.7%	6.6%	26.7%	15%
Other field of study	30.8%	-	35.7%	28.6%

72.2% of the human resource directors who had completed studies directly related to their field of work have formed a human resource strategy in written form, 24.1% an unwritten one, and only 3.7% have not formed one at all. The situation is altogether different with those having completed studies insufficiently related to their field of work, as only 30.8% of them have a human resource strategy in written form, 35.7% an unwritten one, and no less than 28.6% have none. An analysis of how a human resource director's field of study is related to the formation of a human resource strategy shows that managers with an actual education in the human resource management field hold an advantage over those having completed other studies, especially such as do not provide a proper basis for the management of a human resource department (such as engineering, security, education, and similar).

companies belong to the first category, 47.2% to the second, and 10.2% to the third.

Involvement of the human resource director in the formation and implementation of the company business strategy

General managers are usually well aware of the import of their strategic role in the company. What is important is that, in its performance, they do not act in separation from their co-workers but rather involve them in the preparation of strategies and, if necessary, also in deciding which of the prepared strategies to select and pursue. Thus, they will win over their co-workers, making them more committed and ready to pursue the strategies, and greater knowledge and experience resulting from this will enhance the possibilities of success. The extent of an organization's effort to achieve internal congruity, i.e. congruity between its business and human resource strategies, can be judged by the extent to which its business strategy formation process incorporates the human resource function.

One of our objectives was to find out how much the human resource directors were involved in the formation and implementation of their company's business strategy. The answers are presented in Chart 3. The results indicate that such involvement remains insufficient in Slovenian companies. Only 36.6% of the questioned human resource directors* always participated in the formation and implementation of their company's business strategy, 26% did this often, 28.2% occasionally, and 9.2% never.

* The questions concerning the post of human resource director were answered by the human resource director himself/herself in companies employing one, and by the general sector manager in other companies.

Chart 3: Answers to the question: »How often does the human resource director participate in the formation and implementation of the company's business strategy?«

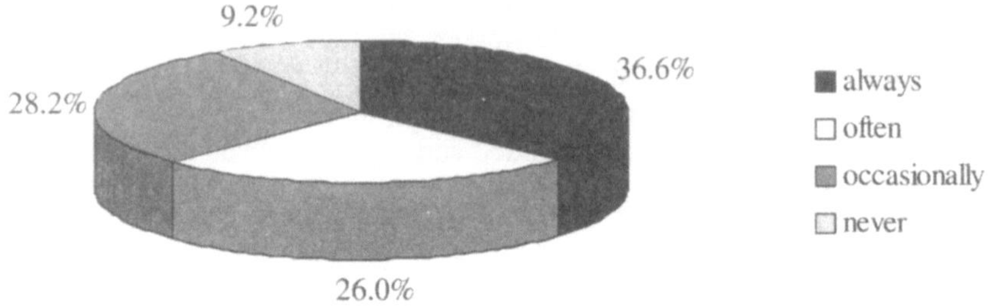

General managers' acquaintance with employee skills and knowledge
Managers must be aware that company goals must be determined so as to commit the employees, thus impacting their behaviour in relation to the achievement of the goals. The strategy formation process therefore requires from general managers to know what kind of skills the employees have and whether they are such as would allow efficient implementation of a particular strategic alternative. Once they decide upon a strategy, they must provide the employees with the skills and knowledge as well as motivation required for its delivery, thus making the best of the existing business skills of the workforce.

The study has shown that general managers in Slovenian companies are still insufficiently acquainted with employee skills and knowledge. 41.8% of those questioned agreed with the statement: »The company's general managers are insufficiently acquainted with the skills and knowledge of the employees,« while 26.1% disagreed with it (Chart 4).

Chart 4: The opinion of the questioned managers as to the statement: »The company's general managers are insufficiently acquainted with the skills and knowledge of the employees.«

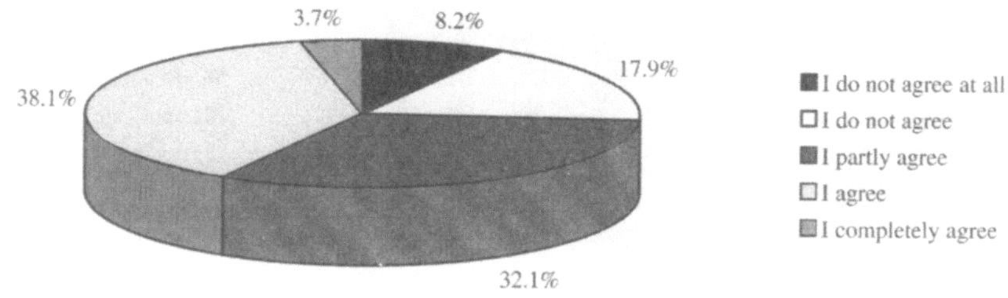

In strategy formation, the general managers must carefully examine and take into account employee skills, thereby participating in the staffing process. Only thus can they select a strategy that would allow the company to gain a competitive advantage over others, as a misassessment of personnel advantages and disadvantages can result in a selection of a strategy impossible to realize.

The human resource director's impact on the strategic plan

According to the study, managers believe that the human resource director's impact on the strategic plan is insufficient. The results are presented in Chart 5.

Chart 5: The opinion of the questioned managers as to the statement: »The human resource director's impact on the strategic plan is insufficient.«

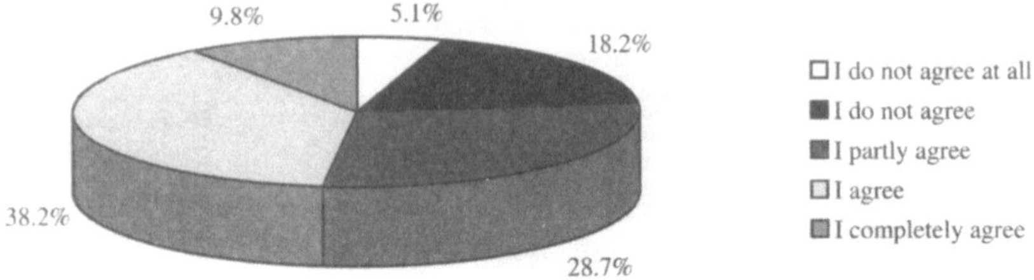

The results are not surprising, as the international study (Svetlik, 2001, p. 158ff) shows that, in Slovenian companies, the person in charge of human resources is much more expected to help implement a given business strategy than to act as a consultant in its development. The human resource director is involved as a consultant in business strategy development in 12.9% of Slovenian companies, while this percentage amounts to 25.3% in the EU, and even to 26.5% in the transitional countries. This might be due to the fact that human resource sectors in Slovenia are understaffed, as there is only 1.14 human resource practitioner per 100 employees, while this figure comes to 2.34 in the EU and even to 2.55 in the transitional countries. Thus, more than twice as less people work in Slovenian human resource departments compared to other European countries.

Integration of the human resource management into the business strategy

Slovenian managers mostly believe that the human resource function is not integrally incorporated into the strategy formation process. The level of their agreement with the statement: »The human resource function is not integrally incorporated into the strategy formation process« is presented in Chart 6. However, almost one third of them disagree with the statement, allowing us to suppose that in those companies such integration is satisfactory. This makes it possible for them to identify all the human resource problems with which they are faced.

Chart 6: The opinion of the questioned managers as to the statement: »The human resource function is not integrally incorporated into the strategy formation process.«

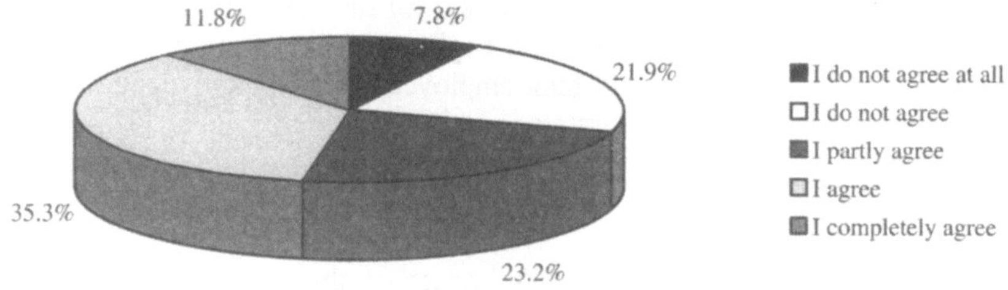

5. Findings

The findings of the study can be summarized as follows:

- 62.5% of Slovenian companies hold a written human resource strategy. The results show that Slovenian managers are aware of the import of a human resource strategy and thus of the basic principle of human resource management, i.e. that a company's human resources are its principal asset and, if managed effectively, a key to business success. However, it should be taken into account (Svetlik, 2001, p. 158) that in Slovenia the human resource director is, rather than being engaged as a consultant, involved in the implementation of the business strategy, which somewhat mars the relatively favourable picture of the situation.

- Human resource directors should be involved in their company's business strategy formation to a greater extent and should be sufficiently acquainted with its developmental orientations and strategic goals, which is extremely important in the formation of functional strategies. A sound acquaintance with strategic goals is thus a sound basis for the achievement of a congruity between the business strategy and the human resource strategy.

- General managers are insufficiently acquainted with employee skills and knowledge in most companies. To be able to form a successful strategy, they should know well what the potentials of the employees are and whether they are appropriate for the delivery of a particular strategic alternative. They must begin to realize how important it is to know and take into account employee skills and knowledge when forming a company strategy, as a misassessment of personnel advantages and disadvantages can result in a selection of a strategy impossible to carry through into practice.

- The human resource director's impact on the strategic plan is too weak in most companies. The results show that the questioned general managers do not make sufficient use of the potential support by the human resource director, whom they should engage as the main consultant in business strategy formation. After all, he/she is the one who knows the human resource situation in the company best and knows whether the skills and knowledge of his/her current co-workers would suffice, in a changing organization, to attain the goals set.

- The human resource function should be integrated into the strategy formation process in all companies. Organizations can only be effective if they ensure congruity between their general management, functional managers and human resource specialists, so that they reconcile their decisions, plan their activities and the allocation of resources, and participate in the implementation and evaluation of all the activities related to the management of human resources. Slovenian managers, too, must realize this as soon as possible, incorporating the human resource function integrally into the strategy formation process.

The results indicate that, in Slovenian companies, the human resource strategy is still insufficiently linked to the business strategy. We go on to propose how a company's human resource strategy should be incorporated into its business strategy to make for a greater congruity within it, which would make the work of individuals and the whole organization more effective.

6. A Proposal of How to Incorporate a Human Resource Strategy into a Company's Business Strategy

Most companies consist of various business units and certain joint departments. For the greatest possible efficiency, the strategies of all units must be brought into accord and interconnected. A company uniting the activities performed by separate and independent units creates synergy.

In a society dominated by information and services, human resources are a key factor of success in the complex, dynamic and bombarded markets. Their management has thus been gaining value continually and it has become necessary to actively incorporate the human resource function into the process of business change, which makes it possible to directly monitor the effects of the human resource solutions by the product and service quality and economic success. Measures concerning human resources taken as the company goes along are thus replaced by planned strategic decisions similar to business decisions of other business functions. This results in a congruity between the material, financial, and human resources, allowing effective realization of the company's goals.

The human resource director shares the responsibility for a company's human resources with its corporate management, for which he/she must have sufficient knowledge and skills to be able to keep up with the change in business practices and contribute sufficient support to the realization of the corporate goals. The connection between the business and human resource strategies is strong and vital (Picture1).

Once a company has formed a business strategy, it must also plan the human resources necessary for its delivery. To do so, it needs to:

- analyse the environment,
- link the business goals and strategies with human resources,
- analyse what human resources are available internally,
- forecast the need for human resources,
- develop ways and programmes for the implementation of individual human resource activities, and
- assess and evaluate goals realization.

Picture 1: The connection between the human resource and business strategies

HUMAN RESOURCE STRATEGY	BUSINESS STRATEGY

INTEGRATION

PRACTITIONERS OF STRATEGIC HUMAN RESOURCE MANAGEMENT WILL:

- monitor, analyse, and forecast change in the company's internal and external environments from both its human resource strategy and its business strategy perspective;
- define the human resource goals and strategies that would support the company's business strategy within individual activities;
- keep the lower operational levels informed of the strategically important goals and tasks;
- define staffing needs from the business strategy perspective;
- determine the present and future human resource supply within and without the organization;
- determine what activities should be undertaken to tackle the discrepancy between human resource supply and demand;
- determine who is in charge of a particular task and what the deadlines are;
- configure an appropriate information system;
- provide financial funds;
- monitor and evaluate the goals achieved.

Attention must be paid to the whole range of human resource activities, including anticipation of the needs of employees and thus of the problems likely to occur at individual developmental stages. In practice, a static approach to the management of human resources is still prevalent in many organizations, and therefore the instruments of individual activities in the staffing process should be interconnected. Considering that some companies have not yet formed a human resource strategy while others have not integrated it into their business strategy, managers must realize that effectiveness of strategic management largely depends on the extent to which the strategy formation process incorporates the human resource function.

A human resource strategy must be defined in such a way as will make it possible to adapt the internal human resource make-up to the requirements of the adopted business strategy, taking into account the change in the environment. Individual human resource activities must be determined on the basis of realizable human resource goals. Recruitment of new personnel should be connected to the company's strategies and not formed as a separate activity.

The human resource and business strategies can be successfully connected in different ways, depending on what is better suited to a given situation and the needs of a company. Regardless of the form the process takes, it must include not only the company's general managers and human resource specialists but also its line managers, who bear responsibility for the implementation of individual tasks related to human resource management. Human resource directors must be primarily concerned with professional aid and consultation, as the managers need information on the employee skills and their potential development as well as other factors important for a successful tasks implementation.

In addition to co-operation between the general, human resource and line managers, what is also needed to connect the human resource strategy to the business strategy is to be aware of how important it is to continually gather data and form databases, to continually monitor the discrepancy between the human resource supply and demand from both the quantitative and the qualitative aspect, to search for, and draw in, the best workers, to find out what employee knowledge and skills are needed, to encourage and create proper conditions for employee development, and to evaluate the achieved results. Hence, it is necessary to develop such a human resource strategy as will fully involve the employees in the realization of their company's strategic goals. Thus, they will be effective and dedicated to the goals, the direction of development will be known, the position in the market will be appreciated, and all the activities will be deployed and extended in a structural and systematic way.

7. Conclusion

The constantly growing dynamics of the environment gives rise to diverse, risky activities, which is why an effective organization must have a creative, highly motivated, and strategically oriented workforce. Therefore the human resource function is no longer merely work done by the human resource directors or practitioners, but rather an essential part of a company's business strategy delivery, and a concern of all those in managerial positions.

If a strategy is to be successfully delivered and the company's goals reached, the employees must be efficient in the performance of certain tasks. To be so, they must have the right skills and knowledge as well as sufficient motivation. No matter how successful a certain business strategy is in theory, it is bound to fail if managers do not concern themselves with human resources, with the choice and further development of their co-workers, and if they lack power and authority, and trust that the adopted strategies would be realized. In this, human resource directors can greatly support and assist general managers, as their knowledge and practical experience enables them to help the latter tackle various kinds of human resource related problems.

It is the increased awareness of how important the human resources are that incites a company to incorporate a human resource strategy into its business strategy, so that managers guide the employees by inspiring them to solve problems in new ways, by communicating visions to them, stimulating them intellectually, and taking into account their particularities.

Bibliography and References

Baron, J. N. & Kreps, D. M. (1999). Strategic Human Resources: Frameworks for General Managers. New York: John Wiley & Sons, Inc.

Beardwell, I. & Holden, L. (1997). Human Resource Management: A contemporary perspective. London: Pitman Publishing.

DeNisi, A. S. & Griffin R. W. (2005). Human Resource Management. Boston: Houghton Mifflin Company.

Florjančič, J., Bernik, M. & Novak, V. (2004). Kadrovski management (Human Resource Management). Kranj: Založba Moderna organizacija.

Guest, D.E. & Peccei, R. (1994). The Nature and Causes of Effective Human Resource Management. British Journal of Industrial Relations, 32(2): 219-242.

Hellriegel, D., Jackson, S. E. & Slocum, J. W. (2001). Management: A Competency – Based Approach. Cincinnati: South – Western.

Heneman III H.G. & Judge, T. A. (2006). Staffing Organizations. Middleton: Mc Graw Hill.

Kreitner, R. (2007). Management. Boston: Houghton Mifflin Company.

Lipičnik, B. (2002). Ravnanje z ljudmi pri delu. V Management: nova znanja za uspeh (Human Resource Management. In Management: New Knowledge for Success). Edited by Možina, S. Radovljica: Didakta.

Možina, S. (2002). Strateški pomen kadrovskih virov. V Management kadrovskih virov (Strategic View of Human Resource Management. In Human Resource Management). Edited by Možina, S. Ljubljana: Fakulteta za družbene vede.

Noe, R., Hollenbeck, J.R., Gerhart, B. & Wright, P. (1994). Human Resource Management. Illinois: Irwin.

Novak, V. & Florjančič, J. (2005). The Role of Managers in the Staffing Process. In Personnel and Management: Selected Topics. Edited by Florjančič, J. & Paape, B. Frankfurt am Main: Peter Lang.

Porter, M. E. (1997). Creating Tomorrow's Advantages. In Rethinking the Future. Edited by Gibson, R. London: Nicholas Brealey Publishing.

Pučko, D. (2002). Strateško planiranje. V Management: nova znanja za uspeh (Strategic Planning. In Management: New Knowledge for Success). Edited by Možina, S. Radovljica: Didakta.

Sadler, T. (1995). Human Resource Management: Developing a Strategic Approach. London: Kogan Page.

Schmitt, N. & Chan, D. (1999). Personnel Selection: A theoretical Approach. Thousand Oaks: SAGE Publication.

Schuler, R. S. & Huber, V.L. (1993). Personnel and Human Resource Management. St. Paul: West Publishing Company.

Stoner, J. A. F. (1978). Management. Englewood Cliffs: Prentice – Hall.

Svetlik, I. (2001). Mednarodne primerjave. V Upravljanje človeških virov: mednarodna primerjalna študija (International comparison. In Human Resource Management: International Comparative Study). Edited by Svetlik, I. Ljubljana: Fakulteta za družbene vede.

Svetlik, I. (2002). Slovenski kadrovski management. V Management kadrovskih virov (Slovenian Human Resource Management. In Human Resource Management). Edited by Možina, S. Ljubljana: Fakulteta za družbene vede.

Ulrich, D. (1997). Human Resource Champions: The Next Agenda for Adding Value and Delivering Results. Boston: Harvard Business School Press.

Wensley, R. (2001). Marketing strategy. In The IEBM Encyclopedia of Marketing. Edited by Baker, M.J. Thomson Learning.

Wheelen, T.L. & Hunger, J.D. (1995). Strategic Management and Business Policy. Addison – Wesley Publishing Company.

About the Author

Vesna Novak is an asistant professor at the University of Maribor, Faculty of Organizational Sciences. Her research fields are human resource management and staffing activities.

Education and Training for Visual Merchandising in Retail Companies

Jure Meglič[1]

jure.meglic@fov.uni-mb.si,

Goran Vukovič

goran.vukovic@fov.uni-mb.si

Abstract

This paper deals with the state of Visual Merchandising in Slovenia and about the opportunities, from the standpoint of educational services, in this untapped sector. At this moment in time, visual merchandising is a competitive advantage and by tomorrow it will be a must for preserving the retail company. The most important issue is that there are numerous retail companies which still need to implement visual merchandising. A low-level of education in retail companies did not surprise us. However, we were hoping for a better result, which then became evident in the research undertaken with Slovenian companies. It is interesting that education and training has fallen onto the shoulders of the employees – sales representatives, who in many cases are not financially capable of covering the costs for such training.

Keywords: Visual Merchandising, Marketing, Retail Company, Consumer

1. Introduction

Every shopkeeper and merchant's primary objective is to sell merchandise. When the giant nineteenth century dry goods establishments like Marshall Field & Co. shifted their business from wholesale to retail, the visual

---

[1] This paper presents some results from doctoral dissertation "Allocation of human resources in product development process according to business strategy" of the author Jure Meglič.

display of goods became necessary to attract the retail customer. The store windows no longer simply allowed natural light to shine into the building or act as storage space for stock; they became important venues to attractively display the store's merchandise (Bell, Ternus, 2001, p. 12; Colborne, 1996, p. 17). Gradually, the design aesthetic used in window displays moved indoors and became part of the overall interior store design; eventually displacing the importance of windows altogether in suburban malls (Darian, 2003, p. 21).

Today, knowledge is wealth, and education means renewing the obtained knowledge over various periods of time. At the moment, the majority of retail companies are fighting to keep their position in the market because the times when demand was greater than the supply have long passed. That is why it is necessary to find ways to keep loyal customers and obtain new customers on the market, because everyone is selling comparable products at almost the same price (Heyd, 2007, p. 37).

Visual Merchandising is quite a new science or tool in Slovenia, one which has been quickly spreading to the consciousness of sellers and retailers, especially after the penetration of foreign brand names. Until recently, the advantages and benefits of this approach had not been recognized in Slovenia - not until it was made aware by consumer behaviour and finally in the till at the end of the day. It is driven into the consciousness that, in a classical sale of a product, the seller must be friendly and, as a result, will be successful (Vukovič, Meglič, 2005, p. 11; Zvonar, 2003, p. 5). This ideology, streaming from twenty years ago, when stores such as Slovenijašport, Veletekstil, Tekstil, Tkanina and others were popular, has – at least for some people – become obsolete in more recent times.

Today, friendliness alone is not enough because, in a turbulent environment, we must offer the consumer a quick service at a good price with all kinds of other offers, and with a smile, which is not an easy task (Bell, Ternus, 2001, p. 21). A quick walk through Slovenia's capital and a visit to its shopping centres reminds us that it is necessary for retail companies and their employees to be trained and educated in Visual Merchandising (Luggen, Koruna, 2004, p. 37). There would be plenty of work involved and the philosophy of Visual Merchandising could be adapted to each individual company or subscriber.

Visual Merchandising is a competitive advantage at this moment in time and by tomorrow it will be a "must" for preserving any retail company

(Bell, Ternus, 2001, p. 19; Colborne, 1996, p. 14; Darian, 2003 12; Heyd, 2003, p. 17). The most important thing is that there are numerous retail companies which still need to implement Visual Merchandising.

2. What is Visual Merchandising?

At the Centre for Public Communication in Ljubljana, the dictionary for advertising terms has interpreted Visual Merchandising as a way of accelerating sales, based on the appearance, and the visual impression a product makes on a potential customer. It wants to import a relaxed and friendly environment (Bell, Ternus, 2001, p. 23; Colborne, 1996, p. 31). Products are designed and created for point sale and window shopping (Darian, 2003, p. 22; Devetak, Vukovič, 2002, p. 37; Kotler, 1998, p. 137; Zvonar, 2003, p. 21).

The director of a reputable retail company in Slovenia feels that Visual Merchandising for her is – "the art of ensuring the right products, which are attractive and presented in certain unifying themes so the chances of a sale are maximised and there is good communication between the retail company, brand name and customer." By all means, Visual Merchandising emphasises the significance of presenting the products on shelves and in windows (Colborne, 1996, p. 32). It is necessary to ensure that those products are offered that customers want to buy, and more importantly, to have an influence on the costumers to buy more than their initial purchase (Meglič, 2004, p. 168).

We could say that Visual Merchandising is a tool with which we can increase sales, decrease operational costs in the store, encourage impulsive purchases, which are usually unintentional, and, by doing so, increase the average value of the purchase and maximise the chances of a sale (Bell, Ternus, 2001, p. 39). It is important that we use products as well as the space for a convincing and informative presentation (Meglič, 2004, p. 169). Now is the perfect time for all those who did not believe in Visual Merchandising until now to make up for lost time and to start preparing studies that will make retailers recognisable and competitive for the current competition in the markets of the European Union.

3. Methodology and Hypotheses

Some previous surveys on the top in-store trends used for Visual Merchandising show the incredible growth of the technological influence. Survey respondents answered the open-ended question asking for the top in-store technological trends (ranked in order) (DDI, 2005, p. 2f) as follows:

1. Interactive kiosks
2. Digital signage
3. High-definition screens (LCD monitors, flat-screen technology, plasma screens, HDTV)
4. Wireless technology, RFID
5. Self-checkout
6. Faster checkouts; increased checkout convenience, Technology's increasing role in environmental branding
7. More interactive devices, such as shopping carts, integrating online and brick-and-mortar
8. Audio; retailers programming their own music
9. Scent technology
10. More customization, such as videos triggered by the customer, biometric authentication, such as fingerprint identification, Corporate network broadcasts on in-store video screens

With this research, we wanted to get to know and to determine the opportunities for preparing Visual Merchandising education and training for different retail companies (Vukovič, Meglič, 2005, p. 29). Prior to the preparation of the questionnaire, we were not aware of how much companies know about Visual Merchandising; whether they would even participate in this kind of education or training, or whether they even need it.

The questionnaire gave us the results on whether a retail company that has been in operation for ten years should also expand its activities in the area of education, as it has adequate terms and conditions, which should not be neglected. We included fifty companies from across Slovenia in the questionnaire, for which we had estimated that Visual Merchandising education and training would benefit them and enable them to become better known in the market.

The questionnaire on Visual Marketing includes fifteen questions which would allow us to determine what the needs of the companies are in Visual Merchandising. We neglected basic company information. Visual Merchandising as a tool for accelerating sales or for communicating with consumers is regarded as a relatively unknown science in Slovenia and, as a result, besides the questionnaire we prepared a short presentation about the advantages of Visual Marketing (Vukovič, Meglič, 2005, p. 31).

The questionnaire was set up in such a way that the participant, in this case we wanted it to be the director of the company, could respond to the questions very quickly. It was not too long, because we had realized that tedious and very long, descriptive questions usually keep participants from filling in questionnaires. This is because it usually takes more time and, as a result, the questionnaire is incomplete. The three basic hypotheses that we wanted to test with our research were as follows:

Table 1: Tested hypotheses

Hypothesis 1:	*Following Slovenia's accession into the European Union, retail companies should implement Visual Merchandising education and training for achieving greater competitiveness because of the arrival of foreign brand names and sales networks, which have already been using these tools for years. We presume that there will be a lot of interest for Visual Merchandising education and training.*
Hypothesis 2:	*Retail companies usually educate and train their employees by themselves and, thus, we presume that there will be a lot of individual education and training tailored to each individual retail company.*
Hypothesis 3:	*We presume that companies receive offers of education and training via e-mail, taking into account that these are usually in the form of leaflets and brochures, which stimulate a need for education and training – something the companies are as yet unaware of.*

3.2 Research and Analysis

Fifty participants filled out the questionnaire. With the first question, we wanted to find out how well people know Visual Merchandising and its function in sales. To our surprise, 30 (60%) of the respondents said that they were aware of Visual Merchandising, while 20 (40%) of them had never heard of it as a tool that could improve their popularity in the market.

The second question was intended to find out about Visual Merchandising education and training and any interest in providing it to employees. The following table shows the results:

Table 2: Results for Visual Merchandising education and training and any potential interest in its provision. (Vukovič, Meglič, 2005, p. 23)

yes	no	maybe
30 companies	5 companies	15 companies
60%	10%	30%

It is evident from the chart that 30 companies, or 60%, of those surveyed replied that they would be willing to participate in such education and training. There is also a high percentage of companies which might be interested in doing so, and only 5% who would not participate in it. It is necessary to present the appropriateness and goals of the training and function of Visual Merchandising more convincingly to the thirty percent of companies who are hesitant about joining in this type of training. In our opinion, Visual Merchandising would be best organized by individually adapting it to the needs of each company. However, with the market research, we wanted to find out exactly what each company wanted.

Ten percent of the companies neglected the next question. From the questionnaire we were able to determine that, here, we could rank companies that were not interested in Visual Merchandising education and training. The majority of the rest of the companies denoted the first option, which included individual training and education adapted to each company in combination with the answer which offers practical workshops in individual shop units (88%) There was no great interest in a general seminar. Let us take a look at the figures:

Table 3: The type of education and training on Visual Merchandising preferred by the selected Slovenian companies. (Vukovič, Meglič, 2005, p. 31)

Individual education and training in the company	General seminar	Workshops in businesses	Other (none of the options mentioned)
44 companies	1 company	44 companies	5 companies
88%	2%	88%	10%

In the fourth question, we were interested in the financial share which a company would be prepared to invest in the types of education and training stated in question three. The companies often answered that they did not know and that it would probably include a certain agreement about the financials. They said that it would be difficult to estimate and that, beforehand, the results would definitely interest them. The graph below shows the number of employees willing to attend training in Visual Merchandising.

Figure 1: Share of the companies that would involve their employees in participation in Visual Merchandising training. (Vukovič, Meglič, 2005, p. 33)

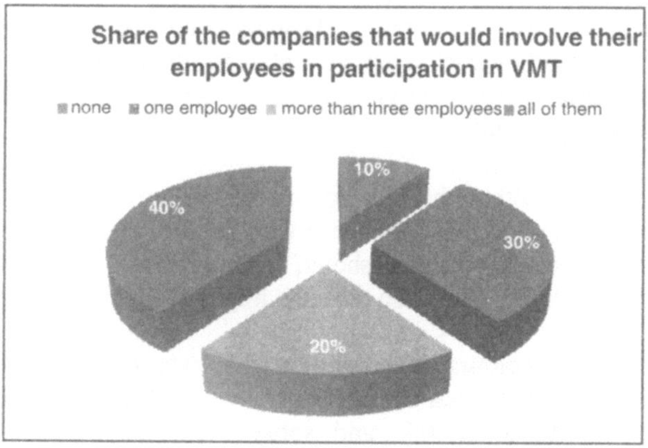

It is evident from the graph that 40 percent of those companies would involve all their employees in Visual Merchandising training. Thirty percent of the companies said that they would train one representative of the company, followed by companies (20%) with more than three participants. The smallest population is represented by the group with no participants – that is, ten percent of the participating companies.

With the sixth question, we wanted to determine the significance of the listed possibilities for the customers of individual retail companies. Let us take a look at the responses below:

Table 4: Mark frequencies of the listed possibilities for the customers of individual retail companies. (Vukovič, Meglič, 2005, p. 36)

Characteristics \ list of marks	1	2	3	4	5
awareness of products	0	2	10	11	27
product positioning	0	0	11	25	14
displays	0	0	30	10	20
promotional material	0	0	0	15	35
price	0	0	10	17	23
parking	0	6	20	14	10
additional benefits	0	0	0	25	25
colours – comfort	5	10	15	5	15
seller expertise	0	2	16	23	9

The key importance for sales in a retail company is, above all, awareness of its products and their positioning. Displays and promotional material, which are welcomed by customers, also play an important role. The price is also an important factor, as almost half of the companies graded it as being the most significant.

Parking is desired although it is not of key importance for making a purchase, which is good news for those who do not have parking facilities for their customers. Research has shown that customers like added services and benefits from their sellers and this also might be the key to success.

The importance of colours and a comfortable atmosphere in stores was answered differently by each company. It is interesting to note that some give great importance to this and some could not care less. Some interesting responses came up regarding seller expertise in that we have the feeling that customers have lost trust in sellers and, as a result, consumers might rather decide on purchasing a product on their own. This is why seller expertise does not even interest them, which can be determined by the given results.

In the seventh question, we were interested in where company representatives recognized the explicit usage of Visual Merchandising for the acceleration of sales. Visual Merchandising was, above all, recognized in foreign brand name franchises such as Benetton, Zara, Max & Co., and supermarkets such as Mercator.

Question eight was intended for thinking about the influence of the Visual Merchandising tool on the success of sales. The results are shown in figure 2.

Figure 2 - The expected influence of Visual Merchandising on sales. (Vuković, Meglič, 2005, p. 38)

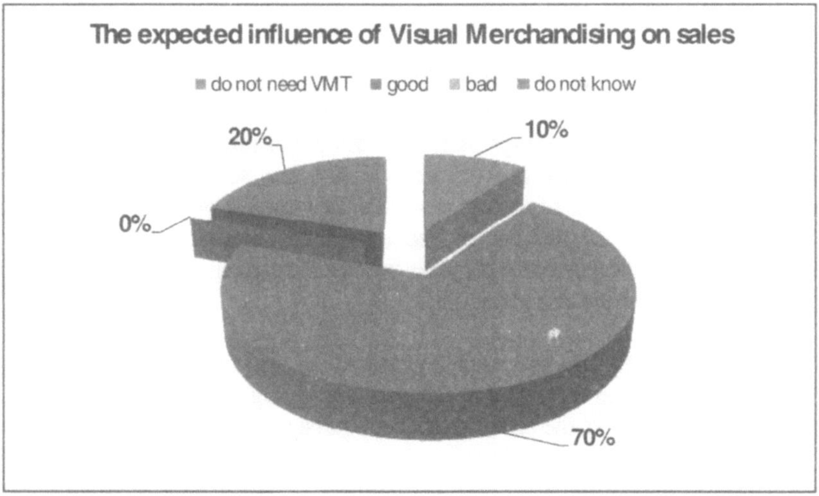

It is evident from the graph that 70 percent of the companies see the beneficial side of Visual Merchandising whereas there are only 20 percent of those that do not know how Visual Merchandising education and training will influence sales. The percentage of those who do not need

Visual Merchandising remained the same, which included ten percent of the participants.

In question nine, we wanted to determine how important education and training were for companies. We were interested to the extent to which and in what way they devote training and education to their employees. The participants had four answers to choose from and the fifth one could have been provided by themselves. The results were as follows:

Table 5: How important are education and training for the companies? (Vukovič, Meglič, 2005, p. 42)

We educate and train them	They procure education and training for themselves	They do not need training and education	We do not have qualified human resources for education and training	other
10	0	5	35	0
20%	0%	10%	70%	0%

The analysis of the results shows that 70 percent of the companies do not have adequate human resources for educating and training the sellers. We expected this high percentage as it includes small retail companies where usually the owner is also head of sales with a few sellers. Ten percent of the companies are still of the opinion that they do not need education and training, whereas 20 percent of the companies educate and train their employees, which means that they are aware of the great competition in the markets of the European Union.

In the tenth question, we were interested in additional education and knowledge and the significance of this for hiring new candidates. The diagram below shows the analysis of the results.

Figure 3 – The significance of Visual Merchandising skills for employment. (Vukovič, Meglič, 2005, p. 44)

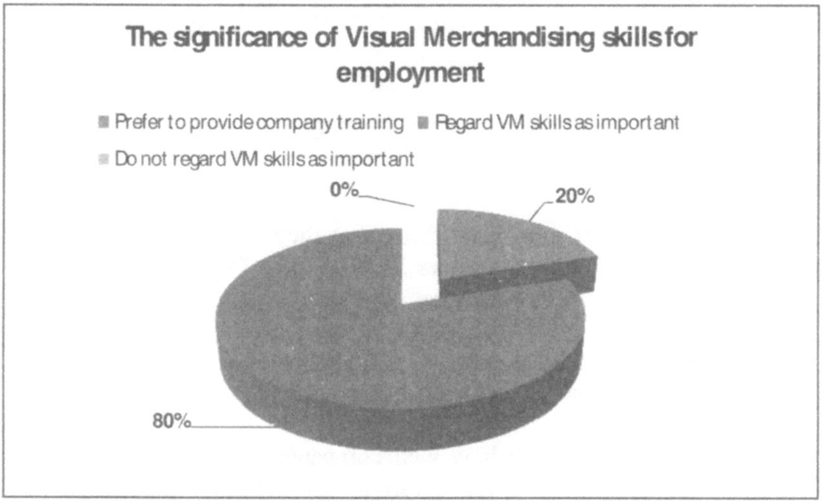

It is evident from the graph that 80 percent of the companies put great importance on additional skills for candidates who are applying for a new position. This is an exceptionally important piece of information for all those looking for new employment. Twenty percent of the companies would rather educate and train their employees themselves and do not demand existing additional skills from new candidates.

In question eleven, we wanted to ascertain employee responses on education and training within the company. The most frequent response was that the employees simply did not like education and training, except for a few who realize the significance for development in their field. A frequent response was also that they themselves were not even aware of this problem because there is no organized formal education and training in their company.

Question twelve dealt with education and training on an employee's own initiative. The analysis showed the following results of employers'' perception of this:

Table 6: Education and training on employee's own initiative. (Vukovič, Meglič, 2005, p. 45)

Yes, everyone would participate	No, it would not interest them	Only a handful would participate	We simply do not know
10	0	5	35
20%	0%	10%	70%

A great percentage of employers think that they simply cannot give an exact figure because they themselves have no idea. Twenty percent of the participants say that their employees would definitely decide to procure education and training for themselves on their own initiative. It is also interesting to note that this population is represented by employees in those companies that also educate and train their employees themselves.

Question thirteen dealt with how well companies know their customers. The most frequent answer to this question was probably "not enough", as they have difficulty in setting up an offer. Many times, they have changed the whole sales program, which means that some brand name groups or some brand names have also been replaced by new ones or have been discontinued altogether.

The fourteenth question also dealt with noticing about declining regular customers. Sixty percent of the participants said yes whereas forty percent of them said that they did not notice a decline.

The last question was intended to deal with education and training via media. The point of interest was in what type of education and training would be most appropriate for advertising education training of a company. Results were as follows:

Table 7: The most appropriate type of education and training for advertising education training in the company. (Vukovič, Meglič, 2005, p. 47)

Type of media	always	never	periodically
Internet, e-mail	15	7	28
Post, brochures, leaflets,...	34	5	11
Television, radio	0	35	15
Audio-visual material	15	12	23
Directories	5	37	8

The best type of media for marketing education and training is the post or brochures and leaflets. They are followed by the Internet and audiovisual material. Radio, television and directories are not types of media that would be used in marketing Visual Merchandising education and training. The Internet is also suitable for marketing, especially for all those who periodically visit Internet.

3.3 Testing the Hypotheses

The entire market analysis has given us different pieces of information, which has helped us to test the hypotheses that were made at the beginning.

Hypothesis 1 – Great interest in Visual Merchandising education and training

We can see that, from the research, the hypothesis was proven to be true. Sixty percent of the companies would decide to engage in Visual Merchandising education and training already at the beginning of a short presentation, whereas it is possible to convince the remaining thirty percent on the basis of individual meetings by company representatives and our Visual Merchandising lecturer. A small group of only ten percent did not show any interest in Visual Merchandising education and training.

Hypothesis 2 – Individual education and training for individual companies

Retail companies usually educate and train employees by themselves and, thus, on the basis of the results, we can prove the second hypothesis and that great interest for individual education and training will be adapted to individual retail companies.

Hypothesis 3 – the best type of marketing for education in Visual Merchandising

The results of the research also prove our third hypothesis. Post, brochures and leaflets proved to be the most used and read for purposes of education.

4. The Marketing Mix (7-Ps) for Services in Education and Training

Education is of key importance for society's development and also for each individual. Since development of service in sales is of key importance, this also coincides with education and training, which often represents a great cost and consumption of leisure time for people. In the past, there were problems with sellers as well as today, especially with those in the most successful companies, whose opinion was that they have finished their schooling and that they already have a career. Motivation, effort and also obtained skills, have convinced them that they must constantly upgrade their skills just as professors, doctors and directors do.

Retailers want to keep the "right" costumers because it is cheaper to keep them than find new ones. Existing costumers increase profit added without additional cost. Loyal customers make referrals to others, reducing a firm's need to spend on getting new costumers. It costs a firm much more to acquire a new customer than to keep an existing one. In terms of profitability, it benefits the firm to analyze the balance between investing to keep clients satisfied and the cost of getting more clients. Regarding upper statements, the 7-Ps diagram is a good illustration of marketing mix for services. The 7-Ps diagram, or Extended Marketing Mix of Booms and Bitner, is a marketing strategy tool that expands the number of controllable variables from the four in the original Marketing Mix Model to seven. It stresses the "mixing" or blending of various factors in such a way that both organizational and consumer (targeted markets) objectives are attained. The 7-Ps Model is very useful for service industries and arguably also for knowledge-intensive environments.

Figure 4 – Marketing mix for services according to the 7-Ps diagram (Devetak, Vukovič, 2002, p. 92)

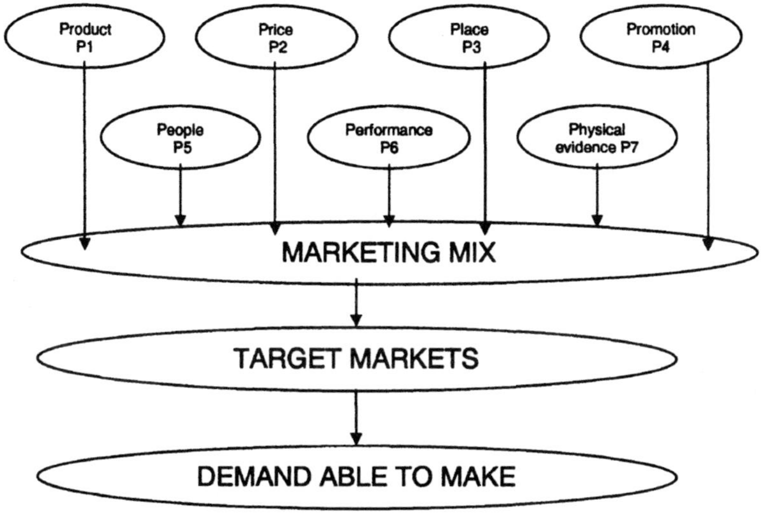

4.1 Education and Training Services P – 1

We often say that the service is the main actor not only in the marketing mix, but in marketing and the marketing philosophy in general. At this point we especially deal with: quality, functionality, characteristics, assortments, style, brand name, service, warranty, image (demonstration, reputation, being renown) and good will (Devetak, Vukovič 2002, p. 93). As we have already mentioned a number of times, the education and training service of a company that wishes to organize education and training for its sellers is of key significance. Visual Merchandising is by all means a tool for accelerating sales and is something of great interest to retail companies.

4.2 Price of Education and Training P - 2

Price is a monetary expression for education and training services. (Devetak, Vukovič 2002, p. 93) Visual Merchandising education and training was desired in different ways in retail companies and by all means it is important that they receive quality education and training for a suitable price because we are aware of the fact that the small companies which were surveyed are not able to pay large amounts of money for education and training. In spite of a small amount of competition and high quality, there is no point in exaggerating the prices because this would mean a loss of many retail companies that cannot pay such high costs for education and training.

4.3 The Place for Carrying Out the Education and Training Services P- 3

Visual Merchandising primarily focuses on place, but product, price and promotion also help fulfil the Visual Merchandising strategies (Colborne, 1996, p. 7). The place for carrying out education and training services is usually determined by the carriers of the training themselves or at the request of the company. It is evident from the market research that, to a great extent, companies would like to have workshops, which means that the education and training would for the most part, take place on company premises.

4.4 Promotion or Market Communication P- 4

Promotion represents one of the methods of communicating with customers because of the acceleration and increase in sales. (Devetak, Vukovič 2002, p. 94). Promotion includes selling, advertising, special events, publicity, window and interior displays. Visual Merchandising utilizes window and specific interior displays to hype and reinforce the event (Colborne, 1996, p. 8). The covering letter and questionnaire is already one form of promotion as the possibilities of Visual Merchandising were presented to the companies. After conducting the research, we found out which forms of communication were most beneficial for companies.

4.5 People Involved in Educational and Training Services P – 5

People have an exceptionally important role in carrying out the services. In education and training they are in the customer role or the lecturers. The education and training field has developed in many companies over the years. The education and training that we prepare for personal needs is interesting and educative and, what is most important, it has brought us better business results, which we all wanted.

4.6 Performing Education and Training Services P – 6

Education and training experts must express their vital enthusiasm, imagination and creativeness when working with people. Safety, quality and promptness should all be taken care of and, what is of great significance is that participants are satisfied with the price (Heyd, 2003, p. 13). The education and training is carried out in a case-study fashion with many practical cases. The participants are actively involved, which is very important because this is the only way we can simulate and become aware of the daily problems of selling.

4.7 Physical Evidence for Education and Training Services P - 7

Physical evidence is what a person sees, hears or feels. The material which the participant receives at the lecture, the place and the appearance of the lecturer etc., are of key importance for participant satisfaction (Bell, Ternus, 2001, p. 11). That is why it is necessary to dedicate a lot of attention to physical evidence, which will prove our skills of expertise, capabilities and success in Visual Merchandising education and training for retail companies.

5 Conclusion

With the aid of the market analysis, we obtained the answers to the hypotheses made at the beginning. At any rate, the research gave us certain directives on how to go forward and on what companies want regarding the topic on accelerating sales for obtaining a competitive advantage with the aid of Visual Merchandising. By all means, education and training are interesting for Slovenian retailers and most of all, Visual Merchandising is some kind of tool, which must be up-graded like any other skill and which means that it is not a onetime form of education and training.

There was great interest from companies for individual consulting and workshops, which is even more interesting for the development of Visual Merchandising in retail companies and means that Visual Merchandising is adapted to each individual company. This is how each retail company can still preserve its own style and image, which customers had already become familiar with in the past. Retail companies have to be a little more market-oriented and up-graded. It might happen that foreign retail companies have strong Visual Merchandising and small Slovenian retailers could get washed up in the sea of offers now that Slovenian is part of the European Union.

Atthough the low level of education and training in retail companies did not really surprise us, we had been hoping for a slightly better result than was evidenced by our research with Slovenian companies. It is interesting that education and training has fallen onto the shoulders of the employees – sales representatives, who in many cases are not financially capable of covering the costs for such training.

In any case, Visual Merchandising education and training has received the green light from retail companies. However, great perseverance and investments will be needed in order for this type of education and training to be started and implemented so that it will have the effect that we want for both those who are going to create it and those who are going to use it and implement it into their sales program.

Bibliography and References

Bell, J., Ternus, K. (2001): Silent Selling: Best Practices and Effective Strategies in Visual Merchandising, Fairchild Books & Visuals; 2nd Sprl edition

Colborne, R. (1996): Visual Merchandising: The Business of Merchandise Presentation, Thomson Delmar Learning; 1st edition

Darian, W. Unger (2003): Product Development Process Design: Improving Development Response to Market, Technical and Regulatory Risks, dissertation, Massachusetts Institute of Technology

DDI (2005): In store technology – industry survey 2005

Devetak, G. (2000): Evropski marketing storitev, (European marketing of services) Moderna organizacija Kranj, Kranj

Devetak, G., Vukovič, G. (2002): Marketing izobraževalnih storitev, (Marketing of education services), Moderna organizacija Kranj, Kranj

Heyd, I. (2007): Visual Merchandising für Praktiker, Eintagesseminar, Irmgard Heyd, Amstetten.

Kotler, P. (1998): Marketing management (Marketing management), Slovenska knjiga, Ljubljana

Luggen, M., Koruna, S. (2004): Development and Application of Core Competencies from a Technology Management Point of View, Int. J. Technology Intelligence and Planning, Vol. 1, No. 1

Meglič, J. (2004): Allocation of human resources in product development process according to the business strategy. In: Jašková, M. (ed.). ECON '04: [selected research papers], (Research works proceedings, Vol. 11, 2004). Ostrava: Technical University of Ostrava, Faculty of Economics

Vukovič, G., Meglič, J. (2005): Visual Merchandising in Slovenian companies – The survey report. Univerza v Mariboru, Fakulteta za organizacijske vede, Kranj, Maj, 2005.

Zvonar, N. (2002): Vodnik uspešne prodaje, (Guide of sucessfull retal), Ljubljana

Zvonar, N. (2003): Visual Merchandising, kot najboljši prodajalec, (Visual Merchandising as bestseller), Ljubljana

About the Authors

Jure Meglič is a higher educational lecturer at the University of Maribor, Faculty of Organizational Sciences. His field of research involves marketing management, product development and manufacturing strategies.

Goran Vukovič is an associate professor at the University of Maribor, Faculty of Organizational Sciences. His field of research involves marketing management, educational and training systems and human resources management.

Foreign Workers in Slovenia

Marko Ferjan

marko.ferjan@fov.uni-mb.si

Eva Jereb

eva.jereb@fov.uni-mb.si

Abstract

Where are people migrating to today, and why? Labour migration has, in the 21st century, moved to the top of the policy agendas of many countries - countries of origin, transit and destination. Most of the world's estimated 150 million migrants are people searching for improved economic opportunities abroad. In the past, there were very strong migration flows from the republics of the former Yugoslavia to Slovenia. 6.2% of the population of today's Slovenia speaks Serbo-Croatian as its native language. Approximately 36,000 foreign workers that are citizens of former Yugoslav republics are employed in Slovenia today. With the entry of Slovenia into the European Union, the opportunities for them to work will be gradually restricted. However, new migration has also arisen with EU entry. In March 2005, there were 2,298 citizens of EU countries employed in Slovenia and, of these, 1,070 were from Slovakia. The bulk of Slovak workers (708) are employed in the construction industry. Their level of education is relatively low. Their wage is also below the average wage in Slovenia. The number of Slovak workers in Slovenia is increasing from month to month. The motivation for this migration is the opportunity for employment and the expectation of higher wages. A phenomenon of new migration is expected, especially for healthcare workers. As yet, this phenomenon of new migration has not affected the wages and employment opportunities of domestic workers.

Keywords: immigrant worker, migration, labour market

1. Defining the Problem

After the last expansion of the European Union, a new labour market opened up in the new Europe. Today there is a mobility of labour forces between countries where this phenomenon had never been observed before.

In the past, numerous citizens of Yugoslavia sought work abroad. This also applied to those living in Slovenia. It was also common for residents of the other republics of the former Yugoslavia to seek work in Slovenia. Following Slovenia's entry into the EU, this situation has changed significantly. As of 1 May 2004, the free flow of labour applies to the new EU member states. Workers from these countries have also received equal rights with domestic workers in Slovenia with regard to employment or seeking employment. This means that workers from these countries do not need a work permit for employment and that an employer that engages such a worker must fill out a labour declaration for an EU worker. The employer must complete the declaration at the Employment Service of Slovenia within 8 days of the beginning of employment.

With the research we have presented, we wanted to find out the following:

- The number of immigrants still entering the Slovenian work force from former Yugoslavia.
- Whether other EU member country immigrant workers entered Slovenia after 1 May, 2004.
- From which EU member countries workers migrate into Slovenia;
- What level of education these workers have.
- How the new migrants influence the employment market (salaries, employment opportunities) in Slovenia.

To arrive at our conclusions, we used a method of collection and interpretation of the statistical data. During the period January to June 2005, we carried out further research involving the Employment Service of Slovenia. Regular meetings were held there with the Representative for Foreign Workers, Ms. Špela Retelj.

2. Theoretical Framework

The concept of mobility is of Latin origin (*mobilitas*) and means "movement" or "adaptability". Here, it especially refers to a change of job, profession, residence, faith and so on. In the context of this article it refers to labour mobility in particular. Labour mobility encompasses all professional changes that persons make while they are part of the active working population. Forms of mobility especially include the following:

a Change of residence: This is also understood as a change of job. This primarily refers to changes in the organization and less so to changes in the function performed by the worker.
b Change of activity: This is a change of function within the same profession. It especially refers to the concepts of promotion and demotion, whether this is in a previous or new organization.
c Change of profession: This takes the educational aspect into account. A worker acquires a new profession with the help of educational activities. One can also advance in a new profession.

Mobility can be separated into the following types:

- Vertical mobility: This is mobility with regard to promotion or demotion (higher or lower pay, status and so on).
- Horizontal mobility: This refers to transfer from one job to another of equal value. (Florjančič et al., 1999, p. 142)

In addition to the two types of mobility cited above, one can also speak of mobility within an organizational unit, between organizational units, and national and international mobility. The factors that influence mobility are various, and can primarily be divided into personal factors (age, family, tradition, education and so on) and environmental factors (national mentality, geographical characteristics, cultural characteristics and so on).

Mobility can also be observed through the prism of social mobility. This means that one observes movements of individuals as well as social groups, in both time and space. Space is understood to include geographical and social space. When geographical space is meant, one speaks of physical mobility or **migration**. When mobility in social space is meant, one primarily thinks of social mobility in the narrower sense of the word or simply of mobility (i.e., the movement of individuals or groups in the structural network of social positions and status).

Migration refers to resettlement or mechanical movement of a population resulting in a change in the place of residence (International Organization for Migration, 2005, p. 462). With regard to the criterion of time, migration is divided into the following forms: permanent migration (resettlement to another place and permanent settlement), seasonal migration (temporary change of residence in order to work a particular seasonal job) and daily or weekly migration (the daily or weekly commute of workers to work).

Migration is also divided by the criteria of citizenship: specifically, into external migration (to another country) and internal migration (within a country). Each person that participates in resettlement is at the same time an emigrant or immigrant.

One may also speak of the vertical and horizontal mobility of immigrants. For example, barriers that are difficult to transcend appear in the transfer from "unskilled" or "semiskilled" labour to "skilled" professions. Normally, only the second generation of immigrants is able to overcome this barrier. As a result, a feeling develops among immigrants that they are limited to low-status ("dirty") work, which does not serve as a stimulus to their efforts to move up in the world. On the other hand, the horizontal mobility of immigrants is very active. A large portion of immigrants change their professions, but they do not change their social status at the same time.

In addition to this, one can also speak of "professional mobility", which is also horizontal. This especially refers to changing employment or jobs without visible professional advancement. This applies in particular to what are known as "staff fluctuations". Of course, various combinations of professional mobility are possible and also actually take place.

As a rule, horizontal mobility applies to a change in employment of the same type (staff fluctuation from one organization to another, to an equal or similar job) or change to employment of a different type unconnected with long-term professional education (e.g., a worker in an automobile factory who is an experienced driver, becomes a truck driver in another organization in the transport industry; a teacher in an elementary school becomes a teacher of students, and so on).

3. New Migration in Europe

Three periods of economic migration can be identified in post-war Europe. The first period started after 1950. At the end of the 1950s, Western Europe began to recruit **labour** from several Mediterranean countries - Italy, Spain, Portugal, former Yugoslavia, later from Morocco, Algeria, Tunisia, and Turkey. Some countries, such as France, United Kingdom, and the Netherlands, also recruited workers from their former colonies.

The second period began with the appearance of an economic crisis after 1973. In 1970, Germany had the highest absolute number of foreigners, followed by France. The total number of immigrants in Western Europe was twelve million. During the 1970s, mass recruitment of foreign workers was abandoned, and only the arrival of their family members was permitted, which led to family reunification in the countries of employment. Europe closed its borders, with the result that clandestine **migration** increased.

The third period began after the fall of communism. The year 1989 was a turning point in the history of international migrations. The political changes in Central and Eastern Europe brought about mass **migration** to the West, which culminated in the so-called "mass movement of 1989-1990" (Winter-Zlatković, 2004, p. 161ff).

Górny and Kępińska (2004, p. 192) report on migration from Ukraine to Poland. Remennick (2003, p. 706) reports that 80,000 engineers emigrated from the states of the former Soviet Union alone to Israel in the 1990s.

The free movement of citizens on the internal market of the EU was introduced the very year it was founded, that is in 1957 in Rome. Article 48 of the Treaty of Rome (in which Belgium, France, Italy, Luxembourg, the Netherlands and West Germany founded the European Economic Community) defines the free movement of workers as one of the fundamental dimensions of the common market.

Today's EU legislation reflects a policy of protection of its member states: the *acquis communautaire* explicitly demands preferential treatment of citizens of EU countries over foreign workers on the labour market (Brucker, 2001, p. 92). A foreign labour force is admitted only if it is shown that EU citizens are not available for a job.

Today, therefore, EU countries must deal with the free flow of persons. However, in actuality, certain countries have introduced a "transition period". Ahead of EU enlargement in May 2004, most EU-15 states introduced transition periods on immigration ranging from two to seven years in order to stem inflows of new workers from the 10 new EU countries. Ireland, Sweden and the United Kingdom did not impose such arrangements, however. Latest available data for the United Kingdom show that between May and December 2004 there were in total 133,000 work permit applicants from new member countries. Of these, nearly 40% were already in the United Kingdom before 1 May 2004.[1]

Now, mobility in the EU is low. Within regions and within the member states, it is lower than within the individual states of the US. Over a ten-year period, this implies there are cross-state mobility flows for one quarter of the population. In the EU, on current trends, it would only be 4 per cent of the population.[2] In 2002, the annual crude net migration rate was 2.8 per 1000 population in the EU-25.[3]

As is shown below, migration is already taking place as a result of EU expansion. Studies of the factors that influence migration most often lead to the conclusion that **differences in income are the key factor that influences an individual's decision to seek employment abroad.** It is also important to keep in mind that, in assessing the difference in pay, a potential immigrant must also take into account living expenses and other expenses connected with moving to another country.

Other factors that influence migration are:

- Position on the labour market, expressed as supply and demand;
- Distance;
- Tradition;
- A network of foreigners;
- Other.

---

1 Source: OECD, 2005, 1.
2 Source: COM (2001) 116, final, 6.
3 Source: COM (2004) 506, final, 14.

4. Foreign Workers in Slovenia

This study has determined that 40,509 persons who were citizens of other countries were employed in Slovenia on 31 March 2005. Of these, 36,209 were citizens of other former Yugoslav republics, 2,298 were citizens of EU countries and 2,002 were citizens of other countries.

From the data it is clear that the largest number of foreign workers in Slovenia are still from other countries of the former Yugoslavia. This is connected with tradition, geographical proximity and the social networks that already exist in Slovenia. It should not be forgotten that 6.2% of Slovenian citizens speak Serbo-Croatian as their native language. Within the former Yugoslavia, there was a great deal of economic migration from other republics to Slovenia. Immigration from other Yugoslav successor states did not stop after 1991, and was strongly connected with the wars in the Balkans. During the war in Bosnia, up to 60,000 refugees lived in Slovenia. Many of them settled permanently in Slovenia. This is also shown by the data presented in Table 1.

Table 1: Number of Workers from Former Yugoslavia in Slovenia as of 31 March 2005[4]

COUNTRY OF ORIGIN	NUMBER
Bosnia-Herzegovina	19,562
Croatia	6,705
Macedonia	3,229
Serbia-Montenegro	6,713
TOTAL	36,209

After Slovenia joined the EU, conditions changed drastically. Slovenia has started to close its labour market to citizens of non-EU member states. However, new trends are arising. **Following Slovenia's entry into the EU, new immigration flows can be observed. The greatest number of workers who are EU citizens come from Slovakia**. An analysis of this

4 Source: Employment Service of Slovenia

trend indicates that their number is growing from month to month. In December 2001, only 77 people from Slovakia lived in Slovenia. In March 2005 alone, the number of workers from Slovakia increased by 148. This can be explained by the beginning of the construction season, because the greatest number of workers from Slovakia work in construction. Table 2 shows the citizenship of workers from EU countries in Slovenia.

***Table 2:** Nationality of Workers from EU Countries in Slovenia in 2005*[5]

COUNTRY	NUMBER 31March	NUMBER 30 April	NUMBER 31May
Austria	203	206	238
Czech Republic	105	112	113
France	103	103	107
Germany	138	140	163
Hungary	145	157	157
Italy	178	183	184
Netherlands	76	31	30
Poland	118	107	136
Slovakia	1070	1192	1289
United Kingdom	64	63	68
Other	156	96	99
TOTAL	2298	2390	2584

This article analyses the reasons for migration from Slovakia to Slovenia. Theory indicates that expectation of higher pay is the main reason for migration.

In Slovenia, a great deal is being said and written about the labour force from Slovakia. There is talk of doctors from Slovakia, workers from Slovakia building Slovenia's motorway network, and so on. We have attempted to determine the actual extent of this phenomenon by means of a study. The questions of interest are how many Slovak workers are actually employed in Slovenia, which areas are they employed in and what is the profile of their educational level?

---

5 Source: Employment Service of Slovenia

In order to obtain relevant data on the extent of the migration of the labour force from Slovakia to Slovenia, discussions were held with companies in which these workers might be employed. Inquiries were also made at the agency (the Employment Service of Slovenia) where foreign workers must be registered. In this way, information was obtained on Slovak workers who were employed in Slovenia as of 31 March 2005.

Slovenia and Slovakia are two countries whose names are very similar, and so Slovenia is often confused with Slovakia, especially in America. Both of these countries became EU member states in the EU's last expansion. This article deals with the mobility of workers from Slovakia to Slovenia, and so Table 3 presents some statistical information that is important for understanding the context of this article.

***Table 3:** Some Comparisons between Slovenia and Slovakia*

INFORMATION	Slovenia[6]	Slovakia[7]
Population	2.0 m	5.4 m
Working population	900,000	2.6 m
Number of unemployed	approx. 110,000	approx. 480,000
Level of unemployment	10 to 11%	just over 13%

Based on information from the Chamber of Commerce and Industry of Slovenia, the average gross monthly salary in 2004 in Slovenia was 267,751 SIT.[8] In 2002, Slovenia achieved 69.0% of the average GDP per capita expressed in purchasing power parity for the euro zone, and Slovakia 45.0% (Bregar, 2004, p. 13). According to the Bank of Slovenia,[9] in 2003, Slovenia achieved 69.1% of the average GDP per capita expressed in purchasing power parity for the euro zone, and Slovakia 47.9%. According to data from the European Commission and Eurostat, in 2004, Slovenia was expected to achieve 85.3% of the average GDP per capita in the EU expressed in purchasing power parity, and Slovakia 55.9%.[10]

6 Source: SI-STAT, May 2005, www.stat.si

7 Source: *Indicators On Economics Development*, May 2005, www.statistics.sk

8 Source: www.gzs.si (June 2005).

9 Source: Bank of Slovenia, Government of the Republic of Slovenia: "Programme for entering ERM II and the Euro Region", Ljubljana, November 2003, p. 10.

10 *Source: Main statistical data on candidate countries: Real convergence: Eurostat data from 2001. The data presented are from 2001. Other sources (e.g., Eurostat in its publication "Statistics in Focus – SIF, no. 37/2004" cites different numbers,*

It is therefore possible to conclude that the expectation of a higher salary has an actual basis and is certainly a factor that influences the decision of workers from Slovakia to seek employment in Slovenia. However, this analysis does not take into account the living expenses of migrants to Slovenia.

Table 4: Professional Qualifications of Unemployed Persons in Slovakia[11]

BRANCH (last employment)	Number of unemployed (thousands)
Agriculture, hunting and forestry; Fishing	33.2
Industry	98.0
Construction	33.8
Wholesale and retail sale; repair of vehicles	38.3
Hotels and restaurants	15.8
Transport, storage, post and telecommunications	12.4
Financial intermediation	2.9
Real estate, renting and business activities	8.9
Public administration and defence; compulsory social security	13.0
Education	8.3
Health, social work	14.7
Other community, social and personal activities	35.4
Private households	1.2
Extra-territorial organizations	-
Not identified	64.5
Unemployed without work experience	100.3

A second, and perhaps even more important, reason for migration is the conditions on the labour market. The problem in Slovenia is what is known

and the Economics Institute of the Faculty of Law in Ljubljana yet others. Regardless of the different values presented in the statistics, it is possible to conclude that significant differences remain in purchasing power between Slovenia and Slovakia.

11 *Source:* Indicators On Economics Development, May 2005, www.statistics.sk

as "structural unemployment". This refers to the fact that the number of unemployed persons in certain professions is very high with regard to the number needed. On the other hand, it is very difficult to obtain staff with specific profiles. As an illustration, the largest medical centre in Slovenia has a shortfall of 800 nurses. Similar problems are encountered in construction. According to Slovak statistics,[12] at the end of 2004, there were 33,800 unemployed persons in Slovakia who had last been employed in construction. Some information on the professional qualifications of unemployed persons in Slovakia is given in Table 4.

It is very interesting that around 9000 non-national citizens were officially working in Slovakia in 2002.[13]

Table 5 shows which activities migrants from Slovakia to Slovenia are employed in.

***Table 5:** Activities in which Slovak Workers are Employed in Slovenia, 31 March 2005*[14]

ACTIVITY	NUMBER
COMMUNITY, SOCIAL AND PERSONAL ACTIVITIES	5
CATERING	102
CONSTRUCTION	708
EDUCATION	6
AGRICULTURE, HUNTING, FORESTRY	6
REAL ESTATE, RENTING, BUSINESS ACTIVITIES	6
UNKNOWN ACTIVITY	1
PROCESSING ACTIVITIES	149
TRANSPORT, STORAGE, TELECOMMUNICATIONS	59
SALES, REPAIR OF VEHICLES	25
HEALTH, SOCIAL CARE	3
TOTAL	**1,070**

12 *Source:* Indicators On Economics Development, May 2005, www.statistics.sk
13 Source: COM (2004) 506, final, 15.
14 Source: Employment Service of Slovenia.

It is also interesting to examine Table 6, which shows the level of education of migrants from Slovakia in Slovenia. Most of these are unskilled workers (Level I means that primary school was not completed and Level IV means that professional skills were acquired).

From Tables 5 and 6 it is clear that primarily unskilled workers are working in Slovenia in the field of construction.

Returning to pay, it has already been shown that it is realistically possible to expect a higher income in Slovenia than in Slovakia. The average monthly wage in construction in Slovenia in 2004 amounted to SIT[15] 218,781[16] (i.e., 81.7% of the average wage in Slovenia). In the case of migrants, this is, therefore, lower paid work. Therefore, the question is whether pay is really the most important factor influencing migration. The main motivation for migration is therefore the possibility of employment.

***Table 6:** Slovak Workers in Slovenia as of 31 March 2005 by Level of Education*[17]

LEVEL OF EDUCATION	**NUMBER**
Unknown	12
I (unskilled)	750
II (semi-skilled)	6
III (2-year vocational school)	13
IV (3-year secondary technical school)	250
V (4-year secondary school)	24
VI (vocational college)	5
VII (undergraduate university)	8
VIII (master's degree)	2
TOTAL	**1,070**

15 1€=239,64SIT

16 *Source: www.gzs.si (June 2005)*

17 Source: Employment Service of Slovenia.

5. Influence of New Migration on the Labour Market

The main concern of migration policies of EU member states has always been:

- Satisfying demand on the one hand; and
- Protecting the interests of domestic workers, especially with regard to pay and employment opportunities.

Of course, in the context of this article the following is of interest:

1. The influence migration has on pay in Slovenia.
2. The influence migration has on unemployment among domestic workers in Slovenia.

Analyses of the influence of migration on the pay of domestic workers have already been conducted in the past in Europe. Brucker presents the results of a number of studies. Brucker (2001, p. 115) summarizes the following findings of studies conducted in various countries.

A 10% increase in the number of foreign workers in Germany would cause:

- In the best scenario, a 0.2% fall in wages for the lowest-paid workers;
- In the worst scenario, a 4.1% fall in pay.

Austrian studies have shown that a 10% increase in the number of foreign workers in Austria would cause a –0.5% to +0.5% change in wages. The majority of studies conducted in America show that migration has a negligible impact on the wages of domestic workers.

In Slovenia, no empirical research has yet been conducted on the influence of migration on the pay of domestic workers.

In the case of migration from Slovakia, a relatively small number of people are concerned. On 31 December 2003, there were a total of 111,000 persons employed in construction in Slovenia, and 59,000 in catering and tourism.[18] Because the share of migrants is small (in construction, less than 1% of all employees in the sector), it is possible to conclude that the

18 *Source: SI-STAT, May 2005, www.stat.si*

influence of migrants on wages and employment opportunities for domestic workers is also small.

6. Conclusion

The entry of Slovenia into the EU very likely marks the beginning of the process of gradually replacing the labour force that in past decades came from other former Yugoslav republics. The question is how will it be possible to make up this loss overall? Currently, the greatest number of new workers come from Slovakia. Although much is being said about this migration in Slovenia, no dramatic trends are discernable.

It is only possible to conclude that migration from Slovakia has actually begun. The trend of migration from Slovakia will certainly continue in the future and, at least for construction workers, will increase. Of course, the extent of migration from Slovakia to Slovenia is limited (i) by the number of unemployed persons in Slovakia and (ii) by the reduction in differences in wages in the two countries. In the future, the greatest number of migrants will continue to be employed in construction. This forecast is based on the following facts:

The value of work performed in construction in 2003 in Slovenia amounted to SIT 342 billion (€1,425,000). The level of growth in construction in 2003/4 was 2.8%. In the period 1995–2003, the number of companies active in construction in Slovenia increased by 26.1%. This trend will continue in the next few years because €4.6 billion is planned for the construction of new motorways alone.[19] In the coming years, the construction of a second rail line on a portion of the Koper–Ljubljana railway is also expected, at an estimated value of €200 million. Funds in the national housing savings plan will also become available. This will represent new opportunities for the employment of migrants.

It is also expected that, in the future, a large number of Slovak workers in the areas of tourism and catering will migrate to Slovenia. The level of growth in catering and tourism in Slovenia in the period 2003/4 was 4.5%.

19 Source: Resolution on the National Programme for Motorway Construction in the Republic of Slovenia, *Official Gazette of the Republic of Slovenia* 50/2004, p. 6715.

The case of workers in catering and tourism will also represent the replacement of workers from other countries of the former Yugoslavia. This will also involve lower- paying jobs.

It is surprising that much is also being said in Slovenia about doctors and nurses from Slovakia. So far, empirical studies have not observed this kind of migration. However, the need for these kinds of workers in Slovenia is great. An inflow of healthcare workers can also be expected in the future in view of this need. The cultural and linguistic barriers between Slovenia and Slovakia are relatively small. Healthcare personnel will be motivated to come to Slovenia by the relatively high salaries paid in healthcare. The average monthly salary in that sector in 2004 amounted to SIT 312,423 (i.e., 116.7% of the average salary in Slovenia).[20] The salaries of doctors in Slovenia are quite high in particular.

Bibliography and References

Banka Slovenije, Vlada Republike Slovenije (2003) Program vstopa v ERM II in Evro območje. (Bank of Slovenia, Slovenian Government (2003) Masterplan for Introduction of the Euro) Ljubljana.

Bregar, L., (2004) Mednarodne in časovne primerjave bruto domačega proizvoda v paritetah kupne moči: končno poročilo (Cross-Country comparisons of gross Domestic Product and Specific Price Indices). Faculty of Economics. Ljubljana.

Brucker, H., (2001) Managing Migration in the European Welfare State: Boeri, T. (2002) Immigration Policy and the Welfare System. Oxford University Press. London.

Commission of the European Communities (2004) First Annual report on Migration and Integration. Brussels, 16.07.2004 (COM (2004) 508 final).

Commission of the European Communities (2001) New European Labour Markets, Open to All, with Access for All. Brussels, 28.02.2001 (COM (2001)116 final)

Eurostat (2004) Statistics in Focus. No. 37/2004. Eurostat. Brussels.

Florjančič, J., Ferjan, M., Bernik, M., (1999) Planiranje in razvoj kadrov (Human Resources Management). Moderna Organizacija. Kranj.

20 *Source, www.gzs.si (June 2005).*

Górny, A., Kępińska E., (2004) Mixed marriages in migration from the Ukraine to Poland. Journal of Ethnic and Migration Studies. 30 (2), 353-372.

Indicators On Economics Development. May 2005. www.statistics.sk.

International Organization for Migration (2005): World Migration 2005: Costs and Benefits of International Migration. International Organization for Migration. Wien.

OECD (2005): Monitoring of Migration Movements and Policies. OECD. Paris. (http://www.oecd.org/document/28/0,2340,en_2649_34709_34606364_1_1_1_1,00.html).

Podlage za izračun stroškov dela (The basis for count up the salaries). Jun. 2005. www.gzs.si.

Remennick, L. (2003) Career continuity among immigrant professionals: Russian engineers in Israel. Journal of Ethnic and Migration Studies, Vol. 29 (4), 701-721.

Resolucija o Nacionalnem programu izgradnje avtocest v Republiki Sloveniji, Uradni list Republike Slovenije (The National programme of building main roads in Republic of Slovenia) 50/2004, p. 6715.

SI-STAT. May 2005. www.surs.si.

Statistični urad Republike Slovenije (2004) Slovenija v številkah. Statistični urad Republike Slovenije (Statistical Yearbook. Statistical Office of the Republic of Slovenia). Ljubljana.

Winter-Zlatković J. (2004) Current Migration Movements in Europe. Migracijske i etnicke teme, 20 (2-3), 161-170.

About the Authors

Marko Ferjan is an associate professor at the University of Maribor, Faculty of Organizational Sciences. His research is in the area of Human Resource Management. He has authored five books and a number of scholarly articles, and he also serves as co-editor of the academic journal Organizacija.

Eva Jereb is an associate professor in the Department of Education–Personnel and Information Science at the University of Maribor, Faculty of Organizational Sciences. She is currently researching personnel expert systems, education and distance education (particularly e-learning and e-examination), office automation and the phenomenon of telework.

Entrepreneurship and Regional Economic Development

Vida Kampuš Trop

vida.kampus-trop@fov.uni-mb.si

Abstract

Regional economic development is subject to the influence of a number of different factors. In the following article, our focus is limited to those related to company development. Numerous studies around the world have proven that, in recent times, the level of economic development of a given country or region can be attributed primarily to the level of entrepreneurship it has achieved.

Regions with a higher level of entrepreneurship, as a rule, also enjoy a higher degree of economic success. For this reason, our initial focus in the article is on the effect of entrepreneurship on regional economic development, in which we have limited ourselves mainly to the small business sector. This is followed by a presentation of the main factors that affect the various levels of development of entrepreneurship within given regions and resultantly also regional economic development. The existing spatial unevenness of regional economic development is further exacerbated by the cumulative relations between the economically more developed and less developed regions. More light is shed on this in the article using the theories of cumulative causation and core-periphery relationships in economic development. Finally, the article presents the results of an applicative study which confirm the conclusions reached based on the theoretical findings of the depicted research on Slovene economic practices.

Keywords: economic development, factors, regional economic development, the theory of cumulative causation, small businesses, the core-periphery theory.

1. Introduction

One of the most important factors of economic development in the 21st century is entrepreneurship. Although implementation of an appropriate macroeconomic policy is one of the preconditions for a successful economy, the latter alone is not sufficient for the achievement of a high level of economic growth. In this day and age, in which the majority of medium and highly developed countries are conducting very similar macroeconomic policies, all of which more or less ensure macroeconomic stability, it is the level of development of entrepreneurship which separates the countries and regions with rapid economic growth from those with a slower growth rate. The results of regional differences in the founding and growth of companies can therefore cause either the preservation or even the deepening of disparities in the levels of economic development of these regions.

The aim of this article is to first present an overview of the effect of entrepreneurship on regional economic development, after which we shall focus on the various factors which might offer an explanation as to the cause of regional differences in entrepreneurship development and the resultant variances in regional economic development. In order to better understand the effects of the cumulative relationships between economically more and less developed regions, which deepen inter-regional disparities, an additional group of explanatory factors of regional economic development was derived from the cumulative causation and core-periphery theory of economic development. Some of the presented findings which were arrived at on the basis of an analysis of numerous theoretical and practical studies conducted around the world were also verified by the applicative research conducted by the author. For this purpose, large amounts of data from the appropriate sources on the characteristics of Slovenian regions and the businesses based in them were accumulated. The results of the statistical analysis of these data led us to a number of interesting conclusions, which are presented in the fifth chapter of this article.

2. The Effect of Entrepreneurship on Regional Economic Development

An analysis of various researches conducted in the entire world's countries with highly developed entrepreneurship has shown the latter to be of key importance for regional and national economic development (see Kampuš Trop, 2000 p. 21ff). The decisive effect of modern entrepreneurship within small and medium enterprises (SMEs) and corporations is evident from the many contributions it makes towards economic development. Further on in the article, our analysis in this area will be limited to the way in which SMEs contribute towards the economic growth of their surroundings.

2.1 The Contribution of Entrepreneurship towards Job Creation

Small business was first regarded as a key factor in job creation soon after the publication of the Birch Report (Birch, 1979 in Kampuš Trop, 2003a, p. 21). In his publication of the results of extensive research conducted on American companies and their employment policies from 1969 to 1976, Birch showed that companies with less than 100 employees accounted for 81% of all net job creation in the USA, while 66% of all net job creation was attributable to companies with less than 20 employees. Later studies conducted in the USA (US Small Business Administration, 1992 in Kampuš Trop, 2003a, p.21; Birch, 1993, p. 93; Davis et al., 1996, p. 118) and the European Union (Commission of the European Communities, 1987 in Kampuš Trop, 2003a, p. 21; Smallbone, 1995 in Kampuš Trop, 2000, p. 24; Drnovšek, 2000, p. 13) also confirmed that the contribution of SMEs towards net job creation was disproportionately large. The above research was conducted over various time spans under normal and recession conditions.

In Slovenia, Vahčič et al. (1998, p. 66) were the first authors who pointed to the meaning of the small business sector as the generator of new jobs in the economic restructuring processes resulting in mass lay-offs in bigger enterprises. These were followed by Kampuš Trop, who focused her research (2000, 2003a, 2005, p. 34ff) on the role of small businesses in mitigating the unemployment issue resulting from lay-offs by big and medium-sized enterprises, and thereby contributing to a net increase in the (national) employment rate.

Research conducted throughout the world has shown that there is considerable disparity from region to region with regard to the contributions of new SMEs to job creation. Since net job creation is generally considered to be one of the indicators of economic growth, we can conclude that regions capable of generating more small and medium enterprises – particularly rapid growth firms – will enjoy greater and more accelerated economic development than the regions in which such entrepreneurial activities are less pronounced.

2.2 The Contribution of Entrepreneurship towards Innovation

Innovation is an important factor in local, regional and national economies, as the opportunities it offers for gaining the competitive edge are potentially more long-term than those based solely on pricing (Porter, 1990 in Kampuš Trop, 2000, p. 24). As entrepreneurship and innovation are already by definition indivisibly interconnected, it often holds true for small companies that they are a source of innovation on all levels, as they are more flexible, more dynamic and also more sensitive to changing demand than larger companies. However, amongst the founders of small enterprises one must differentiate between the inventive and those who merely more or less rapidly and to varying degrees adopt the novelties created by others. Naturally, it is the innovative entrepreneurs who contribute the most towards economic development. In this area, the differences between individual companies can be vast, even in the most developed economies. On the one hand, the most dynamic companies with the highest level of technological development can be likened to the driving force behind a regional economy, as seen in examples such as Cambridge, or Boston (Storey and Johnson, 1987 in Kampuš Trop, 2000, p. 26). On the other hand, there are still many regions throughout the world with large numbers of conservatively managed small businesses working in niches within the traditional fields of production which are almost untouched by technological change and which pay little attention to innovation (Smallbone, 1995 in Kampuš Trop, 2000, p. 25).

A classic example of a high level of technological development is the district of Santa Clara in California, known as Silicon Valley, home to the development of world famous semiconductors and the computing industry. A large part of this development was stimulated by entrepreneurship and the founding of new companies in the classic Schumpeter sense. The main characteristic of the economic development in Silicon Valley was the intent of individuals to change their status from that of employee to small business founder. This process is known as "technological spin-off" and has been well researched and documented (Larsen and Rogers, 1984 in Kampuš Trop, 2000, p. 25).

In addition to innovation in the field of technology, all other forms of innovation also play an important role in maintaining the competitive advantage of a company. As the number of companies with prospects of being truly technologically innovative is rather small, the more crucial question for the majority of small enterprises is what provides them with a fundamental advantage over the competition. Here, Porter puts forward a hierarchy of the sources of competitive advantages based on their duration. The advantages of more simple orders, for example, are the low cost of labour and materials; however such products can easily be imitated by the competition, whereas complex orders are more difficult to copy. The examples given also include differentiation between products based on the uniqueness of the products and services, and the varying types of buyer-seller relationships in which the seller's interests are protected by the potential losses incurred by the buyers in the event that they decide to take their custom elsewhere (Porter, 1990 in Kampuš Trop, 2000, p. 26). This encompasses a whole range of competitive advantages for the development of which small (and medium) enterprises are well equipped, as they offer the possibility to use the flexibility provided by their small size to their advantage and to the advantage of their customers. To this end, successful companies utilize successful and innovative product portfolio management (focused on the development of new products or services) in conjunction with the strategic differentiation of the company in relation to the offer of the competition. This makes them even more indispensable to their buyers, and is further supported by efforts to increase productivity. Seen in this light, every innovation is essential if it can lead to improvements in products and services, development of the technological process, the discovery of new business techniques or assist in the finding of a new market or a new form of the company's offer, organization, leadership and management.

From the above reasoning, one can also deduce that all forms of innovation – not only those based on the latest scientific breakthroughs - are equally important for regional development. After all, every form of innovation increases the regional capacity for exports and/or creating import substitutes. In the same way, companies that acquire highly-developed technological processes and produce high-tech products are important for regional development, even though they may not be innovative in themselves (Sweeney, 1987 in Kampuš Trop, 2000, p. 26). This is because entrepreneurship is not only associated with innovation, but also with the use of innovations discovered by others. Therefore, even the non-innovative use of the most recent technologies is an important factor contributing towards regional discrepancies, as a considerable number of studies have suggested that companies founded on the basis of new technologies or products and/or various other forms of innovations and their use, have a far greater growth quotient over a longer time span (Storey et al, 1987; De Melto et al, 1980; Birly, 1986; Rothweel, Zegveld, 1982, all quoted in Kampuš Trop, 2000, p. 26ff; Kirchhoff, 1994, p. 432ff).

In order to gain a better understanding of the contribution of entrepreneurship to regional economic growth, one must particularly mention also Kirchoff's findings. Kirchoff (1994, p. 456) concludes that, in a dynamic capitalist economy, entrepreneurs penetrate existing markets with the help of innovations. Therefore, it is logical to expect that there will be a direct correlation between the number of innovations created by a company and its economic growth.[1]

In any case, the above conclusions have guided us to the hypothesis that it is those regions capable of producing more companies based on innovation and/or new technologies which will in future generate a greater and more rapidly increasing income - primarily in the field of exports - and create more new jobs, thus achieving greater and more rapid economic development. Oakey emphasises that even one rapidly expanding, technologically highly-developed company can have a significant effect on the employment prospects of a region, and therefore proposes that more active assistance be given to such companies throughout the entire innovative cycle from the initial research and development programme, to production and all the way to the marketing of the final product (Oakey, 1991, p. 30ff).

1 For more details on the results of Kirchoff's research in this area, see Kampuš Trop, 2000, p. 27f.

2.3 Contribution towards Creating Regional Income from Exports and/or Import Substitutes

One of the most important factors affecting the long-term growth possibilities of a region or any level of the economy is the ability of its enterprises to penetrate foreign markets. Sales abroad are an important mechanism for creating revenues, as foreign exports have a conducive effect on economic growth due to a positive multiplier (Kampuš Trop, 2000, p. 28). Exports of small enterprises are becoming increasingly important for a number of reasons:

1. Small enterprises must export in order to achieve rapid growth, as since, if an enterprise is too dependent on the local, regional or even national market, it is not only subject to the fluctuations of domestic economic conditions, but its growth is also constrained by the small local market.
2. The importance of the exports of small enterprises for a region is evident also in the fact that a predominant orientation of new small businesses onto the domestic, regional market results only in transfer effects within the regional economy. This decreases the effect of public expenditure intended for the accelerated creation of new jobs within the small business sector (Hart et al, 1993 in Hanvey et al., 1994, p. 35ff). For this reason, if the aim is to create a growing and competitive regional economy, and not just the game of zero effect of relocating the production factors within the locality, support should be given from public funds to small enterprises with export potential.
3. The introduction of the unified European market brings with it changes in the market structure within regions and sectors. Not only are companies that are not competitive incapable of taking advantage of export market opportunities, but they are also subject to incursions by more aggressive foreign companies into their local market (Foley and Griffiths, 1992, p. 376). Thus, the export strategies of small enterprises not only affect their growth, but in the aggregate also affect the extent of advantages or losses gained by a region from its inclusion in the unified European market or in any other trade grouping. Regions that are more export-oriented are more likely to gain from the effects of the unified European market (Hanvey et al., 1994, p. 38).
4. The data from several studies indicates that employment and sales levels grow more rapidly in exporting small enterprises than in those which sell only on the domestic market. Hanvey found in his study

of Irish companies that the growth level of employment in the period 1989-1992 was 7% in the exporting small enterprises and only 1% in the non-exporting small enterprises, while sales growth had increased by 13% in the exporting small enterprises and by 10% in the non-exporting ones (Hanvey et al., 1994, p. 38).

5. Small companies have a greater potential for export growth than large ones. Size increase in small companies is connected with greater increases in their exports to a far higher degree than similar size increases are connected with company growth in the larger enterprises. (Hanvey et al., 1994, p. 48).

The greatest contributions towards exports are made by high-growth small enterprises, the so-called gazelles, which must inevitably begin exporting and penetrating world markets, or face decline and sooner or later fold.

Case studies from environments where dynamic entrepreneurship is most highly developed only further emphasize the fact that entrepreneurs and those who shape economic policy are only too aware of the manifold importance of exports to small enterprises. In 1991, around 56% of all export companies in the USA had less than 50 employees, while a total of 70% of the exporters had less than 100 employees. In that year also, more than a half of all total USA exports were realised by small enterprises (Birch, 1993, p. 17). This is indicative of a great shift in the structure of enterprises in the USA, in that small companies are becoming multinational already in the early phases of their development.

In the countries of Europe, including those with more highly developed entrepreneurship, small enterprises are in general still orientated towards the domestic market. This is seen as one of the greatest problems of their export strategy, which is based on the growth of domestic newly-founded small businesses.

If Birch's finding that an export capacity is absolutely imperative for the long-term success of gazelles in the USA is correct, then this is all the more an imperative for Slovenia's enterprises, where we have a small and almost saturated domestic market, a relatively high level of unemployment and are facing the imminent direct clash with the competition within the framework of the European Union.

Small enterprises can also supplement regional revenues by substituting imports, i.e. by finding substitutes for goods and services that were formerly imported. However, in order to be able to respond to this challenge, small enterprises must know what is being imported and by whom. Owing to the fact that small enterprises often lack the funds necessary for conducting such market research, public institutions should come to the rescue in such cases as a connecting link between the importers and potential small suppliers.

The size of the contribution of small enterprises to the revenues of a region from exports and/or import substitution will therefore depend on a number of different factors. The most important of these is how many high-growth enterprises exist within a given region, which again depends on the quality of the entrepreneurs (their level of education, experience in company management and implementing strategies of product innovation as well as the market information, i.e. market research they possess). We can therefore conclude that the regions with the better entrepreneurs, better quality and most appropriate government assistance and sector structure, where the greatest amount of new technology is present, will be most capable of achieving greater exports and thus also greater economic development.

2.4 Contribution towards the Building of a Broader Regional Economic Structure

The next way in which small enterprises can contribute towards local and regional economic development is by the extent to which they complement other companies, and through their relations with their suppliers and customers. Small enterprises can decrease some of the disadvantages related to their limited size by means of different forms of cooperation between companies such as vertical cooperation in the production chain, lateral cooperation (where competitors can share joint services), cooperation in the production of complementary products, or through cooperational relations. It has been found that the presence of company agglomeration is a joint characteristic that some of the most successful regional economies have in common (Smallbone, 1995, p. 15). This also includes both suppliers and buyers (customers) which, in addition to achieving external economy of scale also encompasses dynamic competitiveness and an appropriately trained workforce.

One of the roles that small enterprises can play in such agglomerations is the **role of supplier to large companies, by means of which they also contribute towards the external competitiveness of these companies.** Numerous small enterprises function as specialized suppliers for large companies. These enterprises supply parts, smaller units for assembly, components or services, which they often produce at lower costs than the expenses of the larger companies would be, were they to produce them themselves. In this respect, small companies see to the needs of an important part of the infrastructure, on which the competitiveness of the regional economy depends.

The existence of a base of small enterprises/suppliers can also be an important factor for attracting international mobile subsidiary plants of large companies in the technologically advanced sectors, such as the electronics sector, to a region. This can also be an important means of regional promotion (Smallbone, 1995, p. 15). At this point, we feel it is appropriate to point out that caution must be taken when relying on the plants of large foreign companies (Kampuš Trop V., 2006, p. 1372ff). However, whatever the case may be, in order to fulfil this purpose, small enterprises must first achieve the very high levels of quality expected of them in order to satisfy the demanding customers of the large companies.

The effectiveness of the local supply system and the capacity of small enterprises to develop ties with large enterprises within a region does not only have an effect on the external competitiveness of a region, but also increases the growth factors of the leading companies within a region. This means that small businesses not only facilitate, but also supplement internal investment strategies and in this way **function as a channel for effects conducive to the expansion of those companies that invest in the local economic base of a given region.**

In some parts of Europe, entire industrial districts developed through the establishment of small businesses networks. Brusco (1986, p. 184) defines an industrial district as a network of small businesses, which function as cooperators in every production phase. What makes the difference between an industrial district and other groups of small businesses is the high level of innovation and the readiness to apply new technologies. "Parent" companies define their needs and then leave it to the cooperators to satisfy them in innovative ways. An industrial district develops when the economy changes, so that the demand for highly differentiated products exceeds the

demand for items of mass production; and small businesses are more capable of realizing limited series production than larger ones.
These industrial districts have developed to a large extent in the regions of northern Italy such as Venezia, Emilia Romagna, Tuscany, Umbria and Marche. These regions, referred to as the "third Italy" by Brusco (1986, p. 184ff), are of great economic importance, as they generate correspondingly high revenues and contribute significantly to Italy's export capacity. Similarly, such industrial districts also exist in the United Kingdom, a well-known example being the Birmingham Gun Quarter (Barkham, 1989, p. 57).

The above findings lead us to the premise that small businesses can contribute towards the introduction of changes and the construction of a more appropriate broader regional economic structure, and resultantly also towards accelerated economic growth. It has been found that regional economies are more successful as a result of company agglomeration, as this facilitates:

- The development of new activities, particularly in the area of introducing new services;
- Supplementing the offers of larger companies;
- The production of parts and services supply for large companies and subsequently increased external competitiveness of these enterprises;
- Interconnecting small companies and chains of small companies with other large companies, for the purpose of joint market entry and development. To this end, companies form clusters, and nowadays ever more increasingly technological platforms.

2.5 Contribution towards Sowing the Seeds for the Growth of Large Companies

The founding of small enterprises means the entry of new entrepreneurs and a foundation from which medium and large enterprises can grow. However, the empirical results of longitudinal studies conducted on newly established enterprises show that very few new companies actually develop into large ones. One of the studies, for example, showed that the probability of a new small business having 100 or more employees within 10 years of its founding is from 0.5% to 0.75% (Storey et al, 1987 in Kampuš Trop, 2000, p. 34). This is due to the fact that approximately 40% of all new companies cease operating within the first three years after their founding, and because a large number of companies that survive remain small. Another common reason is because they do not wish to expand their operations (Smallbone, 1995 in Kampuš Trop, 2003a, p. 22).

Although they are successful, fast-growing, dynamic companies account for a very small percentage of all companies. These "high-flying" companies, as Smallbone (1995, p. 15) refers to them, are most important of all for the economy. One or two such successful small businesses alone, which expand into large ones through their growth process, can function as supports, role-models, incubators or motors of the regional economy, as their success carries others in its wake. Some emulate them, others provide them as cooperators with the supplies they need, while yet others still provide for their needs in various ways. All this sooner or later leads to a larger or smaller network of new small or medium enterprises forming around the large company, all of which gives rise to new initiatives and significantly contributes towards the development of the region. Although the optimal size structure for such a significant effect on the economy varies depending on the specific characteristics of a given economic environment (sector structures, the size of the domestic market, the degree to which an economy is open to the world market, the economy's levels of development), it depends above all on the technological level of development. However, the general opinion prevails that the most successful market structures are found in those countries with the most effective industrial production, i.e. in the developed countries of the West. In these countries, it has become evident that it is most conducive to economic growth to have a number of very strong and internationally successful large companies, surrounded by a host of small and medium enterprises.

From the above, one may conclude that regions striving to achieve more rapid economic development must ensure that the level of newly founded enterprises remains high and that these enterprises are of good quality, as the seeds and growth potential for large companies are inherent in only a very small number of nascent enterprises.

3. Factors of Entrepreneurial Development

There are numerous different reasons as to why the degree of development of entrepreneurship and subsequently also the level of economic development varies from region to region.

Based on the understanding of the subject matter in the literature pertaining to often cited structural and socio-cultural theories as well as theories on the various agents of development within the environment (Kampuš Trop, 2003a, p. 153), one could list the following as important factors of entrepreneurial development:

1. The sectoral structure of the regional economy
The degree to which a company asserts itself is high in those sectors/activities where the profits are large and the obstacles to entry small. Based on the above findings, one could hypothesize that in the regions where sectors/industries with greater obstacles to entry predominate, the level of founding new companies will be low. Sectors with great obstacles to entry show no tendencies towards the founding of new spin-off companies. This does not mean that there will be no entries into these sectors/industries, but that entries will not be effected by independent entrepreneurs, i.e. small businesses. The situation will be even worse in those industries where, in addition to the obstacles to entry, demand is stagnant or decreasing. On the contrary, however, wherever the demand for products is high and the obstacles to entry are low, one can expect a high level of spin-off enterprises within the sector.[2]

2. The size-structure of the regional companies
The levels of establishing new companies are high in regions where a high percentage of the population is employed in small businesses and low in areas where the working population is to a great extent employed in large companies. There are numerous studies that prove that small businesses generate new companies as spin-offs to a far greater extent than large companies.[3]

3. The occupational structure of the regional population
The levels of establishing new companies are higher in those areas where a

2 For more details on the subject, see the scientific monographic publication by Kampuš Trop, 2003a, p. 154ff.

3 For more detailed research results, see Kampuš Trop, 2003a, p. 158ff.

higher percentage of the region's technological, managerial and other professional employees are located, with regard to the overall occupational structure of the population.[4]

4. The economic strength of the region and its population

The majority of entrepreneurs found their companies very close to the place where they were formerly employed, and therefore the local economic conditions are regarded as important by the majority of potential founders when deciding whether to establish their company or not. An important factor of influence here is above all the level of market demand for intermediate and end products.[5]

5. Research and development activity within the region

Relatively easy access to technological, market, scientific and research and other data has an important influence on the quality and quantity of entrepreneurial activities. In this respect, the research and development institutes in both the private and public sectors are particularly important for the founding of high-tech companies. A greater concentration of research and development within a region means that a proportionately larger amount of its population has access to information on recent findings in the fields of science and technology and other areas than in other regions, and subsequently also greater possibilities for the growth of their enterprises, leading to a greater economic development of the region.[6]

6. The number of information-processing units, including the number of leading staff of the large companies in the region.

Such units or services employ highly qualified experts and managers responsible for the compilation, generation, promulgation and interpretation of various data which are also of strategic importance to small business entrepreneurs. Subsequently, a larger concentration of information-processing units within a region also means easier access to important information for the founding and growth of new companies.[7]

7. Workforce quality and availability

Regions in which newly founded small businesses can more easily obtain

4 For a more detailed explanation of the effects of this factor and research results explaining the above conclusion, see Kampuš Trop, 2003a, p. 162ff.

5 Ibidem, p. 167ff.

6 The effects of this factor are explained in greater detail in the Slovenian case by Kampuš Trop, 2003a, p. 178ff.

7 Ibidem, p. 184ff.

managerial, technical and other professional staff with the appropriate schooling and training have far greater chances of founding high-growth, innovative companies. Important factors influencing this are the education structure, occupational structure and other aspects of the structure of the region's workforce.[8]

8. Availability of financial and other resources in the region
Regions more capable of offering the necessary resources than others significantly reduce the decline of new enterprises and even increase the level of new companies. From this, we can also deduce that a region with a greater income per capita or greater wealth (taking into account its appropriate or equal distribution) and/or financial institutions which are more likely to be prepared to offer more convenient loans or invest in small businesses, and/or entrepreneurs who are more capable of acquiring loans and high-risk capital, will most likely record higher levels of new companies being established as compared to other regions.[9]

In addition to the above-mentioned factors, the results of various different studies also suggest that the following elements also have a significant influence on the development of entrepreneurship:

9. Urbanization / agglomeration. Urban regions can have a significant advantage as incubators for new companies owing to the direct proximity of both potential customers as well as suppliers. Another characteristic of urban regions is a high population density and subsequently also a high number of potential entrepreneurs (Reynolds et al., 1994, p. 446).

10. The local, i.e. regional, political orientation. It is probable that the predominant political relations within a region can have an effect on the founding of new companies, as differing political parties have different attitudes towards entrepreneurship (Reynolds et al, 1994, p. 446f)

11. Government support programmes. Subventions to newly founded enterprises, subventions, loans and guarantees from the regional development funds, and other public programmes for the stimulation, founding and restructuring of existing enterprises (Spilling, 1996, p. 237, 240f).

---

8 For more on the dilemmas related to the effects of this factor, see Kampuš Trop, 2003a, p. 186ff.

9 For more on the effects of this factor, see Kampuš Trop, 2003, p. 171ff.

12. The number and characteristics of already existing entrepreneurs and their socio-cultural backgrounds, motivation, education, know-how and experience, how informed they are, their capabilities and other personal characteristics that separate the successful from the less successful entrepreneurs. (Kampuš Trop, 2002, p. 41ff; 2003b, p. 75).

13. Other important factors affecting regional environments: Institutional system-related conditions of society, the entrepreneurial culture, the entrepreneurial support environment and the market conditions. (Kampuš Trop, 2007, p. 693; 2005, p. 695ff; 2004, p. 258; 2001, p. 196)

In addition to the above-listed factors of entrepreneurial development, other explanations can also possibly be found for the unequal economic development of regions. Amongst these, one must certainly count the elements from the model of cumulative causes of economic development and the mechanisms of functioning derived from the theory of core-periphery relations. The essence of these is presented in the following chapter.

4. The Model of Cumulative Causation and Core-Periphery Relationships in Economic Development

4.1 The Main Elements of the Model of Cumulative Causation and Core-Periphery Relationships in Economic Development

In essence, the core-periphery[10] theory states that economic development once triggered at a particular point, is a cumulative and locationally constrained process. Determining the initial trigger is often very difficult but once it occurs, the mechanisms by which further development is engineered are well documented. The **theory of cumulative causes of economic development** includes the following five elements:

10 The original development of "core-periphery" theory is due to Myrdal (1957) and Hirschman (1958) but much of the discussion is drawn from text book expositions in Lloyd and Dicken (1977) and Richardson (1979), all quoted in Barkham, 1989, p. 140ff.

1. The multiplier. From multiplier theory it is possible to deduce that any initial trigger based on exports from a point will create additional income and employment as export revenues are spent in the locality. This in turn generates a further round of spending and activity. Areas with the lowest leakages (the smallest outflow of incomes) and the greatest tendency towards spending are most sensitive to the initial triggering of the spiral of development.

2. The location of propulsive industries. The presence of a propulsive industry in a region also leads to cumulative development. The most important industries in this respect will be large, fast growing, innovative and have high intensity input/output links. Such industries tend to act as poles of growth and tend to attract other supplemental (ancillary) industries.

3. Economies of scale. Economies of scale, both internal and external to the firm, act to cause industrial agglomeration. External economies arise when firms in the same industry can be supplied more cheaply when clustered together, due to large production runs and economies of scale in input suppliers. Investment in ancillary industries means that economies external to the firms become internal to the region. Internal economies of scale refer to the fact that, in many manufacturing sectors, the minimum efficient scale is very large and so viability often requires sustained growth in a particular location.

4. Innovations. Innovations are associated with successful expanding economies and tend to be centralized in growing metropolitan centres (Barkham, 1989, p. 141). Regions can only continue to grow to the extent that they innovate and capture new markets. A further addition to the cumulative spiral is the tendency for manufacturing industry to require large service inputs.

5. Locational inertia due to uncertainty. Cumulative development has its own inertia in that entrepreneurs operating in an environment of great uncertainty will tend to invest where they have already seen other successful investments even if equivalent profits could be earned elsewhere.

4.2 The Fundamental Findings of the Core-Periphery Theory

The core-periphery theory is an elaboration of the cumulative causation model of economic development and stands in stark contrast to that of the neoclassical school. The latter suggests that, from any given centre of economic growth, spread effects will ensure that this development is also transmitted to other regions. Yet the existence of long-term regional disparities with regard to income and unemployment in different countries as well as in Slovenia indicates that the self-equalizing mechanism does not work (Kampuš Trop, 2006, p. 1371). An explanation for this can be found in the conclusions of the core-periphery theory.

A generalized application of the findings of the core-periphery theory of development in spatial economy suggests, when applied on a national scale, that growth will strongly reinforce one region at the expense of all others. The fundamental findings of the core-periphery theory are derived from the polarizing mechanisms of the "spread" effect. **Backwash or polarizing mechanisms mean that resources flow to the centre to accelerate growth while spread mechanisms diffuse economic development, from the centre (most developed regions) also into the periphery. According to this theory, The problem arises because, in terms of the theory, polarizing effects dominate the spread effects, which leads to the growth of the centre at the expense of the periphery.** It is hypothesized that spread effects tend to have their strongest impact close to **the core** rather than in the periphery.

The most significant **effects of backwash** are the outflow of capital, profits and capable entrepreneurs from the periphery into the core. The high level of skill and education in the economically most developed region has two results. Firstly, the high educational and occupational structure of the employees makes this area more attractive to enterprises locating production units requiring skilled and technical workers. This reinforces the tendency for the labour force to be upgraded and is a powerful agglomeration force. Secondly, of course, a more highly developed educational and political structure ensures that the workforce contains a higher proportion of highly motivated and skilled workers, precisely the kind that make the most successful entrepreneurs.

Spread effects include the increased demand for raw materials and basic products on the periphery, the outmovement of population from the metropolitan core and the movement of capital to the periphery to take advantage of lower peripheral labour costs. Although multiplant enterprises are important channels of growth, they can also hinder an area's development impulses. However, as has been seen, the ability of the system to spread economic growth is somewhat limited, as the demand for basic products and raw materials is also limited. Population movements away from the core occur over very short distances to the edges of the large metropolitan areas. The flow of capital via multiplant companies tends to reinforce the spatial division of labour by introducing low-skill fabricating units to the peripheral regions. In any case, the spatial tendencies of large multiplant enterprises have a significant impact on the socio-economic structure of a region. Their locational orientations are also mirrored in the placement of their research and development functions, which are in general situated in the more developed core area close to the headquarters of the company, due to the need for high-level information interchange and to ensure the availability of a large pool of scientific staff. Nor are there backward linkages for service inputs because these tend to be supplied by or to the head office in the core region. The effect of the locations of the subsidiary factories on the entrepreneurial potential of the peripheral regions can therefore be minimal. Multinational companies and enterprises with several factories can, by locating their operational manufacturing units in less developed regions with cheaper labour forces, become an important element for both preserving the high level of skill in the economically most highly developed regions and maintaining the dominance of the centre over the periphery (Kampuš Trop, 2006, p. 1374).[11]

5. Results of the Applicative Research

In our applicative study, which encompassed the whole of Slovenia, some of the above-mentioned theoretical findings were put to the test. For this purpose, large amounts of data on the characteristics of Slovenia's regions and their enterprises were compiled from primary sources. The results of the statistical analysis of these data led us to the following conclusions:

[1] There is significant variance amongst Slovenia's regions according to the level of economic development. The most highly developed region is the heartland region, i.e. Slovenia's central region, while the Pomurska region is the least developed.

[11] For more on the functioning of the core-periphery mechanism and the possible effects of multinational enterprises and companies with numerous out-sourced factories in this case, see Kampuš Trop, 2006, p. 1371ff.

[2] There was a noticeable connection between the level of development of entrepreneurship and the economic development of each region. Entrepreneurship was most highly developed in Slovenia's central region and least developed in the Pomurska region.

[3] Similarly, the statistical analysis of the compiled data indicated that there was a significant connection between the level of new companies being founded in the Slovenian regions and the following explanatory factors:

1. The sector structure of the regional economy
2. The size structure of the enterprises in a given region
3. The occupational structure of the regional population
4. The economic strength of the regional population
5. The economic strength of the region
6. The research and development activities within the region
7. The number of information-processing units, including the number of leading staff of the large enterprises within the region
8. The education structure of the employees in the region
9. The average number of years of schooling of the employees in the region

[4] The results of our study indicated that Slovenia's central region had the best possibilities for the maintenance and future increase of its current growth level and for the development of entrepreneurship both from the standpoint of the sector and size structures of its enterprises, as well as from the standpoint of the other above-listed explanatory factors (from points 3 to 9) and the resources of the regional environment (markets, finances, information, staff).

[5] Research was also conducted, leading to the conclusion that high-growth companies were founded by entrepreneurs with certain characteristics. Statistically significant amongst these were: motivation for growth, founding the enterprise with a view to creating wealth (and not to ensure survival and/or the improvement of their standard of living or to realize inventiveness), prior experience in positions of management, marketing, or other professional functions and a substantial knowledge of the markets. The results of our study also indicated that the number of entrepreneurs with such characteristics is significantly higher in Slovenia's central region than in the other less developed regions of the country.

[6] The differences between Slovenia's central region and the other regions in the country, particularly the less developed ones, have

increased over the years – with regard to both their entrepreneurial and economic levels of development. (Kampuš Trop, 2003, p. 128ff)
An explanation as to the causes of this can be found by understanding the functioning of the core-periphery mechanisms and the other factors mentioned in this article which are derived from the cumulative causation model of economic development. Their compound effect lies in the fact that they relatively continuously strengthen the economy of central Slovenia - i.e. Slovenia's central region, in contrast with the other regions – especially the least developed peripheral ones.

6. Conclusion

In our article, we have shown that small business has an impact on economic growth, above all by making the following contributions:

1. Job creation
2. The creation of innovations
3. Creating regional income from exports and/or import substitutes
4. Building a broader regional economic structure
5. Sowing the seeds for the growth of large companies

The above leads us to conclude that the founding and growth of small enterprises as a part of the entire entrepreneurial process has a decisive impact on the future development of any given region and subsequently also on the entire national economy. Therefore, regions striving to achieve more rapid economic development must ensure that the level of newly founded enterprises remains high and that these enterprises are of good quality, as the seeds and growth potential for large companies are inherent in only a very small number of nascent enterprises.

For this reason, we continued by searching for the main factors that exert a significant influence on the strengthening of the entrepreneurial potential of a region and through this also its economic development. These factors were listed in three groups:

1. Factors of entrepreneurial development
2. Elements of the cumulative causation model of economic development
3. Core-periphery mechanisms of functioning derived from the core-periphery theory

We found that we were dealing with the complex interaction of a number of intertwined factors. Much of this was also tested within the framework of our applicative research of the entrepreneurial and economic level of development of Slovenia's regions and their entrepreneurs. A brief report on the results of these studies can be found in the last chapter of the article. On the basis of all the conclusions reached in this article, we can say in summary that the establishment of more harmonious regional economic development is not an easy process. Without doubt, this problem will have to be approached in a different way in Slovenia than it has been to date. It is a topical issue - particularly from the standpoint that Slovenia is an economically less developed region of the European Union in comparison with the 15 countries initially included in it. The question then arises as to whether we shall succeed over the years in narrowing the gap between Slovenia and the more developed Europe, or whether it will grow wide. The answer is entirely up to us Slovenians. And in order to achieve the desired answer, we shall need a more appropriate policy and strategy of entrepreneurial development, as well as the implementation of a more appropriate strategy regarding the sale of our companies and banks to foreign corporations than has been conducted to date. Experiences such as the one with Lek d.d. are classic examples of what can happen when the nation's most successful company becomes a subsidiary factory of a multinational corporation (see more information in Turk, 2007, p. 15ff). In any case, there is great need of a change in awareness, a change in the way we think and the way the critical mass of the players shaping Slovenia's economic policy and practices operates – also with regard to entrepreneurship.

Bibliography and References

Barkham, R. J. (1989): Entrepreneurship, New Firms and Regional Development, Submitted for the degree of Doctor of Philosophy, University of Reading, Reading.

Birch, D. (1993): »Dynamic Entrepreneurship and Job Creation: Lessons from the US Experience for Central and Eastern Europe«. In: Abell D. F., Köllermeir, T. (eds): Dynamic Entrepreneurship in Central and Eastern Europe. Delwel, The Hague.

Brusco, S. (1986): »Small Firms and Industrial Districts: The Experience of Italy«, in: Keeble, D., Wever, E., (eds), New Firms and Regional Development in Europe, Croom Helm, London, p. 184-202.

Davis, S., et al.(1996): Small Business and Job Creation: Dissecting the Myth and Reassessing the Facts. Small Business Economics, Boston.

Drnovšek, M. (2000): Slovenian enterprises and the opening of new jobs in the period 1989-1998, University of Ljubljana, Faculty of Economics, Ljubljana

Foley, A. and Griffiths, B., (1992): »Indigenous Manufacturing Enterprises in a Peripheral Economy and the Single Market: The Case of the Republic of Ireland.«, Regional Studies, Vol 26 no 4, p. 375-386, in Hanwey et al, 1994.

Gibb A., Rebernik, M., (1994): "Small Business Management in the New Europe", Proceedings, Ekonomski inštitut, Maribor.

Hanvey, E., Mc Gleenon, M. Barkham, R., Hart, M., (1994): 'Some Characteristics of the »Active« Small Firm Exporter', in Gibb, A., Rebernik, M., p. 35-50.

Hart, M., Scott, R. in Gudgin, G., (1993): »Job Creation in Small Firms«, Northern Ireland Economic Research Centre, in Hanvey, E. et al, (1994).

Kampuš Trop, V., (2000): »Entrepreneurship in Slovenia – Regional differences in setting up and development of new enterprises«, Doctoral Thesis, University of Ljubljana, Faculty of Economics, Ljubljana, 2000.

Kampuš Trop, V. (2001): The importance of market information for founders of small enterprises. In: Jaškova, M. (ed.) ECON: Selected research papers, Technical University of Ostrava, Faculty of Economics, Ostrava.

Kampuš Trop, V. (2002): »Interaction between characteristics of entrepreneurs and growth of their newly established companies in Slovenia« Management and the European Union, 21st International Conference on Organizational Science Development, p. 41-51, Publishing House Moderna organizacija, Slovenia, Portorož.

Kampuš Trop, V. (2003): »New firms creation and growth of enterprises, reasons for regional economic disparities«, Scientific monographic publication, Publishing House Moderna Založba, Kranj.

Kampuš Trop, V. (2003): "The impact of the founder's management background on the enterprise's success". In Kaluža, J. (ed.) Strategic Management and its support by information systems, International scientific conference, Technical University of Ostrava, Faculty of Economics, Ostrava.

Kampuš Trop, V. (2004): "Information of markets – the sources and the influence on small business success. in Florjančič, J., Pütz, K. (eds.) Informatics and management, Peter Lang, Frankfurt am Main.

Kampuš Trop, V., (2005): »Interactive model of entrepreneurial activity influence factors. In Kaluža, J. (ed.) Synergy of methodology: Proceedings of the 24th International Conference on Organizational Science Development, Slovenia, Portorož, March 16 – 18, 2005:«, Publishing House Moderna Založba, Kranj.

Kampuš Trop, V., (2006): Cumulative Relationships "Core - Periphery" and the Economic Development of Regions in Kaluža, J. (ed.) Change Management: Proceedings of the 25th International Conference on Organizational Science Development, Slovenia, Portorož, March 15 – 17:, Publishing House Moderna Založba, Kranj.

Kampuš Trop, V., (2007): "The influence of the Environment on the Formation and Growth of New Enterprises". In Rajkovič, V. (ed.): Creative organization: Proceedings of the 26th International Conference on Organizational Science Development, Slovenia, Portorož, March 15 – 17, Publishing House Moderna Založba, Kranj.

Kirchhoff, B. A. (1994): »Entrepreneurship Economics«, in Bygrave, W.D., The Portable MBA in Entrepreneurship, John Wiley & Sons, New York.

Larsen, J., Rogers, E. M. (1984): "Silicon Valley Fever-Growth of High Technology Culture«, George Allen and Unwin, London.

Oakey, R. (1991): »High Technology Small Firms: Their Potential for Rapid Industrial Growth«, International Small Business Journal, 9, 4, 30-42.

Porter, M. E., (1990): "The Competitive Advantage of Nations", London and Basingstoke; Macmillan.

Reynolds, P. et al, (1994): »Cross-National Comparisons of the Variation in New Firm Formation Rates«, Regional Studies, 28, p. 443-456.

Smallbone, D. (1995): »SME and Regional Economic Developing a Policy Agenda«. In: Plasecki, B., Fogel, D. S., (ed.): Regional Determinants of SME Development in the Central and Eastern European countries, Łódź Univesity Press, Łódź.

Spilling, O. R. (1996): »Regional Variation of New Firm Formation: The Norwegian Case«, Entrepreneurship & Regional Development, 8, p. 217-243.

Storey, D. J., Johnson, S. (1987): »Job Generation and Labour Market Change«, London and Basingstoke: Mcmillan.

Sweeney, G. P. (1987): »Innovation, Entrepreneurs and Regional Development«, Francis Pinter (Publishers), London.

Turk, G. (2007): "Entrepreneurship and Economic Development of Regions, Research Paper, Submitted to Post Graduated Study, University of Maribor, Faculty of Organizational Sciences, Kranj.

Vahčič, et al. (1998): SME and Job Creation in Slovenia in Proceedings of the 28th European Small Business Seminar, Vienna: EFMD.

About the Author

Vida Kampuš Trop, PhD., is an assistant professor at the Faculty of Organizational Sciences, University of Maribor. Her research fields are entrepreneurship and economic development, small business and management of small enterprises.

Increasing SMEs' Efficiency through the Single European Electronic Market as a New Business Model

Andreja Pucihar

andreja.pucihar@fov.uni-mb.si

Kristina Bogataj

kristina.bogataj@fov.uni-mb.si

Gregor Lenart

gregor.lenart@fov.uni-mb.si

Abstract

The different forms of e-marketplaces range from simple catalogue-based online buying and selling to more sophisticated business process integration solutions. Consequently, e-marketplaces contribute to improving efficiency and enhancing the productivity and competitiveness of European enterprises. However, despite the potential benefits of e-marketplaces, the participation of enterprises, especially of smaller and medium sized enterprises (SMEs), in business-to-business e-marketplaces is still relatively low. This paper presents current business models of existing e-marketplaces. Furthermore, significant characteristics of SMEs are presented. Both current business models of e-marketplaces and characteristics of SMEs present main reasons for why e-marketplaces are not used more widely by SMEs. Furthermore, the paper presents the new organizational model of advanced e-marketplace implementation in the common European marketplace, which aims to address specific needs of SMEs and help them to more efficiently participate in the supply chain in the Single European e-market.

Keywords: SMEs, electronic market, business model

1. Introduction

An e-marketplace could be defined as a virtual marketplace where buyers and suppliers meet to exchange information about product and service offerings, and to negotiate and carry out business transactions (Pucihar and Podlogar, 2000, p. 88 ff).

The different forms of e-marketplaces range from simple catalogue-based online buying and selling to more sophisticated business process integration solutions. Consequently, e-marketplaces contribute to improving efficiency and enhancing the productivity and competitiveness of European enterprises. However, despite the potential benefits of e-marketplaces, the participation of enterprises, especially of smaller and medium sized enterprises (SMEs), in business-to-business e-marketplaces is still relatively low.

To encourage SMEs to participate in the e-marketplaces, the European Commission supported the project "eMarketServices" under the 6th Framework programme. The project resulted in a portal with very useful information about e-business issues and about e-marketplaces, with industry reports, SME managers' interviews and with a directory of existing e-marketplaces classified under categories of different industries and presented with most useful information .
(http://www.eMarketServices.com).

In January 2006, the SEAMLESS (Small Enterprises Accessing the Electronic Market of the Enlarged Europe by a Smart Service Infrastructure) project under the 6th Framework was launched. The project is intended to study, design, develop and experiment an advanced ICT-based service to enable a well-identified category of small enterprises, the so-called Craft & Trade companies, to access the common e-business web space created by the Single Electronic Market of the Enlarged Europe (SEEM) and to play an active role in establishing and running frictionless dynamic collaborations (http://www.seamless-eu.org).

The paper presents current business models of existing e-marketplaces. Furthermore, significant characteristics of SMEs are also presented. Both current business models of e-marketplaces and characteristics of SMEs present main reasons for why e-marketplaces are not used more widely by SMEs. Furthermore, the paper presents the new organizational model of advanced e-marketplace implementation in the common European electronic market, which aims to address specific needs of SMEs and help them to participate more efficiently in the supply chain in that market.

2. Current E-Marketplace Business Models

An e-marketplace is a virtual marketplace where buyers and suppliers meet to exchange information about product and service offerings, and to negotiate and carry out business transactions. Furthermore, in the age of the Internet and with the emergence of new information and communication technologies, an e-marketplace is a Web-based information system, where multiple suppliers and multiple buyers can undertake business transactions via the Internet. The e-marketplace uses Internet technologies and standards to distribute product data and to facilitate online transactions (Segev et al., 1999, p.138 ff; Pucihar and Podlogar, 2004, p. 276f).

An intermediary can provide four important mechanisms that cause e-marketplaces to add value (Christiaanse et al., 2001, p. 422 ff; Bailey and Bakos, 1997, p. 7 ff; Pucihar and Podlogar, 2006, p. 88ff):

- Aggregating together a large number of buyers and sellers
- Matching buyers and sellers to negotiate prices on a dynamic and real-time basis,
- Ensuring trust among participants by maintaining neutral position, and
- Facilitating market operations by supporting certain transaction phases.

Intermediary functions may support a multiplicity of activities, including brokerage - auctions payments, logistics, legal, consulting, or may support inter-company communications through third party inter-organizational systems and related systems (Bakos, 1991, p. 1676ff; Choudhury et al., 1998, p. 471ff; Segev et al., 1999, p. 138ff; Kaplan and Sawhney, 2000, p. 97ff; Grewal et al., 2001, p. 17ff).

2.1 E-marketplaces Classification

There are many different types of e-marketplaces operating today. We may divide e-marketplaces into those controlled by sellers, those controlled by buyers and those controlled by neutral third parties (Berryman et al, 1998, p. 152ff):

- E-marketplaces controlled by sellers are usually set up by a single vendor seeking many buyers. Its aim is to create or retain value and market power in any transaction.
- E-marketplaces controlled by buyers are set up by or for one or more buyers with the aim of shifting power and value on the marketplace to the buyer's side. Many involve an intermediary, but some particularly strong buyers have developed marketplaces for themselves. Such e-marketplaces are also called consortium e-marketplaces.
- Neutral or independent e-marketplaces are set up by third-party intermediaries to match many buyers to many sellers.

E-marketplaces might be also divided into horizontal and vertical marketplaces. A horizontal marketplace addresses a specific function (e.g. human resources, office supplies) and serves a wide range of industries, while a vertical marketplace focuses on a wide range of functionalities in a specific industry such as chemicals, steel or automotive (Baldi and Borgman, 2001, p. 629 ff).

We may also classify e-marketplaces into four categories (Kaplan and Sawhney, 2000, p. 98ff):

- MRO (Maintenance Raw and Operations) hubs are horizontal markets that enable systematic sourcing of operating inputs,
- Yield managers are horizontal markets that enable spot sourcing of operating inputs,
- Exchanges are vertical markets that enable spot sourcing of manufacturing inputs,
- Catalogue hubs are vertical markets that enable systematic sourcing of manufacturing inputs.

The appeal of doing business on the Web is clear. By bringing together large numbers of buyers and sellers and by automating transactions, e-marketplaces expand the choices available to buyers, give sellers access to new customers (buyers), and reduce transaction costs for all participants

(Pucihar, 2002, p. 9ff). By extracting fees for the transactions occurring within the business-to-business (B2B) marketplaces, market makers (intermediaries) can earn vast revenues (Kaplan and Sawhney, 2000, p. 98ff).

The success of the e-marketplace depends on the perceived net benefit of buyers and suppliers. From the viewpoint of transaction cost economics, information technology helps to reduce transaction costs, risks, and coordinating costs of e-marketplaces (Clemons et al., 1993, p. 9ff).

2.2 E-Marketplaces Processes

Traditional markets and e-marketplaces consist of many trading processes that create value for both buyers and sellers. For successful e-marketplace operation, trading processes must be transformed from traditional business exchanges to e-marketplaces in an efficient manner. The biggest challenge is how to successfully transmit current business processes from a traditional to a virtual environment (Kambil and van Heck, 2002, p. 26ff). This is possible by information technology that enables business process integration on an e-marketplace (Pucihar and Delina, 2005, p. 132).

These processes, that must be partly or fully integrated into e-marketplaces in order to achieve their successful operation, may be divided into processes related directly to trade executing and processes that enhance trust among trading partners (Kambil in van Heck, 2000, p. 9ff).

Processes related directly to trade executing are as follows (Kambil and van Heck, 2000, p. 9ff):

- Search processes for discovering and comparing trading opportunities,
- Pricing processes for discovering prices,
- Logistics processes to coordinate transfer of goods and services ,
- Payment and settlement processes to transfer funds from buyer to seller,
- Authentication processes to verify the quality of goods or services sold and credibility of trading partners.

Processes for enhancing trust among trading partners and legitimizing the trade are as follows (Kambil and van Heck, 2000, p. 10ff):

- Product representation processes for presenting products and services on an e-marketplace,
- Regulation processes to set market rules and social principles of e-marketplace trading,
- Risk management processes to reduce risks in transaction processes between trading partners,
- Influence processes to ensure that commitments among trading partners are met,
- Dispute resolution processes to resolve conflicts among trading partners and market makers.

E-marketplace processes are shown in Figure 1 (Pucihar and Podlogar, 2006, p. 90ff; Gričar et al, 2006, p. 104ff).

Figure 1: E-marketplace processes

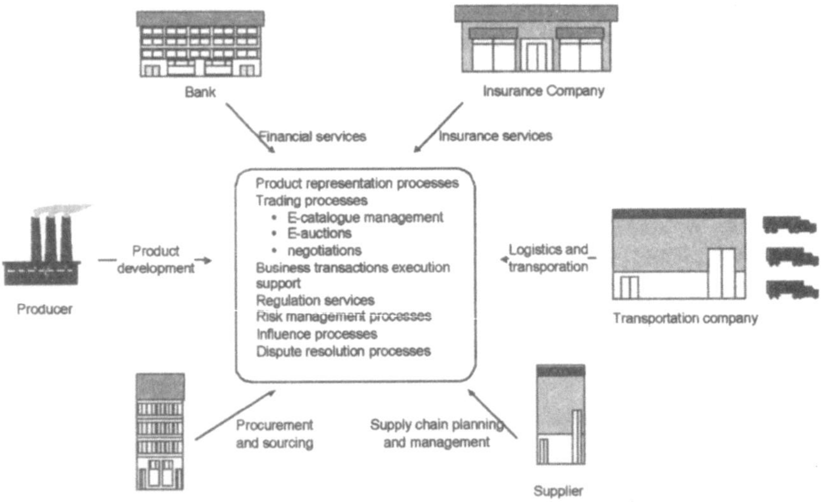

3. Benefits and Threats of Using B2B E-Marketplaces

3.1 The Potential Benefits and Threats of E-Marketplace Use

Benefits of e-marketplace use

Use of the e-marketplace enables many benefits to be gained by organizations. Some benefits for buyers and sellers are described in Table 1 (Bakos, 1998, p. 7ff; Berryman et al., 1998, p. 154ff; Dai in Kauffman 2001, p. 2ff; Pucihar and Podlogar, 2006, p. 90ff).

Table 1: Possible benefits of e-marketplace use

Possible benefits of e-marketplace use for sellers:	Possible benefits of e-marketplace use for buyers:	Possible benefits of e-marketplace use for sellers and buyers:
Easy and fast entrance to new markets	Easy and fast entrance to new markets	Lower transaction costs
Selling at any time	Easy and fast comparison between offers of many sellers	Better co-operation between buyers and sellers in product development processes
Physical store not needed anymore	Fast selecting of best offer	Better image of organization
Less mistakes in order management and fulfillment	Fast purchasing without long-term relationships contracts	Lower marketing costs
Faster detection of new buyers for lower costs	Lower negotiation cycles	Faster time of new product to the market
Possibilities for sales increasing	Lower procurement costs	Lower production time
Lowering of superfluous inventory	Ordering at any time	More efficient production
More efficient production planning	Order status tracking	Lower inventory
More efficient product development	Easy changing of orders	Simplifying of business processes
	Consolidation of minor value orders	Better customer relationship management
		Less mistakes

Threats of eMarketplace use

As well as benefits that organizations may acquire, they may also be faced with threats while using the e-marketplace. Some threats for the buyers and sellers are described in Table 2 (Lee and Clark, 1996a, p. 127ff; Lee and Clark, 1996b, p. 113ff; Bakos, 1997, p. 1677ff; Dai and Kauffman, 2001, 3ff; Lefebvre et al., 2001, p. 2ff; Pucihar and Podlogar, 2006, p. 90ff).

Table 2: Possible threats of e-marketplace use

Possible threats of e-arketplace use for sellers:	Possible threats of e-marketplace use for buyers:	Possible threats of e-marketplace use for sellers and buyers:
Loss of direct relationship with buyers and possibility of loss of existing buyers	Loss of direct relationship with suppliers	Lack of trust between buyers and suppliers, while they first meet in an e-marketplace
Stronger negotiation power of buyers	Possible unreliability of unknown sellers	Lack of trust in e-marketplace intermediary
Reverse auctions (sellers are competing for business with price decreasing),	Lack of trust in products and services quality	Lack of services that would support whole business processes.
Payment of commission to the intermediary (also in trading with existing buyers)	Uncoordinated, different ways of supplying	
Buyers have strong relationship with existing suppliers (are not ready to get new ones)		
Lots of time, knowledge and funds necessary for e-catalogue creation and management		

4. Characteristics of SMEs as Barriers to E-Business Adoption

SMEs have special characteristics, which distinguish them from large businesses. These characteristics are not just the small number of employees, but also the lack of technical knowledge and staff, the lack of resources for information technology investments, the lack of awareness about possible benefits of IT usage, and some other characteristics. Therefore, SMEs need to be addressed differently than large businesses in a means of e-commerce implementation. Not all e-commerce and e-business models are suitable for SMEs and large businesses. These models need to differ and in all ways to address the users' needs.

4.1 Characteristics of SMEs

SMEs are not simply scaled-down large businesses and, although size is a major distinguishing factor, SMEs have a number of unique characteristics that distinguish them from large businesses.

There have been numerous studies carried out in order to establish the characteristics unique to SMEs. Altogether, the main characteristics of SMEs are the following (MacGregor and Vrazalic, 2005, p. 5ff):

- In some cases, SMEs tended to risk more than larger organizations. This results in higher failure rates (DeLone, 1988 p. 51ff; Cochran, 1981, p. 50ff).
- Some SMEs had inadequate records of transactions, especially due to non- using of information technology.
- SMEs often suffer from a lack of trained staff and have a short-range management perspective (Welsh and White, 1981, p. 46f).
- SMEs often suffer from a lack of technical expertise.
- SMEs lack adequate resources to invest in information technology.
- Most SMEs suffer from inadequate organizational planning (Miller and Besser, 2000, p. 68 ff; Tetteh and Burn, 2001, p. 171ff)
- Many SMEs differ from larger organizations in the extent of the product/service range they provide to customers.
- SMEs tend to have a small management team (often one or two individuals) – the owners – or they are strongly influenced by the owner.
- SMEs have little control over their environment (Hill and Stewart, 2000, p. 105f).
- SMEs have a strong desire to remain independent.

4.2 The Barriers of SMEs to e-Business Adoption

The characteristics of SMEs impact on the barriers to e-business adoption. The barriers can be classified as external or internal to the business.

External barriers could be further categorized into the following (Hadjimanolis, 1999, p. 566ff):

- supply barriers, as for example, difficulties of obtaining and exchanging finance and technical information of product and services;
- demand barriers, as for example, e-commerce is not suitable for trading with the range of products/services or not suitable for doing business with existing partners;
- environmental barriers related to security concerns.

Internal barriers might be further divided into resource barriers, as for example, lack of management and technical expertise; and system barriers, as for example, e-commerce not being suitable for the current business practices.

The summarized barriers to e-commerce adoption of SMEs are the following:

- high costs of Internet technologies and their implementation (Riquelme, 2002, p. 276ff; Quayle, 2002, p. 1148ff);
- complex implementation of e-business (Quayle, 2002, p. 1148ff);
- low level of existing technology incorporated into the business processes (Lawrence, 1997, p. 587ff);
- e-commerce is a form of long-term investment and SMEs do not see immediate ROI (McGowan and Madey, 1998, p. 17ff);
- organizational resistance to the change because of the fear of new technology amongst employees;
- satisfaction with the traditional way of doing business, such as paper, phone, fax and face-to-face interaction (Poon and Swatman, 1999, p. 9ff; Venkatesan and Fink, 2002, p. 1136ff);
- lack of technical skills and IT knowledge amongst employees (Quayle, 2002, p. 1148ff);
- SMEs feel that they lack time to implement e-business (Walczuch et al, 2000, p. 561ff);
- e-commerce is not suitable fot the way the SME does business (Hadjimanolis, 1999, 562ff);

- e-commerce is not a suitable way for trading with existing products/services offered by the SME (Kendall & Kendall 2001, p. 2ff);
- lack of awareness about e-commerce and e-business opportunities/benefits (Quayle, 2002, 1149 ff; Lawrence, 1997, p. 587).

5. An E-Marketplace Business Model for SMEs – the SEAMLESS Example

As stated in section 4, significant characteristics of SMEs impact on barriers to SMEs' e-business adoption. As many existing e-marketplaces are supporting industry-specific supply chains, they are, in the main, adopted by larger businesses. However, e-marketplaces offer many opportunities also for SMEs, but as already identified, the business model needs to address specific needs of SMEs and a new approach for e-marketplace business model adoption needs to be developed.

The SEAMLESS project intends to design, implement and assess an advanced ICT-based infrastructure enabling SMEs:

- to access the e-business space created by the Single European Electronic Market (SEEM) considering the enlarged Europe; and
- to play an active role in establishing and running frictionless dynamic collaborations.

The SEEM vision focusses on a web-based structured marketplace, where companies can easily collaborate and do business without geographical and technological constraints. SEEM allows an objective comparison of companies' profiles and offers, which should open up the e-business space to the many SMEs. The comparison of high quality products and services at lower cost and the conducting of on-line business transactions are the main benefits for SMEs which are currently risking being left outside of the electronic market (http://www.seamless-eu.org).

SEAMLESS is focussed on Craft & Trade companies, which are SMEs. Most of them become members of associations (sectoral, regional), that help them to carry out elementary organizational and bureaucratic activities. In other cases, the intended companies find the required support on the market, buying services from ASPs (Application Service Providers), or even at local development agencies, chambers of commerce, technology transfer centres and universities. All these are referred to as "mediators" in the SEAMLESS business model (Lima et al., 2006, p. 2ff).

The ambition of the SEAMLESS project is to create the organizational and technological conditions to enable mediators, from different countries and sectors, to become nodes of the SEEM network and to provide their associated companies with the services needed to access this network and collaborate with other companies.

5.1 The SEEM Concept and the SEAMLESS Vision

The SEEM concept is an e-business space where companies can do business with no technological constraints. Such a concept is less about technology and more about identifying those critical e-business processes which encounter obstacles. Technology must be used properly as an enabler for information flow as required (http://www.seamless-eu.org).

The purpose of SEEM is to ensure the possibility of integrated value chains, where companies, organizations and individuals from different Member States can be linked in a chain without experiencing any access or interoperability problems.

The SEEM vision is towards an Internet-based, structured marketplace where companies can collaborate without geographical and technological constraints, thus overcoming the limits of the hundreds of vertical portals, each adopting its own specific model. It implies, among other things, (http://www.seamless-eu.org):

- creating a self-organizing network of e-registries/repositories (RRs) where companies can classify their own profiles, offers and features so as to gain public visibility for potential customers and partners;
- providing advanced, semantically-based search & find services to discover candidate partners by selecting them from the RRs on the basis of their profiles, qualification and offer;
- establishing the conditions for confident and secure dynamic relations, negotiations and information exchanges with other companies, based on agreed collaboration protocols and reciprocal trust;
- offering compliant web-based applications to manage general-purpose and sector-specific distributed processes, and hide the

SEEM infrastructure complexity under easy and tailored user interfaces; and
- ensuring the interoperability of legacy systems by facilitated information exchanges, to integrate internal enterprise processes (active and passive cycles) with external collaborations.

The success of SEEM depends on the creation of a collaborative environment where SMEs and mediators would come together and interoperate, using e-business practices and mechanisms. The SEAMLESS project intends to provide this collaborative environment and validate it through a series of pilot cases, involving two industrial sectors (construction and textile) at the beginning.

The SEAMLESS framework (Figure 2) is formed of three main parts, namely the collaborative environment itself, the mediators, and the SMEs associated to each mediator. Essentially, the SEAMLESS collaborative environment is the virtual space where SMEs will make e-business operations through the mediators. Each mediator acts as a kind of facilitator between its members and the collaborative environment. Each interaction is considered a business operation that requires, indeed, a perfect understanding between the actors involved, and which is supported by a very particular information flow. Each SME has to be sure about the precise meaning of every single business interaction, not only at the operational level but above all, at the semantic level. SEAMLESS considers that this need can be fulfilled if SMEs share common ontologies managed by the mediator (Lima et al., 2006, p. 3ff).

The SEAMLESS framework is presented in Figure 2.

Figure 2: SEAMLESS framework

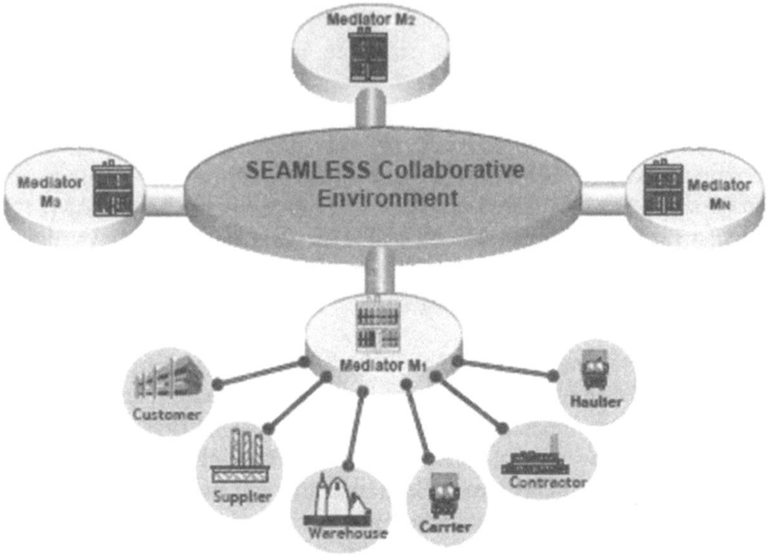

5.2 The SEAMLESS Operational Scenario

Through the SEAMLESS operational scenario, the project goals and expected results that SEAMLESS aims to provide to SMEs are presented.

The focus is Little Ltd, an SME company that is a member of the Small Association (along with many other SMEs like it). The Small Association could be, for example, a Chamber of Commerce or Chamber of Crafts.

- One day in 2008, Little Ltd is invited by the Small Association (SA) to join the SEEM they manage and to become, for the first time, a participant in the SA electronic market. Little Ltd accepts the invitation and receives a Website address, a user code and a password.
- While Little Ltd accesses the Small Association site, it is recognised as a newcomer and guided through the representation of its features to register to the system. It means coding and storing the data in the SA's company registry/repository in a means of its profile, skills and experiences, preferred collaboration forms and contractual templates, as well as its offer (and even demand) of products and services. To this purpose, the Little Ltd is supported by the local ontology

providing lexicon and concepts to associate the right metadata to the stored data. The registration is done in the company (and association) home language.

- A few hours later, Little Ltd receives an unexpected bid request for quotation for the supply of a specific product from Foreign Co, a potential new customer established in a different country. The request is issued according to one of the forms proposed by Small Ltd and made available in its home language.
- The same application suggests to Little Ltd the list of possible reactions the company can take such as, for example accept a request for a quotation, ask for more information, reject, negotiate, etc.. Little Ltd suspends the answer because the requested product calls for the collaboration of partners (suppliers) able to perform special activities that Little Ltd cannot cover itself.
- Little Ltd plans the required activities, indicates as additional resources its usual partners and fixes scheduling conditions and constraints. Based on the scheduler outcome, Little Ltd uses the SEAMLESS system to automatically send the requests for a quotation to the scheduled partners, including Partner Ltd for a certain activity.
- Little Ltd decides that it is time to search for a new partnership as an alternative to Partner Ltd. Therefore, it sends to the Small Association site a request for additional potential partners with a specific profile (region, company size, desired activity, supply time, etc.), which would be able to fulfill the Little Ltd request for quotation. The request is broadcasted to the interesting SEEM nodes, included in the SEAMLESS e-Marketplace.
- Within the fixed deadline, Little Ltd receives indications of three candidate partners discovered by the SEAMLESS system in the respective registries. One of them, New Ltd, is particularly interesting, and Little Ltd starts negotiating with it until a quotation has been obtained.
- Little Ltd takes its time to compare the two quotations coming from (existing partner) Partner Ltd and from (new partner) New Ltd. The day after, it decides and concludes the negotiation with the selected company (while the system automatically closes the negotiation with the other).
- Now all the data needed to answer the Foreign Co request are available. Little Ltd reacts accordingly and the negotiation continues up to the electronic signature of the contract. On this basis, the contract with the scheduled partners is finally signed.

- Following these contracts, a number of information and documents exchanges take place during the following weeks, according to the specific collaboration protocols. Little Ltd is involved, on the one side, in the envisaged collaborative work with the selected partners and, on the other side, in communications with its customer Foreign Co.

The SEAMLESS operational scenario is presented in figure 3.

Both these relations are regulated and supported by the SEAMLESS workflow manager. Although simplistic, the storyboard incorporates a number of very real problems that are still unsolved at the present time and that constitute the ultimate aim of SEAMLESS. They range from easy and fast introduction into the system to guided company self-qualification, up to increased visibility of potential partners and customers, and support in negotiation and collaboration with the identified partners (Lima et al., 2006).

Figure 3: SEAMLESS operational scenario

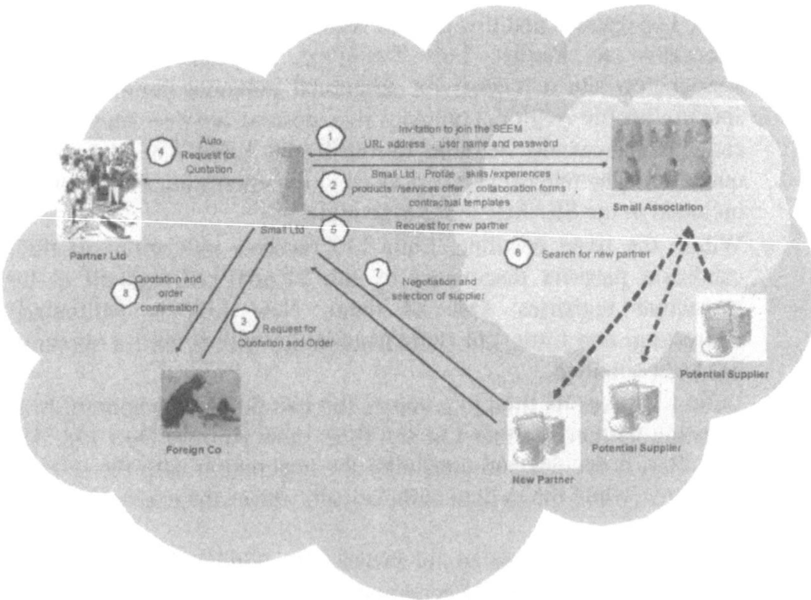

6. Conclusions

SMEs present more than 90% of all of the European enterprises and more than 60% of employees. They represent the base of the European economy and society. As discussed in the previous chapters of the paper, SMEs have specific characteristics, which need to be carefully addressed in order to help them to adopt the newest e-business solutions, which enable them competitive participation in the European and global e-markets.

Because of their limited resources (lack of technical skills, limited funds, lack of awareness), Craft & Trade companies have serious problems in being completely autonomous in an increasingly complex and competitive world and, due to that, they often rely on mediators to help them carry out elementary organizational and business activities.

The situation in New Member States and Associated Candidate Countries, where the percentage of Craft & Trade companies is even larger than in the EU-15, is generally worse, although significant differences are found among countries. Not only are the above figures lower, but there are still problems in the constitution of steady and strong local markets and in establishing fruitful relations with enterprises from other regions and from EU-15 countries.

The support assured by mediators is fundamental to introducing small companies into the SEEM world. The SEAMLESS solution intends to be simple, direct, easy to use and cheap. These characteristics are one of the most important requirements for adoption of any e-business solution by SMEs.

In the SEAMLESS framework, it is perceived that mediators are the only actors that can correctly interpret the company needs, deploy the new solution, and help adapt it to the expectations of every single company. Moreover, mediators can ensure the rapid introduction of a critical mass of companies, to make the SEEM network operate on a large scale (Lima et al., 2006, p. 4ff).

Only integration of all parties – mediators, government institutions, SMEs, large organizations and ISP providers in an open, collaborative environment can assure competitive participation of all in the common European market. The proposed SEAMLESS business model is supported by the European Commission and therefore it promises to address the

SMEs' specific needs and enable them equal participation in the European market.

Bibliography and References

Bailey, J.; Bakos, J. Y. (1997): »An Exploratory Study of the Emerging Role of Electronic Intermediaries«. International Journal of Electronic Commerce, 1.3. Spring, pp. 7–20.

Bakos, J. Y. (1991): »A Strategic Analysis of Electronic Marketplaces«. MIS Quarterly, September, pp. 295-310.

Bakos J. Y. (1997): »Reducing Buyer Search Costs: Implications for Electronic Marketplaces«. Management Science 43(12), pp. 1676-1692.

Bakos J. Y. (1998): »The Emerging Role of Electronic Marketplaces on the Internet«. Association for Computing Machinery, Communications of the ACM, New York, August.

Baldi, S.; Borgman, H. P. (2001): Consortium-Based B2B e-Marketplaces – A Case Study in the Automotive Industry. 14th Bled Electronic Commerce Conference: e-Everything: e-Commerce, e-Government, e-Household, e-Democracy. Edited by: O'Keefe, Bob; Loebbecke, Claudia; Gričar, Jože; Pucihar, Andreja; Lenart, Gregor. Bled, Slovenia, June 25-26, pp.. 629-645.

Berryman, K.; Harrington, L. F.; Layton-Rodin, D.; Rerolle, V. (1998): »Electronic Commerce: Three Emerging Strategies«. The McKinsey Quarterly, 1998, Number 1. http://www.mckinseyquarterly.com/electron/elco98.asp

Cochran, A.B. (1981): Small Business Mortality Rates: A Review of the Literature. Journal of Small Business Management 19(4), pp. 50-59.

Christiaanse, E.; Sinnecker, R.; Mossinkoff, M. (2001): »The Impact of B2B Exchanges on Brick and Mortar Intermediaries: The Elemica Case«. The Proceedings of the 9th ECIS Conference: Global Co-operation in the New Millenium. Edited by:: Smithson, Steve; Gričar, Jože; Podlogar, Mateja; Avegerinou, Sofia. Bled, Slovenia, June 27-29, pp. 422-432.

Choudhury, V.; Hartzel, K. S.; Konsynski, B. R. (1998): »Uses and Consequences of Electronic Markets: An Empirical Investigation in the Aircraft Parts Industry«. MIS Quarterly. 22, 4, December 1998, pp. 471-507.

Clemons, E.K., S. Reddi, P., and M.C. Row (1993): »The Impact of Information Technology on the Organization of Economic Activity: The "move to the middle" Hypothesis«. Journal of Management Information Systems 10(2); pp. 9-35.

Dai, Q., Kauffman, R. J. (2001): »Business Models for Internet-Based e-Procurement Systems and B2B Electronic Market: An Exploratory Assessment«. Thirty-Fourth Annual Hawai'i International Conference on System Sciences (HICSS-34), Maui, HI, January 3-6.

DeLone, W.H. (1988): Determinants for Success for Computer Usage in Small Business. MIS Quarterly, pp. 51-61.

eMarketServices Project. (http://www.emarketservices.com)

Grewal, R., Comer, J. M., Mehta, R. (2001): »An Investigation into the Antecedents of Organizational Participation in Business-to-Business Electronic Markets«. Journal of Markteing. Vol. 65 (July), pp. 17-33.

Gričar, J., Pucihar, A., Lenart, G. (2006): Active learning model for teaching B2B e-marketplaces. J. inf. syst. educ., 2005, vol. 16, no. 1, pp. 103-108.

Hadjimonolis, A. (1999): Barriers to Innovation for SMEs in a Small Less Developed Country (Cyprus). Technovation 19(9), pp. 561-570.

Hill, R. & Stewart, J. (2000). Human Resource Development in Small Organisations. Journal of European Industrial Training 24(2/3/4), pp. 105-117.

Kambil, A.; van Heck, E. (2002): »Making Markets. How Firms Can Design and Profit from Online Auctions and Exchanges«. Harvard Business School Press, Boston, Massachusetts.

Kaplan, S.; Sawhney, M. (2000): »e-Hubs: The New B2B Marketplaces«. Harvard Business Review. May – June 2000, pp. 97 – 103.

Kendall, J. E., Kendall, K. E. (2001). A Paradoxically Peaceful Coexistence between Commerce and Ecommerce. Journal of Information Technology, Theory and Application 3(4), pp. 1-6.

Lawrence, K. L. (1997): Factors Inhibiting the Utilisation of Electronic Commerce Facilities in Tasmanian Small to Medium Sized Enterprises. Proceedings of the 8th Australasian Conference on Information Systems, pp. 587-597.

Lee, H. G., Clark, T. H. (1996a): «Impacts of Electronic Marketplace on Transaction Cost and Market Structure«. International Journal of Electronic Commerce. 1, 1 (fall 1996), pp. 127-149.

Lee, H. G., Clark, T. H. (1996b): »Market Process Reengineering through Electronic Market Systems: Opportunities and Challenges«.

Journal of Management Information Systems. Winter 1996-97, Vol. 13, No. 3, pp. 113 – 136.

Lefebvre, L. A.; Cassivi, L.; Lefebvre, E. (2001): »Business-to-Business e-Commerce: A Transition Model«. Thirty-Fourth Annual Hawai'i International Conference on System Sciences (HICSS-34), Maui, HI, January 3-6.

Lima, C., Bonfatti, F., Sancho, S., Yurchyshyna, A. (2006): Towards Ontology Based Information and Communication Systems in the Single European Information Space for SMEs. e-2006, d-Challenges 2006, Spain 25 - 27 October 2006, Barcelona, Spain.

MacGregor, R., Vrazalic, L. (2005): The Role of Small Business Clusters in Prioritising Barriers to E-commerce Adoption: A Study of Swedish Regional SMEs. CRIC Cluster conference. Beyond Cluster- Current Practices & Future Strategies. Ballarat, June 30-July 1, 2005.

McGowan, M.K. & Madey, G.R. (1998): The Influence of Organization Structure and Organizational Learning Factors on the Extent of EDI Implementation in U. S. Firms. Information Resources Management Journal 11(3), 17-27.

Miller, N. L., Besser, T. L. (2000): The Importance of Community Values in Small Business Strategy Formation: Evidence from Rural Iowa. Journal of Small Business Management 38(1), pp. 68-85.

Poon, S., Swatman, P. M. C. (1999): An Exploratory Study of Small Business Internet Commerce Issues. Information & Management 35, pp. 9-18.

Pucihar, A. (2002): "Entering eMarkets Success Factors". Doctoral dissertation. Kranj: University of Maribor.

Pucihar, A., Podlogar, M. (2004): Characteristics of successful emarketplaces - buyers' and sellers' perspective. V: Jašková, Mária (ur.). ECON '04 : [selected research papers], (Research works proceedings, Vol. 11, 2004). Ostrava: Technical University of Ostrava, Faculty of Economics, 2004, pp. 276-283.

Pucihar, A.; Delina, R. (2005): Academic emarketplace (ACEM) - integration of research and practice for teaching of e-business and e-marketplaces. In: Gričar, J. (ed.). Razvoj e-regije (e-region development), (Organizacija, year. 38, 2005, No. 3). Kranj: Moderna organizacija, 2005, pp. 132-136.

Pucihar, A., Podlogar, M. (2006): E-marketplace adoption success factors : challenges and opportunities for a small developing country. In: Kamel, S. (ed.). *Electronic business in developing countries :*

opportunities and challenges. Hershey (PA) [etc.]: Idea Group, cop. 2006, pp. 88-117.

Riquelme, H. (2002). Commercial Internet Adoption in China: Comparing the Experience of Small, Medium and Large Businesses. Internet Research: Electronic Networking Applications and Policy 12(3), pp. 276-286.

Russ, N. (2001): »E-marketplaces: New Challenges for Enterprise Policy, Competition and Standardisation.« eEurope go Digital. Workshop Report, Brussels, 23-24 April.

SEAMLESS Project - Small Enterprises Accessing the Electronic Market of the Enlarged Europe by a Smart Service Infrastructure (http://www.seamless-eu.org).

Segev, A., Gebauer, J., Färber (1999): »Internet based Electronic Markets«. Electronic Markets, Volume 9, Number 3, pp. 138-146.

Tetteh, E., Burn, J. (2001): Global Strategies for SME-business: Applying the SMALL Framework. Logistics Information Management 14(1/2), pp. 171-180.

Quayle, M. (2002): E-commerce: the Challenge for UK SMEs in the Twenty-first Century. International Journal of Operations and Production Management. 22(10), pp. 1148-1161.

Venkatesan, V. S. & Fink, D. (2002): Adoption of Internet Technologies and E-Commerce by Small and Medium Enterprises (SMEs) in Western Australia. Proceedings of the Information Resource Management Association International Conference, pp. 1136-1137.

Walczuch, R., Van Braven, G., Lundgren, H. (2000): Internet Adoption Barriers for Small Firms in The Netherlands. European Management Journal 18(5), pp. 561-572.

Welsh, J. A., White, J. F. (1981): A Small Business is not a little Big Business. Harvard Business Review 59(4), pp. 46-58.

About the Authors

Andreja Pucihar is an assistant professor of the eCommerce and MIS at the University of Maribor, Faculty of Organizational Science, and the University of Ljubljana, Faculty of Social Sciences. She is head of the eMarkets Laboratory at the former. Her research fields are e-business, e-government, business process reengineering and new business models. She is involved in several EU co-funded projects focusing on eGovernment and eBusiness.

Kristina Bogataj, MSc works for the company "Oria Computers", where she is responsible for managing e-business projects. She graduated from the University of Maribor, Faculty of Organizational Sciences, in e-Business management. She has also been actively involved in several EU research projects which focussed on e-Government and ICT usage in SMEs.

Gregor Lenart is a teaching assistant and senior researcher at the University of Maribor, Faculty of Organizational Science, and the University of Ljubljana, Faculty of Social Sciences. He is also a member of the eCommerce Center and head of the eCollaboration Lab. His current research includes computer supported collaborative work, group support systems and knowledge management. He is also actively involved in several EU research projects focusing on mobile commerce and e-business.